American Intervention in Grenada

Westview Special Studies

The concept of Westview Special Studies is a response to the continuing crisis in academic and informational publishing. Library budgets are being diverted from the purchase of books and used for data banks, computers, micromedia, and other methods of information retrieval. Interlibrary loan structures further reduce the edition sizes required to satisfy the needs of the scholarly community. Economic pressures on university presses and the few private scholarly publishing companies have greatly limited the capacity of the industry to properly serve the academic and research communities. As a result, many manuscripts dealing with important subjects, often representing the highest level of scholarship, are no longer economically viable publishing projects--or, if accepted for publication, are typically subject to lead times ranging from one to three years.

Westview Special Studies are our practical solution to the problem. As always, the selection criteria include the importance of the subject, the work's contribution to scholarship, and its insight, originality of thought, and excellence of exposition. We accept manuscripts in camera-ready form, typed, set, or word processed according to specifications laid out in our comprehensive manual, which contains straightforward instructions and sample pages. The responsibility for editing and proofreading lies with the author or sponsoring institution, but our editorial staff is always available to answer questions and provide guidance.

The result is a book printed on acid-free paper and bound in sturdy, library-quality soft covers. We manufacture these books ourselves using equipment that does not require a lengthy make-ready process and that allows us to publish first editions of 300 to 1000 copies and to reprint even smaller quantities as needed. Thus, we can produce Special Studies quickly and can keep even very specialized books in print as long as there is a demand for them.

About the Book and Editors

Why did the United States invade the sovereign state of Grenada in October 1983, risking world condemnation and the possible escalation of violence outside the borders of the tiny Caribbean island? According to the contributors to this book, the invasion--code-named "Urgent Fury"--was a product of the increasing concern with political instability in Central America in general and especially with the potential for communist destabilization of the region. In this context, the United States became concerned that the construction of the Port Salinas airfield--then being built by Cubans--would lead to the transformation of the island into a Cuban support base. The contributors relate these perceptions of the threat to Grenada's history and internal politics. Aside from assessing the logic of the military option, they also discuss media coverage of the invasion and consider the lessons of the intervention and its aftermath.

Peter M. Dunn is commander, U.S. Air Force ROTC Detachment 440, University of Missouri. Bruce W. Watson is director of publications at the Defense Intelligence College and an adjunct professor in the School of Foreign Service at Georgetown University. They are the coeditors of The Military Lessons of the Falkland Islands War (Westview, 1984).

American Intervention in Grenada

The Implications of Operation "Urgent Fury"

edited by Peter M. Dunn
and Bruce W. Watson

Westview Press / Boulder and London

∞ The paper used in this publication meets the requirements of the American National Standard for Permanence of Paper for Printed Library Materials Z39.48-1984.

Westview Special Studies in Military Affairs

The views expressed in this book are solely those
of the authors and do not represent the positions
or policies of any agency or department of the
United States Government. The following chapters
were derived from unclassified publications and
sources and are intended to neither confirm nor
deny, officially or unofficially, the views of the
United States Government.

Copyright © 1985 by Westview Press, Inc.

Published in 1985 in the United States of America by Westview Press, Inc.;
Frederick A. Praeger, Publisher; 5500 Central Avenue, Boulder, Colorado 80301

Library of Congress Cataloging Card Number: 85-51778
ISBN: 0-86531-868-9

Composition for this book was provided by the editors
Printed and bound in the United States of America

10 9 8 7 6 5 4 3 2

To Jill, Gavin, and Ian Dunn

Contents

Preface

In 1983, we invited a group of experts to contribute to a study on the Falkland Islands War. The resulting work, published by Westview Press as The Military Lessons of the Falkland Islands War: Views from the United States, presented a uniquely comprehensive, American view of that engagement. When the United States landed forces on Grenada seventeen months later, the similarities between the Grenadian and Falklands operations were obvious. As a result, we invited the same team to examine Grenada. Several agreed to participate, and they, augmented by additional authors, have produced the following work.

The similarities between the Grenadian and Falklands operations are certainly noteworthy. In both cases, a traditional power faced a force from the Third World; in both the traditional force had to land on an island held by the opposing side; in both, the traditional power won; in both, the victory was considered a reverse for Third World nationalism; in both, the victory restored faith in the military ability and conviction of the traditional power; and in both, no really new military lessons were learned as a result of the conflict.

However, the differences between the two are even more significant. The British operation was one that lasted weeks as a major test of that nation's military ability. By contrast, the U.S. operation, which lasted only a few days, was a minor engagement. Similarly, while the British restricted the flow of information during the Falklands War, after the war they were quite candid about the military operation, openly admitting where mistakes had been made. Conversely, two years after the U.S. operation, questions remain in the minds of some observers.

This work begins by presenting basic information on the history of Grenada and on U.S., Soviet, and Cuban policies toward the region. To some this information may appear to be pedestrian, but we feel that it is necessary since, before 1983, so little was known about Grenada. The operation itself is then examined, with emphasis on the combat operations, indications and warning, and U.S. decisionmaking. Finally, the study examines the issue of the press, before concluding with a summary of the lessons of Grenada.

Frank Uhlig has cautioned that one should not make too much of a little thing, but one should not ignore a little thing merely because it is small. Though small, the events of Grenada in October 1983 have had and will continue to have significant regional and international implications. If this study contributes to the general understanding of Grenada and prompts additional discussion, then we, the editors, feel that we will have achieved our goal.

Peter M. Dunn
Bruce W. Watson

Acknowledgments

We wish to thank all of the contributors for participating in this study.

We are also indebted to Fred Praeger, Barbara Ellington, Dean Birkenkamp, and the staff of Westview Press for their advice, assistance, and encouragement.

Without the competent and patient support of the individuals who typed all of the drafts and final versions of the chapters of the book, this work would never have been possible. We are thus indebted to Gloria D. Porche, Cynthia A. Wilturner, Norma J. Dorey, Jacquline D. Cooper, and Deborah J. Phillips.

We also wish to thank Jill Dunn, Sue Watson, and Bruce Watson, Jr., who proofread and reviewed the manuscripts. Finally, we are grateful to Ian, Gavin, Bruce, Sue, Jennie, and Ella for their understanding and support.

P.M.D.
B.W.W.

1
The Setting

Courtney Glass

The island of Grenada lies in the Caribbean about 100 miles north of the Venezuelan coast. It is the most southerly of the islands in the Windward chain, and, although only about twice the size of Washington, D.C., it is the most densely populated of the Lesser Antilles. Known as the "Isle of Spice," Grenada is famous for its nutmeg, which it exports along with cacao, cinnamon, mace, sugar, rum, and a variety of other agricultural products. Since 1955, when a hurricane destroyed almost ninety percent of the nutmeg crop, bananas have become an important part of the economy. Although more than a third of the island's population.is engaged in agriculture, tourism has become increasingly significant in recent years. Even though Grenada differs from the majority of its neighbors in that it does not depend upon one single crop as its only source of income, the island faces serious economic problems. It suffers from severe balance of payment problems, high annual inflation, and a high unemployment rate.

About ninety-five percent of the population is of African and mixed descent. There are also a few small enclaves of the descendants of early European settlers, as well as those of East Indians who were brought in to replace the slaves as farm labor when they were freed in the early 19th century. The population of the island is almost 100,000, about twenty to thirty percent of which is concentrated around St. George's, the capital. The annual population growth rate is only about 0.5%, due primarily to a high emigration rate. Most of the population is Roman Catholic, and the offical language is English, although a French patois is still spoken by some of the older villagers.[1]

Grenada, originally called Concepcion, was discovered on August 15, 1498, by Christopher Columbus during his third voyage to the New World. Although the origin of the name "Grenada" is uncertain, it is believed that the Spanish renamed the island for their city of Grenada.

At the time of Grenada's discovery, it was inhabited by Carib Indians, a bellicose tribe of cannibals who had driven away the island's former, more peaceful inhabitants, the Arawaks. For the next 150 years, the island continued to be dominated by the Caribs, who thwarted all efforts to settle the island, including an attempt by a group of British merchants to form a settlement in

1

1609. In 1650 the French finally established the first successful settlement at St. George's when, after several encounters with the Caribs, they brought in reinforcements from Martinique and destroyed them. In 1674 Grenada officially became a subject of the French crown. One hundred years later, the island was captured by the British during the Seven Years' War and was formally ceded to Great Britain in 1763. In 1778, the French recaptured the island for a brief period, but restored it to the British in 1783.

Like the rest of the West Indies, Grenada was originally used for sugar cultivation. Many slaves were brought in from Africa in the 18th century to work the sugar plantations. However, a series of events significantly changed the course of Grenada's history. In the late 18th century, several natural disasters, including a plague of ants followed by a hurricane in 1780, destroyed the island's sugar industry. This led to the introduction of new crops to the island, including nutmeg, which flourished in the island's volcanic soil, as well as cacao and other spices. Since Grenada was much closer to Europe than the Dutch East Indies, the traditional source of spices, the island gained new economic importance. Additionally, the cultivation of the new crops eventually led to the development of land tenantries much smaller than those of the large sugar estates. As peasant proprietorship became increasingly common, a yeoman farmer class developed, establishing the basis of the society found on the island today.

In 1795, a rebellion against British rule was sparked by the abolition of slavery on the neighboring French-ruled islands. The revolt, which was led by a French planter and supported by the French in Martinique, was eventually quelled, but not before the Governor of Grenada and fifty other British subjects had been massacred. Slavery was finally abolished in 1833 and, due to the rapid growth of peasant proprietorship, Grenada experienced far less economic and social turmoil than did its neighbors.

In 1833, Grenada became a part of the British Windward Islands Administration and, in 1855, became its headquarters. The Governor of the Windward Islands ruled Grenada until the end of the colonial period in 1974. The Administration was finally dissolved in 1958 when the Federation of the West Indies was formed. When it collapsed in 1962, another attempt at federation among Britain's remaining dependencies in the eastern Caribbean was made, but also failed. On March 3, 1967, under the Associated Statehood Act, Grenada became a self-governing state in association with the United Kingdom. The act granted Grenada, along with five neighboring islands, full autonomy over its internal affairs, while Great Britain remained responsible for external affairs and the defense of the islands.

In August of 1967, general elections were held in Grenada. The Grenada United Labour Party (GULP) won the election and their leader, Eric M. Gairy, became Prime Minister. Gairy had formerly been a school teacher, a cane cutter, and a laborer in the Aruba oil refineries. He entered politics in the 1950s as a labor organizer, and began his battle against British rule and the island's mulatto elite. Quickly rising to power he was elected to the Legislative Council in the British colonial adminstration in 1951 and again in 1954. He became Chief Minister in 1961. A little more than a year later, however, the British suspended the Constitution and dismissed Gairy and his administration for misuse of public funds. He quickly rallied support, however, and returned to power in 1967 when his party won the general elections and he was elected Prime Minister.

Eric Gairy was a handsome, flamboyant, charismatic, self-educated man. A populist, he found his support among the largely illiterate agricultural workers. Over time, however, he became known for his eccentricities, and his authoritarian style of rule. He was interested in mysticism and spent much of his time studying spiritualism, "psychic" events, extraterrestrial life, and unidentified flying objects. Formerly a Roman Catholic, Gairy believed he had been chosen by God to rule Grenada and attributed the strength of his government to his "relationship with the divine." He professed to have mystical powers and claimed to send out "love waves" to his political opponents. This supposedly kept them from eating and sleeping.[2]

When Gairy came to power, Grenada faced many economic and social problems. The economy, based primarily on the export of agricultural products, was vulnerable to price fluctuations and demand on the world market. The difficulty of finding enough gainful employment for the people on a small island under such economic conditions created serious social problems, including the emigration of skilled labor, growing social unrest, and increasing opposition to the government.

The situation worsened in the late 1960s when middle class youths returned to the island with college degrees from the U.S. and Great Britain, where they had witnessed the turmoil over the Vietnam War and the rise of black consciousness. When they returned to their homeland, they found that there was no place for them in society. They could not find jobs because they were overqualified. The country was led by "aging trade union leaders who sweated it out in European-style clothes and were in awe of the British royal family." These men, to whom the British would soon turn over the reigns of power, had no inclination to go beyond the removal of the colonial officials and the island's colonial status and make any real changes in the political or economic situation on the island.[3] The response of the newly returned youths was increasing opposition to Eric Gairy and his government.

Gairy met this growing opposition to the government with repression. He created a secret police force, which became known as the Mongoose Gang, named after the animal known for the viciousness of its attacks. Many of its members were recruited from the Grenadian underworld. The secret police became the symbol of the brutal authoritarian hand with which Gairy ruled his island.

Meanwhile the economy deteriorated as a result of Gairy's inefficient and dishonest management of the spice and growing tourist industries. Gairy amassed quite a fortune for himself and had become a millionaire by the age of fifty-one. He owned several businesses on the island, including hotels, guest houses, a beauty salon, and a night club.[4]

Although opposition to Gairy continued to mount, he managed to retain power through skillful political maneuvering. He exploited the lack of organization and unity among his opponents, as well as the absence of any clear ideology or strong leader among them. The middle class official opposition party, the Grenada National Party (GNP), was led by the gentlemanly Herbert Blaize. The party was incompetent and ineffective, however, and followed civilized rules which Gairy refused to recognize.[5] It was not surprising that Gairy won the 1972 elections. Although not mentioned during his campaign, Gairy subsequently declared he would lead the island to independence from Great Britain, which was to be granted in 1974. His opponents strongly objected to independence under the Gairy regime, however, which they labeled as despotic and bankrupt, claiming that it would only mean independence for Gairy. Strikes and protests broke out; the island was nearly brought to a standstill. But due to Gairy's political agility and his security police, he managed to survive this threat to his regime.

In spite of Gairy's victory, his support continued to deteriorate, particularly among the agricultural workers who formed the foundation of his following. Meanwhile, a group of dissatified young intellectuals began organizing an opposition movement. In March 1972, Unison Whiteman, a 32-year-old economist with a degree from Howard University, and Selwyn Strachan, a sugar factory clerk in his early twenties, founded a movement known as the Joint Endeavour for Welfare, Education and Liberation (JEWEL). They found enthusiastic support among school teachers and manual laborers. Several months later, Maurice Bishop, a 25-year-old barrister who had recently returned from seven years in England where he had worked among blacks in London; and Kendrick Radix, age 31, founded the Movement for Assemblies of the People (MAP), which advocated a Tanzanian-style grass roots democracy. In March 1973, the two groups merged to form the New Jewel Movement (NJM), and espoused pragmatic nationalism.[6]

When the NJM was first established, it had proclaimed itself to be a nationalistic movement, providing a radical, populist alternative to Gairy. It adopted a socialist manifesto which was based on a variety of socialist theories, with particularly large elements of Tanzanian Christian Socialism.[7] Part of its goal was to educate the peasantry. The group espoused humanitarianism and promoted popular mobilization through grass roots organizations and decentralized village assemblies. In 1974, the NJM decided to move further toward the theories of Lenin, yet did not commit itself to a full Marxist-Leninist position.[8] By 1976, there was pressure from some members for radicalization of the party. For example, Bernard Coard, who was an important figure in the party and would later emerge as Maurice Bishop's rival and eventual enemy, promoted a shift to "scientific socialism" and Leninization of the party.[9]

This ambivalence remained unresolved. By 1979, the NJM still had not formulated a clear and uniform ideology, although at the time of the coup, the NJM described itself as nationalist and socialist-leaning (but not Marxist-Leninist). Maurice Bishop later declared that his government intended to establish "socialist democracy" on the island.

Since the New Jewel Movement was considered leftist by the labor unions and business community of St. George's, it was excluded from the organization of the anti-Gairy strikes and demonstrations during the next year. However, in February 1974, as the date for independence approached, the intensity of the strikes increased. In December 1973, the Committee of 22 Organizations, a broad opposition front composed of trade unions-- including dock workers, utility workers, and civil servants, along with businessmen, clergy, and professional bodies--forced Gairy to agree to disband his secret police force. When he failed to carry out his promise, he was given an ultimatum to resign. When he refused to do so, the general strike was resumed. Demonstrations continued into 1974, and, in late January, Maurice Bishop's father was killed in a violent clash with the police. Gairy meanwhile rushed through Parliament a number of measures aimed at crushing the strike. Bending under government pressure, utility and government workers were forced to withdraw their support from what threatened to be a total shutdown of the island.

On February 7, 1974, Grenada was granted its independence from Great Britain thereby becoming a state within the Commonwealth of Nations with a parliamentary form of government. The event was not a completely joyful occasion, however, as the strikes and violence against the Gairy regime continued. Independence was celebrated by candlelight, because the electric power workers were on strike and Maurice Bishop was arrested by the police and spent independence day in jail. Additionally, due to the unrest on the island, the British cancelled the visit of Prince Richard of Gloucester, who had been scheduled to visit Grenada to participate in the independence celebrations.

Gairy continued as Prime Minister after independence, and, true to the islanders' fears, the political and economic situation continued to deteriorate and became critical. The banana industry was experiencing difficulties due to the declining value of Grenada's currency, and while the nutmeg and cacao exports were still bringing good prices, the once-thriving tourist industry had been crippled by the widespread unrest of 1973 and 1974. Additionally, inflation was sky-rocketing and the country's deficit was enormous.[10]

The political situation also deteriorated as the 1976 general elections approached. The Mongoose Gang was increasingly active and was infamous for its brutality. It violently disrupted the political meetings of the opposition in an effort to intimidate them and beat up or shot anyone who opposed the Gairy regime. However, despite Gairy's efforts to prevent it, the various opposition groups finally managed to unite themselves into a coalition known as the Popular Alliance. This front included the left-leaning NJM and two conservative groups, the Grenada National Party (GNP) and the United People's Party (UPP). The alliance accused Gairy of being erratic and authoritarian and blamed him for the country's economic stagnation. They also charged him with the human rights abuses committed by his secret police force and with forming alliances with "rightist" governments such as that of

Pinochet's Chile, which alledgedly helped train the Mongoose Gang.

In the general elections of December 1976, amidst charges of electoral fraud, Gairy and his ruling Grenada United Labor Party (GULP) were able to win only a narrow victory against the Popular Alliance. Out of a total of fifteen seats, GULP lost five of its fourteen seats in the House of Representatives. Maurice Bishop was elected to Parliament and became leader of the parliamentary opposition.[11] This ended Gairy's near total control of the legisature and marked a significant victory for the opposition.

In the period following the 1976 elections, Grenada drew a great deal of international attention. In 1977, Gairy invited the General Assembly of the Organization of American States to hold its meeting in Grenada, using the opportunity to obtain economic assistance for his island.[12] Gairy's opponents, however, also drew international attention to the island and embarrassed Gairy by holding a demonstration against his regime's human rights record. Gairy had become known for his fascination with unidentified flying objects (UFOs) and, in 1977, he formally asked the United Nations General Assembly to study UFO phenomena thoughout the world and to designate 1978 as "The Year of the UFO." His fanatical concern with UFOs further undermined his credibility among international financiers and foreign governments which might otherwise have served as sources of economic assistance for Grenada.[13] Gairy's mismanagement of the economy had already caused concern among potential local merchants and international lenders alike.

By 1979, the increasing corruption and brutality of the Gairy regime, along with the island's dire economic situation, had alienated many of Gairy's followers and eroded his support in the working class. The NJM now enjoyed much of Gairy's previous support and became an alternative to his oppressive rule.[14]

In March, 1979, Gairy went to New York to discuss UFOs at the United Nations. Informed of rumors that Gairy had ordered his people to kill him, Maurice Bishop, with the NJM, took advantage of Gairy's absence and seized control of the government on March 13, 1979.

Forty-six armed members of the NJM, who called themselves the People's Revolutionary Army, seized the barracks at True Blue Army Headquarters. About 100 soldiers who had been sleeping and were unarmed were arrested, as were Gairy's cabinet members, who were routed out of their beds.[15] The police headquarters at Fort George was also taken. The island's radio station, Radio Grenada, was seized and renamed Radio Free Grenada, and Maurice Bishop himself broadcast the announcement of the overthrow of Eric Gairy. Bishop also stated that all democratic freedoms, including freedom of elections, religion, and political opinion, would be fully restored to the people.[16] However, this was never to happen. Later that week, Bishop stated that the revolution was irreversible, implying that the NJM would not be replaced, democratically or otherwise.[17] This shifting of policy demonstrates an ideological ambivalence that would eventually bring about the downfall of Bishop's revolution.

This ambivalence, however, was unnoticed in March 1979. In essence, the people of Grenada had gone from the tradition of benevolent colonialism under Great Britain to a not-so-benevolent dictatorship under Gairy, but had never become politicized. The majority were probably unaware of the ideological orientation of the group that had just taken over the government. Their primary concern was to be free of Eric Gairy. Thus, the people welcomed the NJM, its revolution, and particularly Maurice Bishop who, to Grenadians and foreigners alike, became the symbol of the revolution.[18]

From that day in March 1979 to October 1983, the political scene in Grenada was controlled exclusively by the NJM; all other political activity was prohibited.[19] The NJM was run by the sixteen member Central Committee but the principal day-to-day Committee decisions were made by an inner circle of eight members which comprised the Political Bureau. This was, in reality, the governing body of Grenada.[20] Maurice Bishop, who was appointed Prime Minister, had the role of approving most (though not all) of the decisions of the Political Bureau. However, in spite of all the organization at the top, any formal link between the party (whose membership in 1979 numbered only forty-five, and only seventy in 1983) and the mass of Grenadians, was unclearly defined.

The direction in which the new leadership wanted to take the country was also ill-defined. The NJM had wanted to establish a new, non-aligned government which would be unique to Grenada. Before they actually came to power in 1979, the party had a program that they intended to implement when they achieved power. But when power came, there were many discrepancies between their goals and reality. First, the NJM initially had wanted to give the grass roots elements of society direct power and establish village assemblies from which power would flow upward. However, when the coup occurred it was actually the Central Committee and the Political Bureau which were given the power to lead the government. There were no village or people's assemblies, only Cuban-style mass organizations, such as workers' councils, national student councils, and women's organizations, and even these were led by members of the inner circle. Thus, there was no direct democracy, but rather a hierarchy of command which flowed downward instead of upward, with power remaining at the top.[21]

The NJM had also originally espoused the idea of collective leadership with no premier. However, after the coup, Maurice Bishop was appointed Prime Minister, apparently without dissent within the party. This issue was to reappear, however, and become a source of conflict that eventually tore the party apart. Nonetheless, in the early stages, it was probably the appointment of the popular Bishop as Prime Minister which kept the people's support for the new government.

Another contradiction was that, in spite of the party's promise to hold elections, none were scheduled and no effort was made to legitimize the government. The NJM suspended the constitution and promised a new one which would be followed by elections. But even the drafting of the new constitution was delayed, allegedly out of concern that the discussion involved would lead to dissension. [22]

This led to another problem. There were no provisions for changing the leadership, nor were vehicles provided for voicing opposition--in fact, no opposition was tolerated. As the aura of the revolution waned, many became aware of the new government's shortcomings, as they found themselves in an increasingly socialist society. Subsequent objections led to numerous arrests and soon the People's Revolutionary Government found itself charged with the same human rights violations with which its predecessor had been accused.

The NJM goals were somewhat clearer in respect to the economy. At first, these were more closely met, but not without certain problems and contradictions. In its original ideology, the NJM emphasized the importance of agriculture and opposed "the typical Third World emphasis on what it called 'prestige dream' projects."[23] This is part of the reason, espoused in its 1973 manifesto, for its rejection of the idea of building a new international airport. But a change of course was taken when it implemented its policy. Rather than grass roots agricultural development, the PRG's energies were taken up by a major airport that became the centerpiece of the nation's development plan. It would serve, they argued, a major new initiative in tourism which had been rejected in 1973 as encouraging "national-cultural prostitution."[24]

Nevertheless, the new government made efforts toward improving agriculture and established food production as a high priority. State farms were begun on idle lands acquired by the government. The new leaders also wanted to increase the number of food processing plants, develop fisheries, and ultimately, reduce dependency on foreign goods.

While the role of the state in the economy became increasingly dominant, the NJM leaders, nonetheless, recognized the value of a mixed economy. However, in spite of the government's efforts to encourage the private sector, the business community was concerned about the government's drift to the left and was hesitant to invest. The result was a significant drop in the level of private business activity. From about 1980 onward, the U.S. Government, which was also concerned about Grenada's leftist drift, made efforts to restrict international economic aid to the island. This further stifled the economy.

In the public sector, however, under the new Financial Minister Bernard Coard, government expenditures were tightly controlled and many of the economic requirements of the International Monetary Fund (IMF) were closely followed. Due primarily to Coard's financial acumen and his honest, efficient, and cautious management of the economy, Grenada's financial position was improved. In fact, Grenada achieved a budget surplus the first year after the revolution and the economy grew by two percent.[25]

Efforts to improve the standard of living began to pay off as unemployment and illiteracy declined. Mass mobilization was used to encourage the people to increase their productivity and to raise their "social consciousness." But this eventually lost its effectiveness however, when economic conditions stagnated and then worsened, and social programs began to suffer. The people become disillusioned with the government and mass mobilization eventually become unpopular.[26]

In spite of the promise it had shown in the early period of the revolution, the economy was faced with many fundamental problems. Its most significant dilemma was essentially the same one which plagued its politics: the conflict between pragmatism and idealism. The party's doctrine was getting in the way of its actions. For example, in order to reach its goal of cooperative farming, the government should have encouraged the most efficient farmers. But they were inevitably the farmers who farmed large tracts of land and to have encouraged them would have been to promote class ideas in the countryside, which was contrary to party doctrine.[27] The result of these contradictions was the existence of the form of socialism without its substance.[28]

It was at this point that some party leaders began to question both the revolution and each other and to accuse each other of responsibility for the shortcomings. Specialists were then invited from Russia, Cuba, and the Eastern Bloc to help them solve their problems.[29] Yet, in spite of this outside assistance, it became clear that the revolution was failing. This recognition of impending failure drove certain elements within the party to extremism.

The leader of the developing extremist element was Deputy Prime Minister Bernard Coard, who had favored a strong Marxist-Leninist approach to the revolution. He also had encouraged an intellectual approach and, in the year before the revolution, had established a study group called the Organization for Educational Development and Research, for the study of socialism. From this developed a strong core of Coard supporters. Additionally, although he did not command the large following which the charismatic Bishop had among the masses, he had a solid following of key elements within the party and eventually garnered enough power that his group became the dominant faction.

Coard impatiently wanted to develop a strong Leninist system. Finally, in July 1982, he resigned in disgust from the Political Bureau and the Central Committee, remaining, however, as Deputy Prime Minister and Minister of Finance.[30]

Bishop, meanwhile, had never retreated from his democratic socialist leanings, but had reservations about moving to a full fledged Leninist system.[31] It was this resistance to full Leninization that was responsible for finally sparking the conflict. Several factors had contributed to building tension within the party. First, there were severe economic problems. This added to the disillusionment of the masses who saw that the government's promises of a brighter economic future were not coming true. Also, some members of the party, particularly the Coard faction, felt that the revolution was moving too slowly; some even feared it was failing. There was disagreement on what direction the revolution should go in order to get it back on course, and this split the party into two factions, the Coard faction, which was pushing for swift movement towards strict Leninism, and the Bishop faction, which wanted to move more slowly and cautiously, and combine elements of democratic socialism into the system. This ideological struggle embodied the personal struggle which emerged between the two leaders: the pragmatic Bishop vs. the idealistic Coard; the charismatic Bishop vs. the intellectual Coard.

It was in the summer of 1983 that the party's leadership became seriously concerned about the revolution. In May and June, Coard went to Moscow, ostensibly for health reasons. While he was away, Bishop went to Washington on a campaign to try to patch up relations with the United States. This was seen by the more extreme elements in the party as a dangerous step, and they accused Bishop of showing signs of "right opportunism." Thus, it was at this point that some members of the party decided that it was time to stand back and reassess where the revolution was going.

In mid-September, the first in a series of meetings of the Central Committee was held. The Coard faction, which took control of the meeting, said that the party was disintegrating, that the Central Committee was showing no leadership, and that its ideological development needed attention lest the party disintegrate altogether. They said that the mass organizations were in trouble and that the masses had regressed ideologically. They placed the blame for these and other woes on Bishop. The basic charges against Bishop were that he had become a "right opportunist," and instead of carefully guiding the party toward Marxism-Leninism, he had allowed it to deteriorate into a social democratic party. They also charged him with failing to tighten ties "with the World Socialist Movement, especially Cuba, the USSR and the GDR."[32]

The solution proposed by Bishop's opponents called for the transformation of the NJM along Leninist lines. The way to do that most effectively would be to establish the joint leadership of Bishop and Coard: Coard would be given charge of the organization of the party and take responsibility for its ideological development, while Bishop would work with the masses and also retain responsibility for foreign affairs.

Bishop and his supporters argued unsuccessfully against this move. On September 25th, the day before he was to leave on a trip to Eastern Europe, and after a great deal of pressure was put on him, Bishop finally assented to the proposition of joint leadership.

The issue was to be reopened in a meeting of the Political Bureau. Before this meeting could be convened, however, the Coard faction moved to take power. While Bishop was still on his trip, Coard, who continued as the Finance Minister, approved a pay raise for the Army. On the night before the meeting of the Political Bureau, Coard's supporters told key members of the Army they were no longer to take orders from Bishop, but only from the Central Committee. "They were to defend the working class as a whole and not the life of any individual leader."[33] The Coard faction also began to demand the expulsion from the party of all the members who opposed joint leadership. These steps went a long way toward undermining Bishop's already weakened position.

In that meeting of the Political Bureau on October 12th, another step was taken to undermine Bishop. This was the discrediting of George Louison, one of Bishop's staunchest supporters. Additionally, Bishop was accused of starting a rumor that Coard planned to assassinate Bishop. Bishop was forced to dispel the rumor by denying it on a radio broadcast that same evening.

The next day, Maurice Bishop was placed under house arrest, was stripped of his positions, and was expelled from the NJM.

The following days were hallmarked by growing tension and confusion. The Coard faction had decided that they would "use force if necessary to impose their will. If the people won't accept it, the people will have to be made to accept it," was their sentiment.[34]

Negotiations continued between the two factions to resolve the crisis. Meanwhile, however, there was growing indignation in the streets over Bishop's arrest. In fact, public outrage reached such proportions that Coard resigned as Deputy Prime Minister.

On October 19th, protests, which had begun the day before, continued. A large crowd went to Mount Royal, the Prime Minister's residence, where Bishop and one of his colleagues, Jacqueline Creft, were being held, freed them, and drove them to Fort Rupert. The small PRA garrison at the fort, unsure of how to handle the situation, allowed the crowd to enter. Bishop then gave orders to some of his followers to distribute weapons so that they could defend themselves in case of an attack.

An attack was indeed on the way. Four of the Army's PRA armored cars sped across town toward Fort Rupert and, when they arrived, began firing into the crowd. Hundreds of people rushed to try to escape.

Bishop, horrified that the soldiers had turned their guns on the people, ordered his followers not to return the fire. He told them to surrender. Some were allowed to leave and return to town, but Bishop and his senior colleagues were detained. They were then taken to a courtyard and there, next to a basketball court and in front of a mural of Che Guevara, Maurice Bishop and several of his colleagues were executed.

Internal political instability followed.

NOTES

1. U.S. Department of State, Grenada: Background Notes (Washington, D.C.: Government Printing Office, March 1980), p. 2.

2. Karen De Young, "Pleasant, Poor Grenada Takes Lead," Washington Post, 25 June 1977, p. A10.

3. "The New Jewel Movement Changes the Rules," Latin American Newsletters, Ltd. (13 April 1979): 119.

4. "Grenada: The Fall of a Warlock," Time (2 April 1979): 47.

5. "Grenada: Confusion Before Independence," <u>Latin American Newsletters, Ltd</u>. (7 December 1973): 389.

6. <u>Latin American Newsletters, Ltd</u>. (13 April 1979): 119.

7. Ibid., p. 84.

8. Jiri and Virginia Valenta, "Leninism in Grenada," <u>Problems of Communism</u> (July-August 1984): 2.

9. Ibid., p. 3.

10. Ibid., p. 119.

11. "Gairy Narrowly Reelected," <u>Facts on File, Inc.</u> (11 December 1976): 925 C1.

12. Ibid.

13. Lewis H. Dinguid, "Logistical Question Mark is Facing OAS in Grenada," <u>Washington Post</u>, 1 May 1977, p. B5.

14. Hugh O'Shaughnessy, <u>Grenada: Revolution, Invasion and Aftermath</u> (London: Sphere Books, Ltd., 1984), p. 75.

15. Ibid., p. 76.

16. <u>Time</u> (2 April 1979): 76.

17. O'Shaughnessy, p. 79.

18. Karen De Young, "Grenada Enjoys Change, Still Keeps New Course," <u>Washington Post</u>, 1 May 1979, p A16.

19. O'Shaughnessy, p. 83.

20. Ibid., p. 84.

21. Anthony P. Maingot, "Options for Grenada--The Need to be Cautious," <u>Caribbean Review</u> (Fall 1983): 27

22. O'Shaughnessy, p 86.

23. Maingot, p. 26.

24. Ibid., p. 27.

25. O'Shaughnessy, p. 86.

26. Valenta and Valenta, p. 5.

27. V.S. Naipaul, "An Island Betrayed," <u>Harper's</u> (March 1984): 70.

28. Ibid., p. 70.

29. Ibid.

30. O'Shaughnessy, p. 109.

31. Ibid., p. 106.

32. Valenta and Valenta, p. 17.

33. O'Shaughnessy, p. 123.

34. Ibid., p. 129.

2
U.S. Policy Toward the Caribbean: Continuity and Change

Robert Pastor

INTRODUCTION

In the twentieth century, U.S. policy toward the Caribbean has been the sum of the answers to a set of recurring questions. These questions were how to ensure stability; discourage foreign penetration; promote economic development, human rights, and democracy; gain respect for U.S. investment, the American flag, and U.S. citizens; and maintain good relations. The answers have differed from one administration to the next, and particularly when administrations represent different political parties. But the change is seldom as great as a new administration claims when it takes office, nor is it as insignificant as an administration suggests when its power is waning or its policy is found wanting, and it seeks additional strength through bipartisanship and assertions of continuity. The task for analysts is to distinguish between the true and false threads of continuity connecting diverse administrations and the genuine and trivial changes.

Though Americans perceive themselves as idealistic, U.S. foreign policy always has been guided by a realistic appraisal of U.S. interests. In U.S. policy toward the Caribbean, these two strands of idealism and realism have been woven together in a most curious way. Americans tend to see only the idealism in the policy while Caribbean people see only the realism, and the reality is neither and both.

In the early 1960s, the Caribbean underwent a profound transformation, and U.S. policy is adjusting only slowly to the new realities. Two-thirds of the "old" Caribbean--Cuba and the Dominican Republic, not Haiti--experienced a change-of-life, as old autocracies collapsed, and a new Caribbean of about a dozen microstates emerged.

This chapter is an examination of the historical reasons for U.S. engagement, the patterns of U.S. involvement, and the changing interests in the Caribbean. Two contemporary strategies--the liberal Democratic and the conservative Republican--are contrasted and finally the Reagan administration's approach to the region is assessed. Although U.S. economic, and to a certain extent, strategic policy has begun to focus on the entire Caribbean basin --Mexico, Central America, and the Caribbean--this chapter is primarily about U.S. policies toward the Caribbean, the islands and those English and Dutch-speaking countries on the rim--Belize, Guyana, and Suriname--which are tied to the islands by a long colonial heritage and recent independence.

MOTIVES VIVENDI

On January 29, 1981, at his first press conference as president, Ronald Reagan was asked whether his meeting with Jamaican Prime Minister Edward Seaga encouraged him to develop a policy toward the Caribbean. He replied that Seaga's electoral victory--four days before his own--represented a "great reverse in the Caribbean situation ... The turn-around of a nation that had gone certainly in the direction of the Communist movement ... This opens the door," Reagan said, finally bringing his answer back to the question, "for us to have a policy in the Mediterranean." Sigmund Freud could have explained Reagan's slip. So could Alfred T. Mahan, an influential naval strategist, who wrote at the turn of the century that the time had come for the United States to act as if the Caribbean were "America's Mediterranean Sea."

Mahan educated the political leaders of his and succeeding generations about the strategic implications of the Caribbean for U.S. interests. Because of the increasing importance of the Atlantic and Pacific areas to the United States, Mahan wrote, "Central and Caribbean America, now intrinsically unimportant, are brought in turn into greater prominence ..." And this is as it has been. Primary U.S. interests in the region have not stemmed from any desire to extract resources or to implant a political philosophy, although history is replete with examples of both.

From Mahan's guiding vision to Reagan's freudian slip, the United States has been motivated not so much to control the region but to keep things from veering out of control where they could be exploited by others viewed as hostile. While some consider this imperialistic or hegemonic, in fact there is no nation in the region or elsewhere that remains passive or indifferent to the possible establishment nearby of a regime which is hostile or tied to a powerful adversary. Of course, the difference between the United States and the other nations in the region are legion, but most stem from the wide disparity in wealth and power. As a consequence of that disparity, the United States has a capability to influence political and economic developments in the Caribbean in a manner and to a degree which no Caribbean nation could contemplate vis-a-vis the United States.

The motive for U.S. engagement sometimes has been altruistic--to promote democracy or development, but more often it has been fear, a seemingly disproportionate fear for such a large power in such a small sea, but a fear nonetheless that events could turn hostile to U.S. interests. It follows that American foreign policy in the Caribbean always has seemed to err on the anxious side. In the nineteenth century, the United States was anxious to prevent "another Haiti," an independent black republic. In the early twentieth century, the United States was anxious to prevent governments in the region from defaulting to European creditors lest that be used as a pretext for European intervention. (On that rationale, U.S. Marines intervened on twenty separate occasions in the entire Caribbean area--including Mexico and Central America--in the twenty years following the Spanish-American War of 1898). During the second World War, the United States was anxious to keep out Nazi Germany, and after that, Soviet Russia. After the Soviets turned up ninety miles offshore, the United States became anxious to avoid "another Cuba," and U.S. interest and activity in the region has intensified whenever there appeared a chance of repetition.

The instruments and strategies used to pursue this interest of avoiding a hostile or unfriendly presence near the U.S. southern border have changed, of course, as the world and the region have changed. From the Spanish-American War in 1898 to the Good Neighbor Policy in 1933, the blunt instrument of U.S. military force was used whenever diplomacy, threats, or nonrecognition failed to achieve U.S. objectives. After a four year occupation and installation of a democratic government in Cuba in 1902, U.S. troops left, but returned four years later for another three year period. U.S. troops landed in Haiti in 1915 and stayed nineteen years, and in the Dominican Republic, the military occupation lasted from 1916 to 1924.

In each instance, U.S. involvement followed a pattern.[2] First, the U.S. warned feuding factions in the nations as well as foreign powers about the consequences of continued violence or instability. If the situation did not stabilize, the United States employed the logic of the Roosevelt Corollary (to the Monroe Doctrine), which asserted U.S. responsibility to correct "wrongdoing or impotence" on the part of Caribbean governments to deny other powers a pretext for intervention. The marines landed with the most vigorous protestations that the United States was uninterested in annexation; the defensiveness doubtless was due to the annexation of Puerto Rico, the purchase of the Virgin Islands, and also the continued need by the United States to distinguish its own expansion from European imperialism. The next turn in the road of intervention was the discovery--each time as if for the first--that it was easier to get in than it was to get out. After much difficulty, the grounds for exit were paved by legitimizing a government in an election supervised by the marines, and the establishment of an "apolitical" military guard, which stayed apolitical only as long as the marines stayed.

The interventions proved more and more costly and less and less effective. The experience in Nicaragua, from 1927 to 1933, finally impelled the U.S. government to recognize the net benefits of nonintervention. Although Secretary of State Cordell Hull's statement on nonintervention at the Montevideo Conference often is cited as the beginning of the policy, the real test was passed by Hull and Roosevelt in 1933 when they rejected at three different times the recommendation of U.S. Ambassador to Havana Sumner

Welles to land marines in Cuba, allegedly to protect American citizens, but really to control events.[3]

Interventions became more costly because of the strengthening of national leaders and institutions in the affected countries, and because opinion in the United States and internationally became increasingly critical. Moreover, the United States could not credibly oppose Nazi and Japanese expansion if it were similarly guilty. Therefore, the United States looked to other instruments and strategies for promoting stability in the region. The most traditional tool was U.S. investment. In addition, during the years of the Good Neighbor Policy, the Roosevelt administration negotiated bilateral commercial arrangements, provided credits, and began some educational exchanges.

However, in the Caribbean, stability was maintained not so much by trade, investment, or mutual respect, but by the strong arms of dictators like Fulgencio Batista in Cuba, Rafael Trujillo in the Dominican Republic, and the Duvaliers in Haiti. With the decline of Batista and the assassination of Trujillo, instability returned to Cuba and the Dominican Republic and so too did the United States--by proxy intervention in the Bay of Pigs invasion in April 1961 and with 23,000 marines four years later in the Dominican Republic.

The resort to military intervention in the 1960s, as in the first decades of the century, underscored the continued physical and psychic presence of U.S. power in the region, but that similarity should not obscure a more fundamental difference. Simply, by the 1960s the utility of U.S. military intervention declined to the point that it had become a blunderbuss, shooting the United States even as it pulled the trigger. The Bay of Pigs was an unalloyed fiasco. While the Dominican Republic did not become a "second Cuba" in the mid-1960s, most students of the intervention conclude that this was never likely; the only outcome with a high probability was that U.S. intervention would damage severely U.S. relations with Latin America, as it did.[4] And finally, while President Kennedy set as one of his priority goals the replacement of Duvalier as president of Haiti, he remained in power long after Kennedy was shot.[5]

Some have interpreted these failures as signifying a decline of U.S. power, or in the case of the Dominican Republic, a departure of wisdom. In actuality, they represent not a retreat for the United States, but rather an advancement of nationalism in the Third World, and a recognition, albeit an extremely reluctant recognition, that even U.S. power could not alter this trend. There are few clearer illustrations of this point than the fact that seven U.S. presidents, representing the full spectrum of legitimate political views in the country, have not used the full weight of U.S. military force to replace Castro's regime.

With the decline in the utility of force and the increase in the importance of economic development and indigenous military capabilities, the United States turned increasingly to new instruments of economic and military aid to influence political developments. These instruments initially provided some leverage, but this too declined over time, as Caribbean governments found other alternatives, and as their economies became more developed and diversified and their politics more sensitive to constituent pressures.

In the mid-1970s the United States began using a new instrument--moral suasion, the mobilization of international public opinion behind the universal norms of human rights. Curiously, this new instrument had more impact on Duvalier in Haiti than any previous one.[6] The mobilization of international opinion by the Carter administration may have helped preserve and indeed institutionalize democracy in the Dominican Republic in 1978--a feat that the U.S. Marines never could achieve. The strength of the human rights policy is that it encompasses the entire debate, thus recognizing that the most effective influence in contemporary U.S.-Caribbean relations is indirect.

A DIFFERENT CARIBBEAN

In the early 1960s, all but Haiti in the "old" Caribbean were brought into the modern era, albeit with considerable internal violence and external involvement. With the establishment of a Communist regime in Cuba tied to the Soviet Union, the first tenet of U.S. policy in the Caribbean was violated and the entire approach impugned so completely that Americans still cannot comprehend the extent to which their vision of the region was rendered obsolete. Whereas Cuba joined the bloc of modern Communist states, the Dominican Republic joined the group of modern democracies, but only after a brief period of regression to violence and instability. The United States also followed the Dominican Republic backwards briefly in time, undertaking its first military intervention in the region in over thirty years.

The last fragment of the "old" Caribbean, Haiti, seems stuck somewhere in history, and neither carrot nor stick by the United States has had much of lasting impact on that country's tragic politics or stagnant economy.

From 1898 until 1962, there were only three independent nations in the Caribbean. Today there are sixteen. Political independence has played a cruel joke on the Caribbean, however, because very few of these nations are economically independent, and some question whether that is even possible.

The Commonwealth Caribbean, representing ten states, has a total population of 5.7 million, about the population of Hong Kong with considerably less economic muscle. If one adds Hispaniola, Suriname, and the Netherlands Antilles, the population increases to 16.4 million, smaller than Peru. Other than bauxite in several nations and oil in Trinidad, the nations generally lack resources, and outside of Hispaniola, fertile agricultural land is scarce.

Even while condemning colonialism, each nation still retains a special link to a metropole. France and Holland have formalized their relationships with their colonies by incorporating them into the mother country; Suriname continues, notwithstanding its revolution, to be closely tied economically and by migration with the Netherlands. Cuba, of course, has a special economic and political relationship with the Soviet Union. Great Britain continues it special bond with its overseas commonwealth countries. To the extent that Haiti has a special relationship with anything other than poverty, it is with France, and also the United States. The U.S. Virgin Islands and Puerto Rico are U.S. territory, and the Dominican Republic remains tied closely to the United States, although the relationship is not formalized. Some might argue that it ended with the demise of the Sugar Act in 1974, which had granted the Dominican Republic such a large and secure share of the U.S. market.

The United States has been ambivalent about the movement toward independence in the Commonwealth Caribbean. While historically supporting movements for independence, the United States also understood that independence for these microstates might represent only a temporary resting place on the way to a new dependency relationship. The United States therefore, hesitated to come to the support of the new nations for fear it would encourage the British to abandon their responsibilities too rapidly. However, the process has been ineluctable.

The fivefold increase in the number of states in the Caribbean in the last two decades is one of several reasons why the United States has been compelled to forge a more complex approach to the area than was needed in the past. Another reason is that the region--together with Mexico and Central America--has become the largest source of migration to the United States, creating new human bonds connecting the United States to the nations of the region and reflecting a mutual dependence which is a new dimension in the historical relationship.

The Johnson, Nixon, and Ford administrations did not feel moved to fashion a governmental response to the emergence of a new Caribbean, nor did events move them. However, both the Carter and Reagan administrations devoted time and energy to formulating and implementing policies. In identifying similarities between the two policies, which are so ostensibly different, one might stumble upon that ambiguous concept, "the national interest." In defining the difference between the two strategies, one might better understand the realm of genuine choice--as opposed to false options--in policymaking.

INTERESTS

U.S. national interests in the Caribbean are not immutable; they have changed over time, slowly, sometimes imperceptibly.[7] Many Americans for example, continue to view the Panama Canal as an invaluable strategic asset and the eastern approach to the canal around Hispaniola and Cuba as critical sealanes. However, with the advent of aircraft carriers which are too large to transit the canal, U.S. interests in the canal changed from strategic to primarily economic, from facilitating the movement of the U.S. fleet to providing a marginal economic advantage in the shipment of supplies. U.S. interests do not change, however, as sharply from one administration to the next as the rhetoric of the incoming administration might suggest; what changes is the value attached to each interest and the strategy for pursuing these interests.

The national interests which guided both the Carter and Reagan administrations include the following: (1) avoidance of the emergence of hostile regimes tied to the Soviet Union; (2) enhancement of the security of the region; (3) promotion of human rights and democracy; (4) encouragement of social reforms; and (5) support for economic development through private investment and public assistance. Although neither administration ignored any of these interests, the Reagan administration has attached the highest priority to the pursuit of the first two interests while the Carter administration gave greater importance to the last three. Both administrations would acknowledge that the security of the United States necessarily takes precedence. In giving less priority to the first two interests, the Carter administration argued that the best way to pursue them, at a moment when the threat to the United States or the possibility of conflict in the region is remote, is by stressing the last three interests.

The difference in the priority given to these interests reflects two divergent tendencies in U.S. foreign policy--a liberal, Democratic and a conservative, Republican tendency. These attained their clearest definition in the policies toward Latin America of the Carter and Reagan administrations. When these tendencies become fixed on one or two interests, excluding others, they verge on becoming ideologies. At that time, political forces in the United States representing the other interests respond with sufficient force to encourage greater balance, in rhetoric if not in policy.

The Reagan administration's policy represents the clearest case of a tendency almost becoming an ideology. The initial strategy of drawing a line in El Salvador and defining the problem exclusively in east-west terms provoked such a strong national (and international) reaction that by 1982, the administration was insisting on human rights and land reforms there, and was trumpeting an economic program--the Caribbean Basin Initiative--to deal with the socioeconomic roots of the problem. Similarly, the Carter administration had placed so much stress on human rights and so little on traditional security concerns that it was pressed even by liberal senators to give an unwarranted amount of attention to a Soviet brigade in Cuba.

THE CARTER TENDENCY AND STRATEGY

The Carter administration was the first in U.S. history to focus on the Caribbean in the absence of a security threat, or as it turned out, before rather than after such a threat.[8] This was due to several policy and personal reasons, but also to the recognition that the region had been changed by the creation of the microstates.

In 1977, Rosalynn Carter began a seven-nation tour of Latin America with a visit to Jamaica where she informed Prime Minister Manley of an increase in economic aid and invited him to meet with the president at the White House at the end of the year. U.S. Ambassador to the United States Andrew Young followed with a much more extensive trip to the Caribbean basin. By the end of the year, Carter had encouraged the World Bank to establish what came to be known as the Caribbean Group for Cooperation in Economic Development, a group of thirty-one nations and fifteen international institutions which increased aid flows to the region. The aim of the Caribbean Group was to encourage regional approaches to economic problems, by being uniquely multilateral at both ends. Donor nations coordinated their individual aid efforts, which quadrupled between 1977 and 1980, and recipient nations decided which regional projects deserved highest priority.

In 1980, the Carter administration encouraged the establishment of a private group, called Caribbean/Central American Action, headed by Govenor Bob Graham of Florida, to assist the private sector (business and nongovernment) in the region through a variety of expanded people-to-people contacts.

The Carter administration pressed for human rights progress in the two dictatorships, Haiti and Cuba, and supported those in the Dominican Republic intent on guaranteeing that the election in 1978 was fair and free. The emphasis on human rights, democracy, and development rested on the premise that the nations in the basin were secure from external aggression because of the Rio Treaty (and the United States), and internal security depended on economic development, political participation, and the wisdom of a nation's leadership. The United States could not guarantee a regime against political instability; all it could do was provide resources and suggest a strategy.

The one exceptional area with an external security concern was the Eastern Caribbean, where many small nations were coming to independence with no armies, and were therefore vulnerable to attacks by mercenaries, religious or political radicals, or narcotics traffickers. There was reluctance on the part of the Carter administration to address this "security gap" for bureaucratic reasons, but also for two other reasons. First the United States did not want to take steps which would have encouraged the British to reduce their responsibilities for the security in the area any sooner than necessary. And second, the United States did not want to promote military establishments that could become threats to the parliamentary democracies rather than their protectors.

Changes in the region and the world in 1979 and 1980 made the Carter adminstration more sensitive to traditional security concerns. The coup in Grenada in March 1979 and the collapse of the Somoza dynasty in July both brought new leaders to power who tended to see Castro's Cuba as the answer, or in the words of Grenadian Prime Minister Maurice Bishop, "the beacon," and the United States as the problem.[9] Both regimes moved rapidly to consolidate one-party rule by building up large military establishments, internal security operations, and "popular" organizations. Simultaneously, an economic decline in the region and a more aggressive Cuban posture--exemplified by the obstrusive role played by the Cuban ambassador in the 1980 Jamaican elections--further unsettled the region. The instability naturally was viewed in the United States in the context of other more ominous international developments--the invasion of Afghanistan, hostages in Iran, uncertainty in the Persian Gulf, and Soviet threats against Poland.

While the Carter administration's interest intensified because of the global concerns, it, by and large, chose to respond to the "crisis" of Grenada as a regional, not a global problem, and to consult often with leaders in the region. The United States followed the lead of CARICOM and recognized the new regime in Grenada only after the other nations did, which was after they received assurances from Bishop--later broken--of early elections. When Bishop sought confrontation to justify the suppression of his opposition, the United States cooled the relationship and sought to expand aid to Grenada's Caribbean neighbors as a signal that only democracy would be rewarded in the region.

In the security area, a task force was established in Key West to coordinate naval exercises in the region, and there was a modest increase in security aid. Economic assistance also continued to increase, as did the numbers and quality of official personnel stationed in the area.

THE REAGAN TENDENCY AND STRATEGY

While the Carter administration started with an interest in promoting economic development in the Caribbean but eventually returned to a concern for national security, the Reagan administration, reflecting a more traditional approach, made the same journey in the opposite direction. But the different points of departure mandated a different tone and approach. President Reagan believes that "instability is being inflicted on some countries in the Caribbean" by Cuba and the Soviet Union.[10] As he told the Wall Street Journal during the campaign: "The Soviet Union underlies all the unrest that is going on. If they weren't engaged in this game of dominoes, there wouldn't be any hot spots in the world." And in his speech announcing the Caribbean Basin Initiative on February 24, 1982, which was, in many ways the culmination of his journey toward recognizing the importance of economic development for the region, President Reagan still repeated the point that the instability in the region was due to "imported terrorism." The military/security perspective which moved the Reagan administration to develop the CBI was woven throughout the speech and the policy. The single-minded pursuit of anticommunism by the Reagan administration makes John Foster Dulles' world-view seem almost catholic in comparison.

The Caribbean was literally of two minds about the Reagan administration's ideological offensive against communism; both views were articulated eloquently by Jamaican Prime Minister

Edward Seaga and Barbado's Prime Minister Tom Adams, at a
conference in Miami soon after Reagan's election in November 1980,
and repeated again during President Reagan's trip to the area in
April 1982. Jamaica's Prime Minister Seaga argued that communism
was on the offensive in the Caribbean, and that the Reagan
administration would need to undertake a development effort on the
scale of the Marshall Plan to defeat it. Having just emerged from
his own election where the smear of communism had worked so
effectively, Seaga thought the United States needed to be
frightened if it were going to extend massive aid to the region.

Aware that six elections in the eastern Caribbean had led to
defeats of radicals and victories by moderates, Barbado's Prime
Minister Adams was much calmer about the threat to the Caribbean
than he was about a new administration in the United States which
looked at the region strictly through east-west lenses. He feared
the United States either could lose interest when it discovered
that the threat was not that real or show only military interest
if it failed to discover that fact.

All of Seaga's and Adams' observations have been proven
correct. Reagan's fixation on the communist threat has led him to
request more aid from Congress although almost all of it was aimed
at where the threat was most urgent--Central America. The eastern
Caribbean was budgeted a total of $10 million out of the $350
million supplemental requested in the administration's Caribbean
Basin Initiative. Ironically, just as the Carter administration
focused early on Manley's Jamaica to make a broader point about
its respect for "ideological pluralism" in the region, the Reagan
administration similarly has showered special attention and aid on
Seaga, but to make the opposite point--that the Reagan
administration respects and supports only those whose views of the
east-west struggle coincide with its own. This disrespect for
ideological diversity is evident also in Reagan's specific
reference in a press conference on March 31, 1982 to Manley's
social democratic government as "virtually Communist."

After his first meeting with Seaga in January 1981, President
Reagan pronounced himself "unrelaxed" about the Cuban threat to
the Caribbean. His mood apparently had not changed by the time he
reached Barbados for a vacation in April 1982. Referring to
Grenada, Reagan said that "it will attempt to spread the virus
among its neighbors." The opposite occurred. Three years after
the Grenada "revolution," the Commonwealth Caribbean seems to have
been innoculated effectively by Grenada rather than infected by
it. More than a dozen elections have occurred since then, and in
every case, radicals were defeated decisively; moderates
triumphed.

Using a military-security perspective, the Reagan
administration quite naturally divides the world between communist
and "free world;" it concentrates its efforts on "targets," such
as El Salvador, and "sources" of instability, such as Cuba,
Nicaragua, and Grenada, and relies heavily on traditional
instruments to project power.[11] Thus, military manuevers and
exercises in the region have increased in numbers and in size,

including a NATO operation in March 1982, the first such exercise in twenty-three years.[12] Military aid increased for the eastern Caribbean from less than $100,000 (for Coast Guard training) to a total of nearly $17 million for Fiscal Years 1982 and 1983. Similarly, the requests for the Dominican Republic have increased from less than $3.5 million in Fiscal Year 1981 to a total of nearly $16 million for Fiscal Years 1982 and 1983.

Has the traditional approach enhanced the security of the region? With respect to Cuba, the results of the Reagan administration's strategy are, according to the State Department, first, that Cuba received three times as much military equipment from the Soviet Union in 1931 as in any other year since 1962, and second, that the level of arms flow to the guerrillas in Central America from Cuba and other sources is as high in the spring of 1982 as just before the so-called "final offensive" in early January 1981. With respect to the eastern Caribbean, the principal security need is for a regional coast guard, and the Reagan administration moved very slowly on that until the intervention in Grenada.

With respect to Grenada, between 1981 and October 1983, the administration's heavyhanded approach to trying to get the Caribbean Development Bank to veto a loan to Grenada not only weakened this key regional institution, but also impelled other governments in the area who were unsympathetic to that regime to defend it. The key event which affected the region was the invasion of Grenada in October 1983, the subject of the rest of the book. The executions of Prime Minister Maurice Bishop and several of his Cabinet--the veritable self-destruction of the Grenadian revolution--so enraged Grenada's neighbors that several of them requested U.S. assistance to overthrow the regime. The Reagan administration was pleased to oblige. The invasion was popular in the states that participated, but it divided the Caribbean Community (CARICOM) internally and widened the gap between the English-speaking Caribbean and Latin America and the rest of the world. Grenada had an opportunity to restore democracy, which it did in a free election a year later, on December 3, 1984, and the Organization of Eastern Caribbean States had an opportunity to re-invigorate their integration movement and create a regional security force. Unfortunately, they have had less success in this area.[13]

The Reagan administration's repeated use of the term "backyard" to describe the Caribbean has antagonized the nationalistic sensibility of the region. In 1977, long before President Reagan resurrected the term, Barbadian Prime Minister Adams found general agreement when he said that such language is "no longer appropriate in an increasingly interdependent world in which all the countries of the region, in spite of their small size seek to be active and independent participants."[14] There are few in the region, outside of Haiti and Cuba, who find the east-west framework, which defines to a great extent the administration's view of the region, as either relevant to their problems or anything but condescending.

Partly to mollify critics who argued in early 1981 that the administration was insensitive, or worse, unaware of the socioeconomic roots of the instability in the region, work began on an economic program. After nearly a year of consultations with Venezuela, Colombia, Canada, and Mexico, and fierce bureaucratic battles, President Reagan unveiled a comprehensive and bold Caribbean Basin Initiative (CBI) on February 24, 1982.[15] The "centerpiece" of the program is one-way free trade for all exports from the region except textiles, apparel, and sugar. The other elements in the CBI include expanded balance of payments support, bilateral aid, technical assistance to the private sector, and special assistance to the Virgin Islands and Puerto Rico. If the U.S. economy improves, then the CBI could stimulate important investments in the region, creating jobs and pressing the economies beyond the import-substitution plateau on which most of them currently are sitting.

There are also some negative aspects of the CBI, which can be anticipated merely by examining the effect of Puerto Rico's Operation Bootstrap, which is essentially a prototype for the CBI. Bootstrap encouraged investments by "enclave" industries, which imported almost all their raw materials and exported their products; it created half as many jobs in manufacturing as were lost in agriculture; and it ignored the population problem. Unless corrective action is taken in all three areas, the benefits of the CBI could be dissipated. This is particularly true for a population program since forty percent of the population of Puerto Rico moved to the United States during Bootstrap.

Though born of the struggle in Central America, the CBI will be of limited use there. However, it will help the stable democracies in the Caribbean who need and can use investment, technology, and new jobs. Haiti also will benefit because of its relatively cheap labor force. All would benefit even more if there were clearer support for regional projects and for regional institutions. The Caribbean Group already has established a Project Development Facility aimed at identifying promising new medium-sized instruments; together with the trade and investment incentives of the CBI, this facility could have a rapid and positive impact on economic development, and ultimately, the security of the region.

THE UNITED STATES AND THE CARIBBEAN

U.S. policies toward the Caribbean have been anchored in a set of interests which have changed much less than the strategies formulated to pursue them. All U.S. administrations want to avoid the establishment of a hostile regime in the area; all want the region to be secure so that democracy, human rights, and development can flourish. In the pursuit of these interests, the United States has faced a recurring set of problems--instability, dictatorship, poverty, and foreign involvement--and has offered similar kinds of threats and promises, aid, and support. From the

Caribbean perspective, U.S. policy has been a problem and occasionally a promise. Two different foreign policy "tendencies"--one conservative, one liberal--have developed which give greater attention and assign higher value to some interests rather than others. Each tendency uses instruments suited to these interests--the liberal tendency stresses human rights and development; the conservative tendency views threats as more immediate and relies on more direct uses of power. Both tendencies, however, have to cope with a world which is less responsive to the concerns of big powers; neither tendency has been comfortable with this fact nor capable of fashioning a strategy which fully takes it into account.

NOTES

1. This chapter is adapted and updated from my article, "U.S. Policy Toward the Caribbean: Recurring Problems and Promises." in Jack W. Hopkins (ed.), Latin America and Caribbean Contemporary Record, 1981-1982 (New York: Holmes and Meier, 1983): 79-89. Reprinted with permission.

2. For the most authoritative and detailed histories of U.S. intervention, see the two books by Dana G. Munro, Intervention and Dollar Diplomacy in the Caribbean, 1900-21 (Princeton, NJ: Princeton University Press, 1964), and The United States and the Caribbean Area (Boston: World Peace Foundation, 1984). Also see Bryce Wood, The Making of the Good Neighbor Policy (New York: Columbia University Press, 1961).

3. For an excellent account of U.S. policy toward Cuba when Welles was ambassador, see Wood, chapters 2 and 3.

4. See Abraham F. Lowenthal, The Dominican Intervention (Cambridge: Harvard University Press, 1972).

5. Edwin Martin, "Haiti: A Case Study in Futility," SAIS Review 2 (Summer 1981): 68-70. Martin, who was President Kennedy's Assistant Secretary of State, describes Kennedy's views and directives on Haiti.

6. For a compelling description of the personal impact of Carter's human rights policy on Haiti, see Patrick Lemoine and Erich Goode, "Living Hell in Haiti," Inquiry (March 3, 1980). In late 1976, the treatment of political prisoners improved dramatically, according to Lemoine who was arrested in 1971 and released in February 1977. By September 1977, after a visit to the island by U.S. Ambassador to the U.N. Andrew Young, all 104 political prisoners were released and amnestied. Some of those and others were re-arrested in December 1980 after Carter lost the Presidential election.

7. For comparative reasons, the reader might wish to see my analysis of the evolution of U.S. interests in Central America in "Our Real National Interests in Central America," The Atlantic (July 1982).

8. Reagan's Ambassador to the United Nations argued that Carter's policy toward the Caribbean made U.S. friends easy targets for Cuba and the Soviet Union. (Jeane Kirkpatrick, "U.S. Security and Latin America," Commentary (January 1981)). In defending the lack of communication between the Reagan administration and the Cuban government, Assistant Secretary of State Thomas Enders implied, in testimony on Capitol Hill, that the fact that the Carter administration negotiated with Cuba might have encouraged them to be more aggressive.

9. In a speech to the Second Congress of the Cuban Communist Party on December 19, 1980, Grenada's Prime Minister Maurice Bishop said, "Cuba has been a beacon for us in Grenada ... It has reminded us of the central role of the party in building the revolution. It has reminded us of the critical importance of being the genuine vanguard of the people ... Imperialism must know and understand that if they touch Grenada." Foreign Broadcast Information Service, December 24, 1980, pp. Q9-14.

10. From remarks by President Reagan on the departure of Prime Minister Seaga, January 28, 1981. Reagan also said he was "unrelaxed" about the Caribbean.

11. Robert Pastor, "The Target and the Source: U.S. Policies Toward El Salvador and Nicaragua," Washington Quarterly (Summer 1982).

12. James McCartney, "Reagan Decides to Step Up Military Presence in Caribbean," Miami Herald, 30 January 1982.

13. For the implications of the invasion see Robert Pastor, "The Impact of Grenada on the Caribbean: Ripples of a Revolution," in Jack W. Hopkins (ed.), Latin America and Caribbean Contemporary Record, 1983-84 (New York: Holmes and Meier, 1985).

14. Adams cited in Don Bohning, "Policies Revised in Caribbean," Philadelphia Inquirer, 6 July 1977.

15. Foreign Policy (Summer 1982) has a large section devoted to the CBI; also Robert Pastor, "Sinking in the Caribbean Basin," Foreign Affairs (Summer 1982).

3
The Effects of Culture on Cuban Influence in Grenada

Dorothea Cypher

Despite appearances to the contrary, Cuba's effort to increase its influence in Grenada between 1979 and 1983 was less than successful. Social and cultural differences between the two peoples were serious detractors to effecting significant Cuban influence, notably at the popular level. This influence, especially in terms of ideology and policy, was basically only effective at the party level of the relatively small New Jewel Movement (NJM). This chapter discusses the common bases of the two countries, briefly describes the Cuban involvement in Grenada, then explores the social and cultural differences which hampered Cuban influence and speculates what this experience may mean for future attempts at extending Cuban influence in the Caribbean.

Cuba and Grenada are Caribbean island nations located at the extreme northern and southern ends of the West Indies, respectively. Both were discovered in the 1490s by Christopher Columbus and subsequently colonized by European powers who exploited them for similar agricultural purposes over a period of centuries. The colonial masters of both islands found it necessary to introduce and later rely extensively on African slaves to facilitate this exploitation.

The colonial period was extremely important in determining the unique character of both Cuba and Grenada. These qualities derive in large measure from the differences in geography, demography, and colonial masters. Cuba is an island of 46,300 square miles with a population exceeding ten million. The people reflect their colonial heritage in their peculiar form of Spanish. The Spanish legacy also accounts for most of the white population and accounts for the mestizo population, which is an even larger force today. Black descendents of the African slaves make up the largest segment of contemporary Cuba, accounting for somewhere between thirty and forty percent of the total.[1] The Spanish heritage is evident throughout Cuban society, but as with the language, which is an unusual blend of the Andalusian dialect of Cuba's settlers and African slurred pronunciation, the manifestations are uniquely Cuban.

Grenada, on the other hand, encompasses only 120 square miles and supports a population of about 110,000. Today a very few

Grenadians speak a French patois, reminiscent of the 112 years that France ruled the island. The vast majority speak English, a function of Great Britain's stewardship from 1763 to 1974. The Grenadian population is ninety-five percent black, with a small percentage of mulattos included in that figure. French and English colonial descendents number only in the hundreds, as do a conglomerate of other whites. Grenada's culture has definitely retained an African flavor.

An enduring shared colonial vestige, evident throughout the Caribbean as well, is the traditional dependency on foreign nations. This dependency is linked with a related psychological inadequacy which resulted in extensive European and North American identification and placed a great significance on metropolitan values, attitudes, assumptions, and institutions.[2] When the colonial period ended the United States filled the Cuban void and Great Britain continued in Grenada, although their formal relationship was altered. Even today, Cuba's dependency is manifested in reliance on the Soviet Union, while Grenada's recently had been subsumed by Cuba and, by extension, the Soviet Union.

Cuba may have considered Grenada a target for expansion as early as 1976. The coup by Maurice Bishop and the NJM which ousted Sir Eric Gairy in March 1979, radically altered Grenada's political orientation. Some scholars would assert the coup also began a leftist Grenadian experiment which attempted to break from the traditional Caribbean dependency.[3] Subsequent events suggest that the Grenadians only traded one master for another.

The leader of this experiment was the charismatic Grenadian, Maurice Bishop. Educated in Britain, he returned to Grenada in the early 1970s fired with socialist political attitudes which were similar to many of his contemporaries.[4] He led activists there who took over JEWEL (Joint Endeavor for Welfare, Education, and Liberation), a rural workers' organization. This organization eventually became the now familiar New Jewel Movement (NJM). Bishop and other leaders of the NJM linked themselves to Castro's brand of Marxism-Leninism by seeking training in Cuba and developing ties there, eventually cemented by a close personal relationship between Fidel Castro and Maurice Bishop. Like Castro, Bishop had tremendous popular appeal. Unlike him, however, it appears that Bishop was unable to successfully transfer that appeal from his person to the New Jewel Movement.

Grenada's new prime minister and his attendant party were a decidely welcome change for Grenadians weary of the autocratic Gairy, his Mongoose Gang strongmen, and his obsession with UFOs and witchcraft. The new People's Revolutionary Government (PRG) by contrast turned their attention to literacy drives, agricultural cooperatives, health care improvements, and a new international airport. Cuban aid, especially in the latter two areas, was critical.

This aid was facilitated by the arrival of Julian Torres Rizo, a senior Americas Department and DGI official, who had been appointed as the Cuban charge d'affaires and later full ambassador to Grenada. Both he and his wife, had direct contact with the leaders of the NJM. Between them, they prepared a daily "survey of the world press" for Bishop and his ministers which could have been caveated "according to Cuba."[5] In addition, Torres constantly advised Prime Minister Bishop on the optimal course of action for Grenada.

A stream of Cuban advisors came in Torres' wake. They were most evident in training the People's Revolutionary Army (PRA) and the militia. A large number directed the educational and medical efforts. Other advisors assisted in the fishing, transportation, general industry, and other areas. Probably most important were the party organizers who helped establish the communist party structure at the government and mass organization levels. The approach was for the advisors to initiate the programs and train Grenadian leaders to maintain them.

In short, Grenada became a "Little Cuba" in the mold of post-1959.[6] One of the first actions of the NJM was to dispense with the constitution and to rule by People's Laws. The Communist Party apparatus was established from Central Committee, Politburo, and Secretariat on down. An extensive youth indoctrination program was attempted. The PRA and militia were strengthened. Grenada's two independent papers were banned. Elections were suspended. Political prisoners were jailed without legal charges. Grenadian students were sent for training in Cuba and·the Soviet Bloc. In the U.N., Grenada voted with Cuba in support of the Soviet invasion of Afghanistan. Treaties were signed with the Soviet Union. The transformation seemed complete.

Yet the Central Committee meeting notes of September 14-16, 1983, clearly acknowledged failure. They noted that the populace had ideologically regressed and mass organizations were enjoying less participation. In fact, the women's movement and youth organizations collapsed. A cultural abyss existed between the Cuban and Soviet teachings and what the majority of Grenadians could or would absorb.[7]

The Cuban model had been adopted structurally as well as ideologically at the party level of the NJM, but could not be sustained at the popular level. The NJM, although numbering only around 300 full and candidate members, was less than completely effective. The failure of the party mirrored Bishop's lack of ideological success. Failures were evident in military training, education, and even the fishing industry. Explanations cited most often for the failures were lack of ideological fervor, motivation, discipline, and qualification on the part of the Grenadians. The job of the NJM had been to sustain the programs initiated by the Cuban advisors. Both Bishop and the NJM failed, but why?

Basically the Cuban revolutionary ideology and fervor clashed with the predominantly gentle, religious, conservative Grenadian populace. Grenada did not have the revolutionary base of the Cubans, nor was it readily adaptable to it. In fact, the Grenadian response was one of bewilderment, intimidation, and resentment. Many Grenadians called the Cubans the "new masters."

The Cubans, for their part, reportedly reciprocated the lack of respect, as reflected by their habit of simply taking items from the small grocery stores around the island without paying for them. Actually the populace at large had very little direct contact with the Cubans. When they did, at the Point Salines airport construction site, for instance, fighting often erupted.[8]

Evidently the Cubans and Grenadians often clashed on an interpersonal level •(although a number of them married Grenadians), but since the interaction appears to have been limited, the answer must lie elsewhere. That answer appears to lie in the fact that the Grenadians were not culturally suited to the Cuban's programs, at least not with the way they were presented in Grenada. The cultural clashes appear to have occurred in three key areas: ideology, work, and education.

Revolutionary Marxist-Leninist ideology is all pervasive in Cuba. Grenada, on the other hand, appears to be somewhat apolitical, and most Grenadians were happy to confine themselves to personal matters during Bishop's rule.[9]

Essentially the preliminary evidence indicates that Grenada was a situation where Cuban influence was very effective and far-reaching at the top, but with basic differences at the bottom. This finding is supported by the obvious relief of the Grenadians at the Cuban departure and their welcome for U.S. troops. It also appears credible that cultural differences impeded Cuban success considerably. As more of the captured Grenadian documents are analyzed and as the post-invasion situation develops in Grenada, more light will undoubtedly be shed on this question.

Certainly one can speculate, despite the lack of definite answers, on the effect of Cuba's Grenadian experience on their future involvement in the Caribbean. The Joint U.S. Carribean operation on Grenada was obviously a blow to Cuban expansionism in the region. The peak of Cuban influence in the Caribbean occurred in 1979 with their heavy involvement in Guyana, Jamaica, and Grenada. Guyana has remained relatively low key, Seaga's election in 1980 caused a reversal in Jamaica, and the Grenadian attempt was foiled by discord between Coard, Austin, and Bishop.

Cuba is likely to continue its involvement in the Caribbean Basin, although the Grenadian outcome has moved it into an apparent period of reassessment which will slow further operations for the immediate future. One would expect that the social and cultural aspects of Cuba's target countries will receive more attention in view of Grenada, especially because of Cuba's particular brand of "person to person" aid.

Cuba will face new obstacles in the future as a result of Grenada. Grenada's neighbors clearly evidenced their suspicion of its Cuban-aided non-conformist socialist experiment by calling upon the United States for assistance. Fear is also evident. Perhaps fear of a fate similar to Bishop's prompted Prime Minister Bouterse to oust the Cubans from Suriname after the Grenadian invasion. The island neighbors are particularly conscious of their vulnerability, especially to takeover by small groups. As social conditions in these Caribbean nations worsen, notably in the economic arena, these concerns will undoubtedly grow. Evidence of dissatisfaction and deeply rooted pessimism about the future is already apparent.[10]

Despite the speculative nature of the preceeding paragraphs, Cuba will assuredly continue to look for targets of opportunity throughout the Caribbean. The tactics for entrenching influence in the future are not yet obvious. A few lessons will probably be incorporated from the Grenadian experience. A less rigid Marxist-Leninist approach appears more conducive to Caribbean cultures, at least initially. In this regard an emphasis on state-to-state versus party-to-party relations may develop. The initial focus of Cuban involvement is also likely to shift to the economic area to minimize those prevalent destabilizing factors which detract from Cuban objectives. Finally, a longer period of involvement may be necessary on the part of Cuban advisors to ensure the success of various educational and mass organizational endeavors before relinquishing them to local leaders, especially since these institutions are crucial to the Cuban program. Future events in the Caribbean are necessary to prove, disprove, or modify these projections. The resolution will certainly provide food for thought for all students of the region.

NOTES

1. Jan Knippers Black, et. al. Area Handbook for Cuba (Washington, DC: The American University, 1976), p. 100.

2. Tony Thorndike, "The Grenada Crisis," The World Today (December 1983): 471.

3. Timothy Ashby, "Grenada: Soviet Stepping Stone," US Naval Institute Proceedings (December 1983): 30; and Thorndike, p. 473.

4. Trevor Fishlock, "How Maurice Bishop Changed from Devil to Saint," The Times (London), 21 November 1983, p. 41.

5. Interview with Herbert Romerstein, co-editor of Grenada Documents (Washington, DC: U.S. Department of State and U.S. Department of Defense, 1984), 29 February 1984.

6. "Serpent in Caribbean's Island Paradise," U.S. News and World Report, May 19, 1980, p. 25.

7. Michael Ledeen, "Grenada's Captured Documents," (Presentation delivered at Georgetown Center for Strategic and International Studies, Washington, DC, January 17, 1984).

8. "Serpent in Caribbean's Island Paradise," p. 25; and Peter Hnatiuk, (personal interview, 8 March 1984); and interview with Herbert Romerstein.

34

9. Ledeen, "Grenada's Captured Documents, and interview with Captain Peter Hnatiuk, U.S. Army.

10. Juan Williams, "Grenada Isn't Our Only Caribbean Problem," Washington Post, 18 December 1983, p. C-1.

4
Soviet Involvement in the Caribbean Basin

Bruce W. Watson

INTRODUCTION

The radicalization of Grenada, the use of Cubans to build the Grenadian airport, the caches of Soviet-supplied weapons, the secret agreements between the U.S.S.R. and Grenada, and the visits of high ranking Soviet military and civilian personages have all been discussed elsewhere in this book. The purposes of this chapter are two-fold. The first is to examine Soviet military operations and intentions in the region. Here it will be shown that these maneuvers have focused upon Cuba and have involved both providing for the island's security and using it as a base of operations. The second purpose will be to demonstrate the relationship between Cuba and Grenada by showing that this development is consistent with previous Soviet operations in other areas.

In conducting such an examination, it is best to begin by looking at the major types of Soviet involvement in Cuba; these contributed to the Soviet military threat.

SOVIET MILITARY INVOLVEMENT IN CUBA

Here Soviet military activity has included deploying groups of Soviet naval combatants, constructing a naval facility at Cienfuegos, staging Soviet naval aircraft and detailing elements of the Soviet Air Force to the island, delivering arms, stationing a brigade, and assisting the Cuban efforts in Africa and Latin America.

The Cuban Missile Crisis

Soviet involvement began shortly after the Bay of Pigs invasion in April 1961 and increased in the summer of 1962. This activity included aid, which was delivered by a massive sealift from June to October 1962 of over 100 shiploads of men and material. The U.S. discovery of Soviet medium- and long-range ballistic missiles in October led to the Cuban Missile Crisis. When the United States reacted by establishing a naval blockade, the Soviets, who were unable to project sufficient naval power to the region to challenge this force, removed the missiles and **Beagle** strike aircraft in return for highly conditional U.S. guarantees not to invade Cuba. [1]

Following the missile crisis, the Soviets proceeded cautiously in an attempt to develop a military presence in the Caribbean. This was accomplished by dispatching naval, air, and ground forces to Cuba.

The Soviet Naval Combatant Deployments

The first Soviet naval combatant deployment to the Caribbean began on July 10, 1969. Twenty-three such voyages have occurred, the last one concluding on May 11, 1984. The Soviets have consciously altered the groups' compositions so that they could introduce a variety of cruise missile-equipped surface combatants and submarines, which are ideal for anti-shipping operations and interdicting the sea lanes. The time between these deployments has varied from six weeks to more than eighteen months, and the lengths of the deployments have also fluctuated.

The activities of these groups include probing U.S. defenses by making counterclockwise circumnavigations of the Gulf of Mexico. During these maneuvers, the Soviets have, on occasion, lingered off the Mississippi delta, Galveston, Texas, and other points along the U.S. Gulf Coast. The Soviet Navy also often exercises with the Cuban Navy and has made many visits to Cuba.

Generally, these excursions amount to an assertive use of naval power in order to weaken the U.S. stance vis-a-vis Soviet military power in the region. This is most evident in the composition of the various combatant groups. For example, Golf II ballistic missile-equipped submarines, strategic weapon platforms, were included in the eighth and eleventh deployments. In addition, the deployments are an impressive show of support for Castro and his Cuban regime. Finally, they support Soviet foreign policy through port visits and other activities. Two impressive examples of this support are the timing of the seventeenth deployment to coincide with a visit by Admiral of the Fleet of the Soviet Union Sergei G. Gorshkov, the Commander-in-Chief of the Soviet Navy, to Cuba, and the timing of the twenty-first deployment in April-May 1981 to coincide with the twentieth anniversary of the Bay of Pigs.

In summary, the naval combatant deployments have been quite successful to the extent that they have been accepted by the United States as a routine part of Soviet naval operations on the high seas. Whereas the first deployment prompted a considerable reaction in the U.S. press, by the time of the tenth deployment, such Soviet naval operations were no longer reported in the national news media. It was not until the Reagan Administration that the White House again emphasized the importance of these deployments and they again received national attention. The Soviets have not been as successful in desensitizing the United States to other aspects of their involvement in the region, as the controversy over the naval base at Cienfuegos clearly demonstrates.

The Naval Base at Cienfuegos

Soviet interest in Cienfuegos began in 1970. In the summer of that year, the United States learned that a highway was under construction between Havana and Cienfuegos, that a barracks and recreational facilities were being built in Cienfuegos, and that an existing pier was being refurbished and moorings were being laid. When some ships of the third Soviet combatant deployment group to Cuba remained after that group left for home, the United States became deeply suspicious that the Soviet Union was developing a base at Cienfuegos. In late September, the United States warned the U.S.S.R. against building such a base, and in November, the Kennedy-Khrushchev understanding of 1962 was extended to include the staging of ballistic missile submarines from Cuba. The U.S.S.R. did not lose completely in this incident--the highly qualified Kennedy promise of 1962 not to invade Cuba was further defined so that while the Soviets were denied access to Cienfuegos, they won additional guarantees concerning Cuba's defense.[2]

Construction was stopped at Cienfuegos after November 1970, raising questions concerning whether the Soviets truly intended to use the base. However, in the late 1970s, construction began anew and, in 1980, the State Department announced that it was watching the construction of a facility which had deepwater piers and naval support buildings. Foxtrot diesel attack submarines, which the Soviets had delivered to Cuba, were at the facility, but there were no indications that the Soviet Navy was using the base.[3]

Although the Soviets are not currently using Cienfuegos, several factors support the belief that they may use it in the future. First, the Soviet-Cuban relationship is such that Castro will allow the Soviets whatever access they desire. Secondly, the Soviets use several foreign port facilities worldwide to support their naval operations and Cienfuegos would fit in well with this network. Third, the Soviets will need a base if they wish to increase the tempo of their naval operations in the Caribbean. Finally, naval power has traditionally been deployed to safeguard Soviet policy initiatives in the Middle East, Africa, and South and Southeast Asia. Given the intensity of current Soviet initiatives in Latin America, traditional practice indicates that such naval power should already be deployed. That it has not been probably reflects a Soviet deference to U.S. sensitivities. However, should insurgent activity in Latin America expand, then the Soviets may well establish a constant presence in the Caribbean. Should this occur, then Cienfuegos would be an ideal facility to support such operations.

The Soviet Naval Aircraft Deployments

The first pair of Soviet naval aircraft to deploy to the

Caribbean landed in Cuba on April 18, 1970. Each has been composed of a pair of aircraft. For years, these were Tu-95 Bear D long-range reconnaissance aircraft, which, for the first several years, landed at Jose Marti airport near Havana. Recently, the Soviets began staging Tu-142 Bear F antisubmarine warfare aircraft from Cuba, which increases significantly their antisubmarine warfare capability in the region. Like the combatant deployments, the Soviets have varied the length of the aircraft deployments and the intervals between them. However, when they were forced to move the African staging area from Conakry, Guinea, to Luanda, Angola, they were compelled to route all Tu-95 flights to Africa through Cuba. This was necessary because the distance from the U.S.S.R. to Angola exceeds the range of the Tu-95. As a result, the presence of Bear Ds in Cuba has increased markedly in recent years, with no significant reaction from the United States.

The Soviets enjoy several advantages by staging these aircraft in Cuba. First, they enhance their reconnaissance capability over the North Atlantic. By concurrently staging such aircraft from Cuba, the Soviet Union, and Luanda, Angola, the Soviets can surveil almost the entire North Atlantic. This provides them with information on U.S. and NATO naval and merchant activity in the Atlantic, permits spying in the Caribbean and off the U.S. East Coast and the African West Coast, and allows for effective crew training over the Atlantic. The value of this surveillance capability is so great that many of these deployments have occurred during periods of tension or of major U.S. and NATO exercise activity in the North Atlantic. Secondly, the deployments permit a probing of America's defenses. This occurs when aircraft are staged from Havana, operate along the U.S. East Coast, and return to Cuba. These aircraft have penetrated the U.S. Air Defense Identification Zone (ADIZ). One such operation caused a U.S. reaction in April 1977 when the Soviets came within seventy-five miles of the Carolinas, but generally these operations have occurred so often that the U.S. considers them routine.[4] Finally, like the naval combatant voyages, the naval aircraft deployments visually demonstrate the Soviet commitment to Cuba. As such, they are of value to Soviet foreign policy.

The Soviet Brigade

Soviet Army personnel have been stationed in Cuba since before the Cuban Missile Crisis of 1962. However, until 1979, either the number of Soviet Army personnel was so small or they were so dispersed that they were not identifiable as a brigade. In August 1979, however, Senator Frank Church of Idaho stated that a Soviet brigade of from 2,300 to 3,000 personnel was stationed in Cuba, thereby beginning an incident in U.S.-Soviet affairs.

The results of the incident were far reaching. First, it weakened U.S. policy as defined by the Monroe Doctrine. In this respect, the fact that the troops had been in Cuba since 1962 may have been relevant, but what was more important was that in 1979 the United States identified them as a brigade, stated that their presence was unacceptable, and then failed to force their removal from the island. The result, was a major weakening of the American posture under the Monroe Doctrine, and it is with this liability that President Reagan took office in January 1981.

Today the brigade is located near Havana and numbers between 2,600 and 3,000 motorized rifle, armor, and artillery personnel equipped with about forty tanks, 100 armored personnel carriers, rocket launchers, and antiaircraft weapons.[5] It is a force which must be considered in any assessment of Cuban defensive capability and is a political factor favoring the survival of Castro's regime.

The Involvement of the Soviet Air Force

The presence of the Soviet Air Force in Cuba began in 1976, when Soviet MiG pilots began flying air defense missions over Cuban airspace, freeing Cuban Air Force pilots for duty in Africa. These Soviet pilots returned in 1978 to substitute for Cuban pilots then fighting in Ethiopia.[6]

Indications that the Soviet Air Force might play a greater role in Cuba in the 1980s emerged when it was announced that several Cuban air bases had been improved. Today many Cuban airfields have runways long enough to stage Soviet Backfire bombers.[7]

The Arms Deliveries

Soviet military assistance to Cuba dates back to the early 1960s. However, the tempo of these deliveries increased significantly in 1976 when the Cubans began sending troops to Africa, and Cuba received $87 million in military aid. This assistance may have been part of Cuba's reward for its African operations, and also may have been provided because the Cubans, seasoned from their combat experience in Africa, could now use it. Resupplying Cuba's African combat losses would also partially account for the increase.

By 1979, Cuba had received $1.6 billion in arms. These have been such that Cuban military forces now enjoy such a vast military superiority in the Caribbean that only the United States could defeat them in battle. The Cuban Army, extremely well equipped, has been armed with tanks, armor, and missiles. The Cuban Air Force has received a wide variety of aircraft, most recently MiG-23 fighters and ground assault helicopters, and is the best equipped air force in Latin America. Likewise, the Cuban Navy is a small but highly effective coastal force. Equipped with Osa and Komar missile equipped boats, it was the first navy to receive Turya hydrofoil patrol boats.

Deliveries of military equipment to Cuba continued to increase in 1980 and 1981. The U.S.S.R. delivered 63,000 tons of arms to Cuba in 1981, the highest yearly total since 1962. In 1982, the deliveries increased to 68,000 tons and were worth about a billion dollars. In 1983, the New York Times reported that the

U.S.S.R. intended to transfer four more Foxtrot submarines to Cuba, which would give Cuba a total of six Foxtrots. The Soviets also intend to transfer additional Koni-class frigates to Cuba. Furthermore, they have helped the Cubans convert a large trawler into an intelligence collection ship and continue to operate their intelligence center at Lourdes, Cuba, intercepting communications in the eastern United States.[8]

Although a portion of this equipment is intended for transhipment to insurgent forces in Latin America, much of it is earmarked to upgrade Cuba's Armed Forces. More significantly, recent arms deliveries, such as the Foxtrot submarines and the Koni frigate, indicate that the Soviets have varied from the traditional practice of supplying Castro with defensive weapons and are now providing him with a limited offensive capability.

A similar trend has occurred in aircraft deliveries. The southeastern portion of the United States is well within the combat radius of Cuba's MiG aircraft, and Cuba's MiG-23 Floggers can reach bases in Nicaragua, where they can refuel and proceed further into the region. In 1978 and 1979, they received An-26 Curl short-range transport aircraft which can be used to airdrop troops on the Bahamas, Belize, Jamaica, Haiti, and most of the Dominican Republic. That the Cubans may conduct more offensive operations was demonstrated in July 1981, when on two occasions U.S. naval aircraft intercepted Cuban MiG-21s in the Florida Strait as they approached the aircraft carrier USS Independence.[9]

Delivering such offensive systems further insures the defense of Castro's Cuba. It is also risky, because it provides Castro with the ability to exert greater influence in the Caribbean. This contributes to the instability of the region by enhancing an established force with which the other Caribbean states must contend.

SOVIET ASSISTANCE TO NATIONAL LIBERATION MOVEMENTS

In recent years, the Soviets have drastically increased their support for Caribbean and Latin American national liberation movements. This optimism has not always existed. In the 1960s, for example, the U.S.S.R. was pessimistic concerning the chances for successful national liberation revolutions in Latin America, and offered only lukewarm support to Cuban involvement in insurgency.

In the 1970s, the Cuban and Soviet views converged in Africa. Soviet assistance in the Angolan Civil War in 1975-6 was considerable. A naval force of seven ships was stationed in the Gulf of Guinea to insure the earliest detection of any U.S. reaction. Meanwhile, the Soviets launched a massive assistance program to arm and supply insurgent forces and also assisted Cuban convoys of troops as they proceeded to Angola. Likewise, in Ethiopia in 1977-78, the Soviets supplied military equipment, stationed a naval force of as many as twenty-two ships in the area, conducted reconnaissance, and transported Cuban troops from Angola and Cuba to Ethiopia. As mentioned earlier, the Soviet Union also sent pilots to Cuba so that Cuban pilots could fight in Ethiopia, and they sent General Vasiliy Petrov to Ethiopia to help direct the Ethiopian/Cuban effort.

Africa provided an opportunity for closer Soviet-Cuban cooperation and demonstrated Cuban proficiency in Third World wars. Meanwhile, the Soviets perceived that several factors in the Caribbean basin, including the British withdrawal, U.S. neglect, poor economic conditions, and the caliber of insurgent forces, made the area ripe for revolution. As a result, the Soviets began to more actively assist insurgent national liberation forces in several nations of the region.

The Grenadian, Nicaraguan, and El Salvadoran cases revealed a great deal concerning Soviet strategy in the region, in that they demonstrated that the Soviets intended to remain removed from national liberation movement forces until each had gained control in its respective country. However, experience has shown that after a movement succeeds in a country, Soviet assistance becomes more open and more substantial as the revolutionary force attempts to consolidate its gains. This is traditional Soviet policy and provides them with two advantages. First, it minimizes the chances of a U.S.-Soviet confrontation, and second, it permits the insurgent forces to appear as truly indigenous factions because their connection with the Soviet Union remains concealed.

Even operating under these self-imposed restrictions, the Soviet role in the Caribbean basin has been considerable. In the 1960s and 1970s, insurgent Latin American forces were trained in Cuba. Given the number of Soviet military advisors and Soviet KGB personnel on the island, it is reasonable to conclude that the Soviets helped to train these forces.

An even more important role is the financial support the Soviets have given these groups. In essence this assistance has been such that it amounts to financing the insurgent movements. Soviet aid has been provided through Cuba and has accounted for an undetermined portion of the military assistance which the Soviet Union has provided to Castro. Once in Cuba, many of these arms were transhipped to insurgents in the region. This tactic, which allowed the Soviets to support and yet remain divorced from the national liberation movements, has previously been used in Africa (particularly during the Angolan civil war) and in Asia. It allows the Soviet Union to integrate its revolutionary activities with its stance as a legitimate nation in the international community, thereby synchronizing Soviet regional and worldwide goals.

Finally, it is important to note that the Soviets move their protected enclave from one nation to another as the national liberation revolutions succeed. In the Caribbean, this means that in the future the Soviets may attempt to establish additional transshipment and training bases in Central America, and have prepared Nicaragua as such a base of operations.

THE CONSISTENCY WITH SOVIET OPERATIONS IN OTHER REGIONS

For two reasons, the Soviet-Cuban relationship is unique and therefore can be distinguished from the Soviet Union's relationship with other Third World nations. The first is that Cuba, as a communist nation, enjoys an extremely close relationship with the Soviet Union. This has led to a greater Soviet willingness to finance the development of the Cuban military than would be the case if Cuba were merely a Third World nation. The second reason is that the Caribbean is a region to which the United States assigns great importance and is extremely sensitive to military intrusions by foreign powers. As a result, the Soviet Union has proceeded much more cautiously in extending its military power into the Caribbean than it has in the Mediterranean Sea, West Africa, the Indian Ocean, or Southeast Asia. In spite of these factors, the Soviet relationships with Cuba and Grenada bear great similarity to Soviet relations with their other Third World clients, and, in this sense, they conform to an established Soviet pattern.

This pattern usually begins by an initial Soviet military intrusion into a region. This force is almost always the Soviet Navy. Sometimes the Soviets are invited into the region by a client or potential client, as in the cases of Cuba in the Caribbean, Guinea in West Africa, Somalia in the Indian Ocean, and Vietnam in Southeast Asia. In other cases, such as the Mediterranean and the southern Indian Ocean, the U.S.S.R. begins naval operations because it perceives an opportunity to advance its influence.

Once in a region, the Soviets seek to establish a base to support their naval operations. Such facilities were established at: Conakry, Guinea; Luanda, Angola; Alexandria, Egypt; Tartus, Syria; Berbera, Somalia; Dahlak Island, Ethiopia; and Camranh Bay, Vietnam. Here Cienfuegos differs from the others in that the Soviets have not opted to operate constantly in the Caribbean, probably in deference to U.S. sensitivities.

In addition, Soviet naval involvement at a base is tied into a complex program of military, economic, political, and cultural initiatives with the goal of extending Soviet influence in the nation. Here, again, Cuba was the exception because it already had a communist regime.

Fourth, the Soviets also strengthen the regional power of their client through arms assistance. Here, Cuba differs from the others only in terms of the amount of military aid that Cuba has received, which far exceeds that delivered to other nations.

A fifth aspect of the pattern is that the Soviet Union uses these clients to support insurgent national-liberation movements in the region. The U.S.S.R. carefully conceals this sponsorship in order to provide the movements a degree of legitimacy that they would not enjoy if they were identified as a part of Soviet-assisted insurgency. The Cuban case is different from Guinea,

Angola, Ethiopia, and Syria due to Castro's commitment to revolution. However, in respect to the Caribbean, the Soviets are content with their relationship with Castro, since it provides them with surrogate military forces to be used in insurgent wars, and because the identification with Castro, a Third World revolutionary rather than an imperialist leader, has propaganda value.

A sixth aspect is that once established in the client state, the Soviet Union attempts to expand its influence to other nations in the region. This approach often makes use of insurgent movements, as in El Salvador, but can take the form of clandestine aid to a new client, as in Grenada and Ethiopia. If possible, the Soviets will conceal their relationship with the new nation until a radical government is firmly in power and the security of the nation has been bolstered. It is at this stage in the Soviet-Grenadian relationship that the United States intervened.

In the final stage, the new nation is given legitimacy through Soviet diplomatic support. Economic aid and military assistance are offered openly, the regional power of the nation is enhanced, the U.S.S.R. begins to use the nation's facilities to support Soviet military operations, and the cycle continues as still other nations are targeted. As the secret agreements captured during the Grenadian operation and the construction of the airport vividly demonstrate, the Soviets intended to progress to this stage and would have done so had the United States not intervened.

SUMMARY AND FORECAST

From a strategic perspective, the U.S. and Organization of Eastern Caribbean States' joint action in Grenada effectively ended Soviet influence in Grenada. In this respect it must also be viewed as an effective U.S. counter to a Soviet strategy which has been effective time and again in other regions of the world. To this extent, then, Grenada is important because it demonstrated that the United States can counter Soviet strategic moves in the Third World, even when these moves are about to achieve their goals. Thus Grenada's ultimate significance is that it has demonstrated again that the Soviet strategy is vulnerable and can be countered if the United States has the resolve to do so.

But one should not overestimate the significance of Grenada. The Soviet initiative has been thwarted, and the Soviet threat in the eastern Caribbean has been contained for at least the immediate future. Beyond this, little has changed. The security of Cuba remains intact, Soviet progress in Nicaragua continues unabated, and Soviet military operations in the Caribbean will continue. To be sure, Moscow and Havana will continue to apply pressure, possibly a little more cautiously, because, in the end, Grenada merely represents a tactical setback in a Soviet strategy that has been extremely successful toward the Third World.

44

NOTES

1. G. Scott Sugden, "Public Diplomacy and the Missiles of October," Naval War College Review (October 1971): 30; and Raymond L. Garthoff, "American Reaction to Soviet Aircraft on Cuba, 1962 and 1978," Political Science Quarterly (Fall 1980): 428, 436.

2. Martin J. Scheina, "The U.S. Presence in Guantanamo," Strategic Review (Spring 1976): 86-7; Barry M. Blechman and Stephanie E. Levinson, "Soviet Submarine Visits to Cuba," United States Naval Institute Proceedings (September 1975): 33; George H. Quester, "Missiles in Cuba, 1970," Foreign Affairs (April 1971): 493; and Garthoff, pp. 436-7.

3. Scheina, p. 87; U.S. Congress, House, Committee on International Relations, Impact of Cuban-Soviet Ties in the Western Hemisphere, Hearings before a subcommittee of the Committee on International Relations, 95th Cong., 2nd sess., 1978, p. 7 (hereafter referred to as "Impact of Cuban-Soviet Ties"); and U.S. Congress, House, Committee on Foreign Affairs, Impact of Cuban-Soviet Ties in the Western Hemisphere, Spring 1980, Hearings before the subcommittee on Inter-American Affairs of the Committee on Foreign Affairs, 96th Cong., 2nd sess., 1980, p. 67 (hereafter referred to as "Impact of Cuban-Soviet Ties, 1980").

4. "Impact of Cuban-Soviet Ties," p. 7.

5. "Impact of Cuban-Soviet Ties, 1980," pp. 14, 23.

6. Jiri Valenta, "The Soviet-Cuban Alliance in Africa and the Caribbean," The World Today (February 1981): 47.

7. "Impact of Cuban-Soviet Ties, 1980," pp. 20-1.

8. New York Times, 15 March 1983, and 28 March 1983.

9. "Navy Jets Intercepted Cuban MiGs," The Washington Star (31 July 1981): 4.

5
Grenada: Indications, Warning, and the U.S. Response

Dorothea Cypher

INTRODUCTION

On Tuesday, October 25, 1983, the airwaves crackled with the news of U.S. troops landing on Grenada. However, the reports did not help us to understand why the troops were there. A number of explanations for their presence were offered to the U.S. public. The actual decision to intervene in Grenada was a function of many different inputs and considerations at the national level, all of which were available but not necessarily obvious to the public. The decision was basically a response to the perception of a threat. This chapter will first establish a framework for this case based on applicable indications and warning (I&W) concepts. Then it will attempt to identify the indications which led to the determination of threat, describe the setting for the decision to intervene, and deduce the lessons to be learned.

The case of Grenada, October 1983, does not present a classic I&W problem from the U.S. perspective. Traditionally, Party A achieves surprise by attacking Party B with the entire situation characterized by a web of complex alliances and interrelations. It seems that the United States frequently assumes the role of Party B or is allied with Party B. Grenada appears to fit one of Knorr and Morgan's frameworks for case studies in strategic surprise where "the surprise is initiated by a great power A against a small power B associated with another great power."[1] This framework suggests unique opportunities and incentives for Party A and affects Party B's vulnerability, both of which are illustrated in the case of Grenada.

Within this framework, U.S. actions in Grenada can be viewed as a response to a threat, although again, not completely in accordance with the classic model which would suggest a direct threat to the United States. Although some debated whether the 1,000 U.S. medical students were in danger in Grenada, a perceived threat to U.S. citizens in an unstable and unpredictable situation appears clear. A rescue operation was conceived as a counter to this danger.

In addition, Grenada's neighbors perceived a threat to their own well-being. This perception, exacerbated by the tumultuous conditions in Grenada in October 1983, caused the organization of East Caribbean States (OECS) to request U.S. assistance. Finally,

45

although not cited as a reason for the Grenada operation, there was the perceived long-term threat posed by an unfriendly military buildup on the island as well as the possible establishment of a strategic base of operations for the Cubans and Soviets in the southern Caribbean. Intervention as response to this last menace specifically could conform to Betts's concept of "preventive war" where a military response is initiated "in anticipation of eventual vulnerability, not against immediate threats, and is designed to engage the enemy before he has improved his capabilities."[2] The various indicators and indications of enemy intentions and capabilities which described all three of these threats will be discussed as a function of the formula: I + C = T, where the I represents the intentions of the opponent, C represents their capabilities, and T is the probable threat. [3]

The final basis of this study is the view that U.S. and Grenadian actions, decisions, and reactions exemplify Belden's interactive warning cycle.[4] In this cycle, indicators are discerned by intelligence, then analyzed and presented to decisionmakers who make a decision and authorize appropriate action. This action, in turn, provides an indicator and signal of intentions--or even a warning--to the opponent. For instance, as mentioned above, threats were perceived in Grenada on the basis of indicators discerned by the United States, analyzed, and presented to national decisionmakers who initiated the Grenadian operation. It can be argued that this operation acted as an indicator to Cuba and the Soviet Union of U.S. intentions in the Caribbean and perhaps in an even wider arena.

HISTORICAL BACKGROUND

Many trouble spots which become I&W problems have long histories of tension and conflict between the eventual players in a confrontation. As Betts notes there have never been any "bolts from the blue."[5] The history of tension between Grenada and the United States is relatively short by comparison. Sir Eric Gairy, who ruled even before Grenada became independent of Great Britain in 1974, was on friendly terms with the United States and maintained an ambassador in Washington. No one would argue, however, that Gairy's rule was anything but authoritarian; his was an authority largely enforced by his infamous "Mongoose Gang." In many ways, the coup by Maurice Bishop and the leftist New Jewel Movement (NJM) in March 1979 was a welcome change for the Grenadians. The coup also marked the downturn in Grenadian/U.S. relations.

Although the history of conflict between Grenada and the United States is relatively short, a much longer and more explosive history exists between the United States and Cuba, largely attributable in modern times to the latter's close relations with the Soviet Union. That history is beyond the scope of this study but serves as the basis for the tension with Grenada since Cuban influence in Grenada has been pervasive.

INDICATORS

The NJM was formed in the early 1970s and openly developed ties with Cuba, cemented by an eventually close personal relationship between Bishop and Fidel Castro. A team of black Cuban commandos from the Cuban intelligence service's Directorate of Special Operations (DGI) allegedly helped in the coup in 1979.[6] A month later Julian Torres Rizo, a senior American Department of Intelligence officer, was appointed charge d'affaires and later full ambassador to Grenada. Cuban "advisors" in many arenas, especially those of the military and militia, soon followed. That November, Prime Minister Bishop announced that Cuban aid would enable construction of a new international airport at Point Salines.

Overt political, military, and economic indicators like these, in addition to a tradition of human rights abuses dating back to Gairy's regime, exerted a tremendous influence on U.S. policy toward Grenada. For example, requests to extradite Gairy were not honored, President Carter refused to accept the ambassador proposed by the Bishop government, and President Reagan refused to consider the subsequent ambassadorial candidate. But where the United States most hurt Grenada's People's Revolutionary Government (PRG) was in the financial sphere. Washington excluded Grenada from its aid programs and pressured the United Kingdom, the International Monetary Fund (IMF), the Caribbean Development Bank, and other international aid organizations to take similar measures.[7]

Grenada's neighbors also became increasingly alarmed over Grenada's militarization and close ties with Cuba. Only a few weeks after Bishop's coup, St. Vincent complained of an attempted landing by a small group of Grenadian soldiers. In January 1980, Trinidad and Tobago charged that approximately 200 dissidents from their nation were being taught sabotage and guerilla warfare by Cubans in Grenada. St. Vincent also reported similar terrorist training of some of its dissidents in the Cuban DGI school on Grenada, while Kenrick Radix, later Grenada's Minister of Justice, was deported from Antigua for attempting to foment revolution in that nation.[8]

Overt Soviet links became apparent in 1980 through a number of political indicators. In May, Grenadian Deputy Prime Minister Coard made his first official visit to the Soviet Union. The Grenadians received several million dollars worth of trade credits and machinery and scholarships for Grenadian students from the Soviet Union, Czechoslovakia, and Bulgaria.[9]

At home Maurice Bishop continued his attack on "American imperialism." As the first of many such accusations, he blamed the U.S. Central Intelligence Agency (CIA) for a bomb blast at a rally in Grenada in June 1980, which killed two children and wounded twenty others. Similar political indicators continued the following year. Prime Minister Bishop declared there would be no elections because these are "incompatible with a revolution," and "the Grenadian people are giving full support to the new socialist regime." In the same statement, Bishop again accused the CIA of attempting to destabilize his government. Further evidence of the NJM establishing a repressive Marxist-Leninst regime in Grenada came in June 1981, when the PRG banned the third and last independent newspaper operating in Grenada. This ban left only the Free West Indian, a propoganda arm of the PRG for which printing equipment and technical assistance were provided by the East Germans.[10]

Another round in the interactive relations between the United States and Grenada started with Ocean Venture '81, a U.S. naval exercise in which the scenario described the invasion of the island nation of "Amber and the Amberines" to rescue American hostages there and prepare the nation for free elections. Although the exercise was conducted in August 1981 against Vieques Island off Puerto Rico, the Grenadians clearly perceived themselves as the target of that operation. In fact they were so sure they were about to be invaded that Bishop enjoined the United Nations to protest to President Reagan. Just two months later Mr. Bishop again accused the CIA of attempting to subvert the PRG.

Economic indicators came to the forefront in 1982 with President Reagan's proposal of the Caribbean Basin Initiative (CBI) from which Grenada was excluded because of its close relations with Cuba. Mr. Bishop criticized the CBI as "chicken feed." Instead, Grenada turned to the Soviet Union for aid. The May 1982 conference in Moscow netted Grenada $1.4 million for the purchase of 500 tons of steel, 400 tons of flour, and other essential goods, and a ten year credit of $7.7 million to finance construction of a satellite earth station. This accord was politically reinforced by establishing a Soviet embassy in Grenada in September 1982 headed by Gennadiy I. Sazhenev, a high-ranking military intelligence (GRU) official who had previously been stationed in Argentina and Colombia. Ambassador Sazhenev promptly established a Tass office upon his arrival to "inform the Grenadians of world events."[11]

Grenada received major publicity in March 1983, when President Reagan displayed photography of the Point Salines airport construction, asserting that its intended use was military and unfriendly. He also accused the Cubans of building a military operations base on Grenada for storage of arms and ammunition and military and terrorist training. In addition to the photography, some compelling supporting evidence had come directly from the Grenadians. In December 1981, the Grenadian Minister of National Mobilization publicly stated in a speech to Jamaica's official Communist Party that "Cuba would eventually use the new airport to resupply troops in Africa and that the Soviet Union would also find it useful because of its 'strategic location' astride vital sea lanes and oil transport routes." This statement was made despite repeated protests by Grenadian officials that the new international airport was necessary to expand the tourist industry, although the island clearly did not have more than 400 beds to support that industry--or evident plans for more. The next day, in response to this latest accusation by Mr. Reagan,

Prime Minister Bishop promptly accused the United States of planning an invasion of Grenada or a CIA-backed counterrevolutionary operation, and put his forces on alert for the imminently feared attack.[12]

That attack never materialized. But in retrospect the Grenadians probably regarded it as only one in a series of false alarms. Prime Minister Bishop responded to this particular false alarm by making diplomatic overtures to Washington at the invitation of the U.S. Congressional Black Caucus. Following a speech to the OAS in which he denied that his country posed any threat to the United States, criticized Grenada's exclusion from the CBI, and proclaimed a desire for normal relations between the two countries, Bishop met with President Reagan's national security advisor William Clark. Later he claimed to have established "some sort of a dialogue" with the United States at that meeting but was still convinced of a CIA plot to destabilize his government. A few days later, in June 1983, a further indication that the PRG might be changing, or at least moving slightly away from its leftist orientation, was the announcement that a five-member commission had been formed to draft a constitution to be submitted to a popular referendum. Elections were tentatively planned for the end of 1984 or mid-1985.[13]

These indicators appear to have only been noise or distractions since they were offset by a number of contracts between Grenada and the Soviet Union, which were developed in June and July 1983. Most of these were in the areas of education, communications, water supply, and seaport development. The most interesting, perhaps, provided for the Soviet Union to build a ground communications station on the island as part of the Soviet Intersputnik satellite system. Coincidentally, an almost identical agreement had been signed in Managua the previous day.[14]

One lone economic indicator appeared in August 1983. The International Monetary Fund announced that it had approved $14.5 million in foreign currency purchases. This decision was based on the fact that Grenada had been unusually adversely affected by the world recession in 1983, contrasted with an average three percent rise in real gross national product each year from 1980-82. The annual inflation rate concurrently declined from an average of twenty percent in 1980-81 to five and one half percent in the twelve months preceeding April 1983.[15]

The press was curiously quiet about Grenada for the next six weeks, a time which was fraught with internal conflict within the NJM and PRG. The first mention of any conflict is on October 13, 1983, when officers of the People's Revolutionary Army (PRA) deposed Prime Minister Bishop, accused him of not being a "true revolutionary," and placed him under house arrest. The army took power and sources suggested that former Deputy Prime Minister Bernard Coard would take Bishop's place. Six days later army commander General Hudson Austin announced that Maurice Bishop and five of his ministers and officials had been killed after they themselves had first killed two soldiers. At the same time Austin ordered a twenty-four hour shoot-on-sight curfew. Unsubstantiated allegations of Cuban complicity in the coup appeared in the U.S. press on October 20th. The next day, unnamed Grenadian officials reported that on October 19th, in addition to Maurice Bishop, as many as forty people may have died. A few other deaths in the ensuing days were also reported.[16]

The U.S. response became evident when the press reported "a ten-ship U.S. task force, carrying 1,900 Marines and headed by the helicopter carrier Saipan, had been ordered toward Grenada to signal U.S. intentions to protect its citizens there in the wake of the recent coup."[17] That was the last report made before the U.S. invasion started on the morning of Tuesday, October 25, 1983.

ANALYSIS

Whether or not the decision to intervene in Grenada was an example of successful analysis or warning can never truly be proven, only debated, due to the "paradox of warning." Perhaps the intervention squelched the threat in Grenada or at least slowed it down; perhaps there was no threat to squelch. The indications in this case seem to prove the former.

As stated at the outset, the indicators discussed here are not all inclusive. Their selection emphasizes the information available to the United States prior to Bishop's house arrest. They are gleaned from the open press, and although fundamentally comprehensive, have been compiled to demonstrate the chronological interactions between the two players. The understanding of the interactive nature of these indicators is extremely important. A very simple example of this interaction occurred when Prime Minister Bishop signalled lots of indicators to the United States by voting with Cuba in support of the Soviets in Afghanistan. The United States analyzed this, decided that Grenada intended to continue to strengthen its ties with the Soviet Bloc and decided to reply by continuing to oppose that alliance by cutting off financial aid.

With that interactive quality in mind, a look at the indications that are collectively suggested by the myriad of political, economic, military, and other factors is in order.

First, the information concerning diplomatic, political, and economic ties to the Soviet Union, Cuba, and other Soviet Bloc countries was a clear signal that Grenada did not intend to be either friendly or neutral toward the United States and its allies.

Second, the excessive buildup of air and communications facilities in addition to the huge arms and armament stockpiling, implied a monumentally increased military capability. In conjunction with the first indication, this increased capability also signalled an intention to use this capability in a manner contrary to U.S. interests.

Third, the evidence of guerrilla training of neighboring island dissidents, combined with the stockpiling of arms, suggested an intention to operate as a base for exporting subversion throughout the region.

Fourth, the deteriorating economy suggested an unstable situation conducive to some sort of revolution. This preliminary indicator was borne out by the subsequent coup, bloodshed, and anarchy.

THREATS

Obviously three factors interacted to suggest intentions and capabilities. In a similar fashion, they are combined to determine threats as a function of the formula: $I + C = T$. When the deteriorating Grenadian economy is combined with Grenada's closer ties to the Soviet Union, as well as with the inability of State Department officials to assure the safety of U.S. medical students after a visit to Grenada on October 22nd, they amounted to a threat to the safety of U.S. citizens.[18]

Evaluation of the second and third factors above suggest a culpable threat to Grenada's neighbors.

Finally, the addition of all four of the above factors demonstrates the third and perhaps most alarming threat in the eyes of the United States: the long term threat of a military buildup on Grenada which might easily be used as a strategic operations base by the Cubans and Soviets against U.S. interests.

DECISION

Confronted with these threats, U.S. decisionmakers at the executive level had to play their role in the warning cycle, that is, to make a decision and authorize appropriate action, if necessary. Had it not been for the threat to the safety of the OECS and Grenada's Governor-General, Sir Paul Scoon, both of which developed very late in the situation, the United States might well have opted for an alternative, probably diplomatic, action.

In light of the existing situation and keeping the Knorr and Morgan framework in mind, the incentive for the United States to win cheaply and quickly in Grenada was obvious. Surprise did not play as crucial a role in the Grenada operation as would normally be expected. In fact, the American people were much more surprised than the Cubans, who were allegedly tipped off by an OECS meeting.[19]

Considering the overwhelming U.S. military superiority, surprise was an even less important factor. Grenada was particularly vulnerable at the time due to the chaotic internal situation on the island. The United States could also make the reasonable assumption that Grenada's allies would not significantly lessen that vulnerability. This assumption was supported by Castro's criticism of the PRA coup and Bishop's execution.[20]

These factors all contributed to the U.S. decision to intervene militarily. Possibly one of the driving factors, however, was the desire to signal to our opponents our capability and intention to use arms if necessary to protect our vital local and strategic interests.

CONCLUSIONS

The best an indications and warning case study can do is to present the events and circumstances of the situation as objectively as possible and to analyze them in order to discover useful lessons. No two cases are exactly alike and the tendency to force one case into the mold of the last must be avoided. General conclusions can be formulated and are useful in slightly different ways to two categories of professionals. Intelligence analysts can apply the lessons to anticipating and predicting future sites and characteristics of crises. On the other hand, understanding past crises and their general characteristics helps the decisionmakers to forestall or manipulate crisis situations for the best interests of their nation.

The primary lesson of the Grenada case lies in the tiny island's inherent lack of importance. In fact, Grenada is like many other small developing Third World nations, which are increasingly the settings for crisis situations. When the current situations in Nicaragua, El Salvador, Guyana, and the recent example of Grenada are considered, the Latin American subset of the Third World is becoming the most critical arena in which to remain alert.

The nature of a complex and increasingly interdependent globe imparts critical significance to these Third World areas which are otherwise of little note. With direct confrontation between superpowers growing ever more costly, more emphasis is placed on superpower allied and surrogate activities. From this perspective, Grenada is an example of second party surrogate activity. Analysts of these problems must look beneath the surface to recognize such underlying forces at work.

As described here the Grenadian case, although subtle, was certainly not a "bolt from the blue." Methodical attention to readily available indicators can provide the basis for highly accurate analysis. Other cases in which surrogate influence is suspected can be compared to cases like Grenada for historical insight.

Finally, the interactive nature of the entire warning cycle is particularly important. Intelligence professionals must understand the interactions to develop accurate insight into the warning problem. Decision and policymakers must be even more conscious of the phenomena since the decisions they make to act (or not act) will often determine the opponent's next move and have far reaching consequences, as demonstrated on a small scale in Grenada.

NOTES

1. Klauss Knorr and Patrick Morgan, eds., <u>Strategic Military Surprise</u> (New York: National Strategy Information Center, Inc., 1983), p. 7.

2. Richard K. Betts, Surprise Attack (Washington, DC: The Brookings Institute, 1982), p. 145.

3. Timothy M. Laur, "Introduction to Warning Intelligence," Book of Readings: Introduction to Indications and Warning Intelligence and Terrorism (Washington, DC: Defense Intelligence College, 1984), p. 14.

4. Thomas G. Belden, "Indications, Warning and Crisis Operations," International Studies Quarterly 1(1977): 183.

5. Betts, p. 145.

6. Timothy Ashby, "Grenada: Soviet Stepping Stone," U.S. Naval Institute Proceedings (December 1983): 30.

7. "Grenada: Defiance After U.S. Snub," London Times, 13 March 1982.

8. "Grenada, 9 Jan 1980," Deadline Data on World Affairs, (Greenwich, Conn.: DMS, Inc., January 1980), p. 1; Ashby, p. 30; and "Deep Concern Over Cuban Plans Reported by Caribbean States," The Washington Forum, 28 October 1983, p. 6.

9. Ashby, p. 30.

10. 1980 Reuters Ltd., June 20, 1980, Friday, PM cycle, International News, St. George's, Grenada, 9 January 1980, p. 1; Deadline Data, 25 March 1981, p. 2; Deadline Data, 19 June 1981, p. 2; and Ashby, p. 31.

11. Deadline Data, 14 April 1982, p. 3; and Ashby, p. 3.

12. The Associated Press, March 10, 1983, Thursday, AM cycle, Washington; United States Information Agency, Grenada: A Preliminary Report (Washington, DC: USIA, 1983), p. 18; and 1983 Latin American Newsletters, Ltd.,; Latin American Weekly Reports: Caribbean, March 31, 1983, RC-83-03; p. 1.

13. Deadline Data, 1 June 1983, p. 4; and Deadline Data, 4 June 1983, p. 4.

14. Ashby, p. 32.

15. Deadline Data, 25 August 1983, p. 4.

16. Ashby, p. 32; Deadline Data, 19 October 1983, p. 5; United Press International, October 20, 1983, Thursday, PM cycle, Washington; and Deadline Data, 21 October 1983, p. 5.

17. Deadline Data, 22 October 1983, p. 5.

18. <u>Grenada: A Preliminary Report</u>, p. 3.

19. Charles W. Corddry, "Strategically 'Ideal' U.S. Base on Grenada Favored by Admiral," <u>Baltimore Sun</u>, 27 November 1983, p. 1.

20. Alan Berger, "Grenada, According to Castro," <u>Boston Globe</u>, 20 November 1983, p. A23.

6
Policy Without Intelligence

Gerald Hopple and Cynthia Gilley

The United States invasion of Grenada in October 1983 provided a dramatic illustration of policymaking without intelligence. The objective success of the operation--and the toppling of a regime which had evolved into rule by what Barry Levine refers to as an elite committed to "Creole Leninism" and "Creole Stalinism"--should not be permitted to obscure this fundamental and disquieting lesson of the invasion.[1]

BACKGROUND

This chapter addresses several themes which emanate from an intelligence post mortem.[2] The emphasis is on precrisis political and strategic intelligence rather than tactical or combat intelligence, and it should be emphasized that the assessment is tentative in nature. Unfortunately for the researcher interested in evaluating the intelligence dimension of the Grenada operation, nothing comparable to the Franks Report on the precrisis phase of the British response to Argentina's attack on the Falklands has become publicly available for Grenada.[3]

An indications and warning (I&W) stocktaking of the Grenada case involves issues linked to both military and political intelligence. In the military intelligence sphere, five substantive issues emerge: the nature and scope of the Cuban presence in Grenada; the Soviet role (and particularly Soviet arms and advisors); the overall extent of communist penetration of the country; Grenada's military capability and intentions; and pre-attack intelligence related to invasion planning. As a backdrop to these specific questions of evidence and interference, the strategic threat posed by Grenada surfaces as an analytical arena where intelligence and policy decisions and concerns overlap and shade together.

The realm of political intelligence raises a host of issue areas, but two particularly intractable topics are at center stage: the Grenadian elite and the larger question of the relative causal influence attributable to internal versus external determinants of developments within Grenada between the coup of March 1979, which installed the Marxist regime, and the invasion of October 1983. The political intelligence issues will be deferred until a later section of this chapter.

OVERALL ASSESSMENT

Generally, the conclusion is inescapable that intelligence available to U.S. policymakers was deficient in volume and quality. Given the importance accorded to Grenada and the perceived strategic threat associated with it since the early days of the Reagan administration, this finding is surprising. If anything, evidence unearthed after the attack provided justification that was lacking prior to the decision, underlining Stephen Andriole's conclusion elsewhere in this volume that the Grenada invasion decision was an instance of military action shaping a policy, rather than the latter setting the stage for invasion.

The Chairman of the Joint Chiefs of Staff, General John Vessey, admitted, "We got a lot more resistance than we expected."[4] General John A. Wickham, Jr. pointed to military intelligence shortcomings, noting that more adequate knowledge of the Cuban antiaircraft capability might have averted some helicopter losses.[5] Advance intelligence was, according to Vice Admiral Joseph Metcalf III, the U.S. forces commander for the operation, "not what we would have desired."[6]

Perhaps the most striking deficiency in military intelligence was the underestimation of the Cuban presence in Grenada. Intelligence information well before the U.S. invasion showed evidence of extensive Cuban involvement. On March 9, 1983, for example, Nestor D. Sanchez, the Deputy Assistant Secretary of Defense for Inter-American Affairs, told a group of educators, "In Grenada, Cuban influence has reached such a high level that it can be considered a Cuban protege."[7] There was also awareness of some Cuban buildup in the several weeks prior to the operation.[8]

However, in a "lesson learned" report, U.S. Navy Commander Michael F. O'Brien said that advance intelligence data claimed that "an estimated 50-60 Cubans are present in Grenada," while the U.S. forces discovered about 800.[9] In the aftermath of the invasion, one Republican Senator asserted:

> I can understand that there wasn't time to provide the kind of intelligence information you'd like to have before launching an invasion, but if it turns out that Cuba was in fact planning to turn the island into base, that Castro was moving massive amounts of arms and large numbers of troops to Grenada, then I'd like to know why our intelligence agencies couldn't detect that until we landed 6,000 troops on the island.[10]

Administration officials attributed the Cuban strength estimate error--and an array of other intelligence inaccuracies and inadequacies--to the limited time available for pre-invasion planning. This, however, is simply indefensible in the light of the policy priority accorded to the Grenada threat for several years. This heightened interest (and a perceived security threat), in fact, dated back to the Carter administration.[11]

Administration spokesman Nestor Sanchez expressed surprise at the weapons and documents uncovered in Grenada, pointing out that there was no foreknowledge of the amount of military hardware stockpiled on the island.[12] Since all Soviet arms aid was apparently transshipped to Grenada from Cuba, it is curious that fairly precise arms delivery estimates did not exist--especially in the light of understandable concern about the increased level of Cuban activity in the Caribbean and Central America in recent years. Why was collection tasking not upgraded?

The overall extent of communist penetration of Grenada is an intelligence topic where the policy community had fairly accurate information. While there is no evidence to support the early claims that Cuba and/or the Soviet Union inspired or orchestrated the hardliners' coup and the murder of Maurice Bishop and others in October 1983, it was clear that Grenada was moving rapidly toward a prototypical Marxist-Leninist Third World state.[13] The documents captured after the invasion confirmed this and filled in the details, but this kind of supporting evidence was hardly necessary to establish what was apparent even in the open source literature.

However, the question of Grenada's capabilities and (especially) intentions is a murkier analytical issue. Administration spokesmen repeatedly referred to the danger that Grenada was being transformed into a base for "exporting terrorism." No definitive or even convincing evidence has emerged to substantiate this charge. Debates about capabilities have recurred between critics and defenders of the invasion. Those skeptical of post-invasion official interpretations have asserted that force projections for the Grenadian military were not that alarming.[14] Not surprisingly, of course, those on the other side of the fence have tended to take a diametrically opposed position. However, this is a _post_ _hoc_ interpretive issue. The real question from an intelligence post mortem vantage point is how well Grenada's then-current and projected capabilities were assessed, and the available public evidence--including, of course, pre-invasion intelligence on Cuban, Soviet, and other external arms flows and advisor estimates--suggests that the data were simply not very impressive. The general threat was clearly perceived (but Grenadian statements and other public indicators would have warranted and buttressed this global inference); the specific contours and the magnitude of the threat were hazy at best.

The political intentions underlying military capabilities are a distinct--and vital--element of the I&W analytical equation.[15] It is well known in the literature on intelligence that preconceptions or stratgic assumptions account for intelligence failures and surprise attacks. This has been demonstrated across a series of cases (most recently with respect to the Falklands, where Britain and Argentina both had faulty but seemingly sensible strategic assumptions which led each side to conclude that the other would not attack or go to war in retaliation for a preemptive strike).[16]

Analytical preconceptions apparently exerted a similarly profound impact on the administration's assessment of Grenada's intentions. The policymakers assumed that the intentions were offensive in nature. Even without a lengthy excursion into the many post-invasion discussions which argue that Grenada's buildup was fully compatible with a defensive posture (and that the impetus was fear of a U.S. invasion, not a desire to export terrorism or revolution), it can be asserted that a consideration completely unrelated to external political intentions motivated Grenada's rulers: the use of the military to institutionalize the revolutionary process. Robert Pastor points out in his chapter in this volume that communism in the Third World typically evolves into the militarized revolution. The armed forces are harnessed to sustain the revolution and enforce internal political coercion. This domestic function of the military leads to a society that is both militarized and totalitarian, but the process may have little or nothing to do with aggressive external intentions.[17]

Finally, pre-attack intelligence as the foundation for invasion planning can be evaluated. It is generally agreed that the active planning process was unusually brief. Bishop's fall on October 14, 1983 and his murder on October 19th--with the accompanying apparent collapse of law and order and pervasive uncertainty about what exactly was going on in Grenada and who was in charge--created a need for some kind of decision. The next day, October 20th, Vice President George Bush, State's Inter-American Affairs Secretary Langhorn Motley, and Secretary of State George Shultz met at an urgent White House meeting. The three assessed intelligence reports on the new rulers and ordered the Joint Chiefs of Staff to prepare a contingency plan to evacuate U.S. citizens.

All accounts agree that, during the several sessions of the decisionmaking group, there was "little intelligence" available about conditions in Grenada. It was unclear who was running Grenada; Deputy Prime Minister Bernard Coard was widely believed at the time to be responsible for Bishop's arrest two weeks earlier, but there was no way to determine whether he or General Hudson Austin, head of the new sixteen-member military council, was now in charge.[18]

Secretary of State Shultz's characterization of the atmosphere at the time as one of "violent uncertainty" may be quibbled with if one takes the luxurious--and invariably misleading--vantage point of hindsight. But if the situation is viewed in the context of the pre-invasion state of affairs, there was no way intelligence could have penetrated the fog of uncertainty, clarified the ambiguity, or disquieted the understandable anxiety in Washington.

Legitimate concerns and criticisms can be raised, however, about pre-attack tactical intelligence. The Joint Chiefs of Staff endorsed the invasion option, but expressed misgivings about inadequate intelligence, hasty planning, and strained logistics.

Defense Secretary Caspar Weinberger referred to military concerns about the quality of intelligence reports on Grenada's forces in the context of discussing an admitted "lack of total intelligence."[19]

THEORETICAL CONTEXT

The portrait sketched out above indicates clearly that intelligence on Grenada was generally inadequate and all too frequently inaccurate. This generalization applies with particular force to the two issues which were both tied to relatively hard rather than squishy evidence bases and were absolutely crucial to the success of an invasion: the size of the Cuban presence and the amount and nature of military hardware from the Soviets and other foreign sources. Why was this the case?

One interpretation of any intelligence failure would indict "foolish intelligence" as the culprit.[20] Flawed estimates and other analytical errors and biases constitute the essence of foolish intelligence. The most dramatic example of this kind of intelligence failure--decidedly symptomatic of analysis rather than a collection failure--is the consistent underestimation over a period of a decade and a half of Soviet forces and intentions in the realm of strategic weapons and of the magnitude of the Soviet Union's overall military effort. This analytical miss prompted the CIA to retroactively double the estimate of the percentage of the Soviet Union's GNP devoted to defense in 1976. For too long, North Korea's capabilities had been similarly underestimated, triggering an analogous analytical about face.

A second and competing interpretation offered in the intelligence literature is Ray Cline's well known "policy without intelligence" argument.[21] Cline juxtaposes the October 1973 Defense Condition 3 alert (in the aftermath of the outbreak of the Yom Kippur War) with the Cuban missile crisis of 1962, maintaining that the former exemplifies a classic case of policymaking without inputs from the intelligence community whereas the latter typfies the ideal of synergism between the policymaking and intelligence communities. The October 1973 U.S. alert decision was made without involving the intelligence analytical or lower level policymaking components of the bureaucracy. This was intentional and, as Cline points out, reflected Secretary of State Henry Kissinger's penchant for making crucial decisions via extra-bureacratic means. Kissinger was convinced that ". . . the only way secrecy can be kept is to exclude from the making of the decision all those who are theoretically charged with carrying it out."[22] The upshot of such an approach to policymaking is, as Cline contends, that the President fails to get the benefit of a full and careful presentation of the relevant intelligence.[23]

In contrast, the Cuban missile crisis decisionmaking process reflected the operation of close cooperation between the intelligence and policy communities. In striking contrast with the October 1973 alert decision, senior policymakers were willing to share key intelligence data and diplomatic correspondence with the intelligence bureaucracy at suitable levels. The 1962 crisis is an almost textbook example of "policy with intelligence."

The available evidence, which is marshalled below, indicates clearly that the Grenada invasion decision fits Cline's policy without intelligence perspective rather than Ellsworth's and Adelman's foolish intelligence explanation.[24] It should be emphasized that policymakers certainly have the right to make decisions without an adequate intelligence foundation, that exigencies of the situation and overriding policy dictates may force such a decisionmaking process to prevail. However, policy without intelligence can lead to disaster. Overwhelming U.S. military power and a unique constellation of other favorable factors maximized the prospects for success. As one Department of State official noted afterwards, "Grenada came too close to our worst-case scenario. The top brass can see how hard it would be to do on a bigger scale."[25]

None of the official justifications for the invasion "now stands up to scrutiny."[26] Three claims formed the case for the invasion: that the U.S. students on the island were endangered; that the Soviets and Cubans were about to make Grenada a base of subversion in the Caribbean; and that Sir Paul Scoon, the governor general, the only legitimate authority in the country after the assassination of Prime Minister Bishop, had requested U.S. intervention.

Regarding the threat to U.S. citizens, the evidence indicates that the medical students and other Americans in Grenada were threatened by the invasion itself, not before the military action. Lives of U.S. citizens were certainly not in imminent danger. The White House acknowledged after launching the invasion that, two days before the U.S. intervened, Grenada's new rulers offered the United States an opportunity to evacuate U.S. citizens, but the administration viewed the offer with distrust.[27] Significantly, pro-U.S. governments refused to allow the local airlines company to fly to the island to evacuate foreign nationals at a key point prior to the invasion.[28] The day after the invasion, Charles Modica, chancellor of the U.S. medical school in Grenada, described the action as a measure which was "very unnecessary" as an operation to save U.S. lives.[29]

The Cuban-Soviet plans for Grenada are murky even with hindsight and, as noted, no support for a Cuban and/or Soviet role in the fall and murder of Bishop and his supporters has come to light. In March 1984, the British House of Commons released a report on the invasion which, with respect to the governor general's alleged request for the rescue operation, concludes that both the timing and the nature of this appeal "remain shrouded in some mystery, and it is evidently the intention of the parties directly involved that the mystery should not be displaced."[30]

The policy context in both the longer term and pre-invasion senses further reinforces the argument that the Grenada decision was a manifestation of the policy without intelligence syndrome. The Reagan administration policy toward the Caribbean has been aptly described as "conservative and not innovative. It is based upon perception of the region's significance to the United States which has deep historical roots and involves the employment of traditional measures to safeguard American interests there."[31] This kind of automatic application of a long standing policy posture minimizes the perceived need for intelligence inputs; policymakers simply draw on a specific mix of policy instruments from the available repertoire.

Interestingly, from a policy perspective, the Grenada operation looks very much like a rerun of the Dominican intervention in 1965.[32] In October 1983, a more extreme group had overthrown a left-wing regime and the prime minister was murdered. As with the similar Dominican scenario, U.S. intervention was explicitly undertaken to forestall a communist takeover. In both cases, the United States claimed that its action was designed to safeguard lives given the breakdown of law and order. Policymakers often reason and decide on the basis of powerful analogies, and this seems to be the case for Grenada.

This general interpretation is strengthened by the unfolding and escalating sequence of events from shortly after the March 1979 coup.[33] The Senate Intelligence Committee ordered the CIA to refrain from direct political action in Grenada as early as July 1981. From August 1st to October 15, 1981, the United States coordinated the largest naval maneuvers since World War II--in the Caribbean. As part of the exercises, U.S. forces liberated Vieques Island, off Puerto Rico, under a code name suggestive of Grenada: "Amber and Amberdines." Subsequent naval maneuvers in 1982 and 1983 were clearly directed at the perceived threat from Grenada, with the 1983 exercises accompanied by a presidential statement that Grenada constituted "a threat to the security of the United States." The policy context leading up to the invasion, then, was characterized by a clear trajectory in which U.S.-Grenadian relations were set on a collision course.

Pre-invasion policymaking also reflects the predominance of policy goals over intelligence inputs. In the immediate aftermath of the operation, U.S. officials said that the overriding reason for the invasion was to prevent the United States from being perceived as a "paper tiger" in the eyes of both friendly and hostile Latin American nations.[34] According to administration officials, the United States began to discuss the use of military force in Grenada with friendly Caribbean governments as early as October 15th, one day after Prime Minister Maurice Bishop had been arrested. Officials also said that the decision to launch the invasion was heavily influenced by the swirl of events on Sunday and Monday, according to the New York Times.[35] The decision to authorize plans for the invasion occurred while public concern was focused on the terrorist attack on the Marine Corps headquarters in Beirut, Lebanon.

The tragedy in Lebanon provided the immediate backdrop to the decision. The desire to send a signal to Cuba, Nicaragua, and the Soviet Union clearly entered into the decision, as did the powerful symbolism of Vietnam and the Iranian hostage crisis. These kinds of higher level policy concerns shaped the decision to invade. The rationality or justifiability of the policy premises which undergirded the decision process and the quality of the decision calculus are subjects well beyond the scope of this chapter. But it is clear that Grenada was a case of policymaking essentially without intelligence.

POLITICAL INTELLIGENCE

Political intelligence can be of critical importance for policymaking. A clear understanding of the dynamics and trends of political processes within a foreign country provides an indispensable foundation for decision choice and action. Compared to military intelligence indicators, political intelligence indicators can increase the lead-time dramatically, enabling policymakers to confront and resolve a problem before it explodes into a crisis.

Generally, political intelligence analysis is much more demanding intellectually than military intelligence analysis, although the two components of strategic intelligence must be meshed to produce accurate and valid assessments and estimates. The evidence and reasoning earlier in this chapter suggest that military intelligence with respect to Grenada was deficient. Quite a few indirect but indisputable indicators imply that political intelligence was of even lower quality (for example, the apparent lack of knowledge about the nature of the fissures within the Grenadian leadership, a lack of detailed information about General Hudson Austin, etc.).

Some post mortems have maintained that the paucity of HUMINT (human intelligence) agents accounted for this. While HUMINT can be a valuable adjunct to the more technical INTs (such as SIGINT (signals intelligence) or photographic evidence) in certain contexts, lack of analysis seems to play a greater role for Grenada than a failure to collect information. Public indicators and indications--if analyzed carefully and cautiously--can be exploited very effectively to develop an accurate intelligence portrait. Furthermore, prior analytical evidence can be mined for insights; the New Jewel Movement was formed in 1973, and Bishop, Coard, and many of the other key players after 1979 were involved in this movement from the outset.

In analyzing a Third World society specifically or any foreign power generally, two realms of political intelligence are central. First, what is the leadership like? Elite analysis and biographic intelligence provide insights into the personal characteristics and beliefs of leaders and leadership cliques and factions. Bureaucratic politics--the interaction and clashes of different parts of the bureaucracy or different elements of a country's leadership--is a pervasive aspect of policymaking within almost all nations. Even decisionmaking in communist countries like Cuba and the Soviet Union, which look like such homogeneous and united processes from the outside, is characterized by difference of opinion--and sometimes even sharp disagreement over fundamental policy strategies.36 Post-invasion evidence has demonstrated that this generalization applied to Grenada, a homogeneous country with a population of only a little more than 100,000, and that differences within the ruling elite predated the crisis events of September and October 1983.

The second question concerns internal societal and political trends and processes. To understand a foreign society, it is necessary to analyze domestic patterns in the light of alternative and explicitly posited hypotheses. In the Caribbean Review's post-invasion issue, Aaron Segal revisits two classic books on Grenada.[37] One was published in 1965 and the other in 1968; both dealt with what the intelligence community would regard as political and sociological intelligence topics--for the years from 1951 to 1953.

The two studies accurately projected the dynamics of Grenada's economic and political landscape: the bleak economic prospects; the steady population growth; and the manipulation (under Gairy) and repudiation (under Bishop) of elections. With hindsight, the view of Grenada as an essentially conservative society is supported. Despite political crises in 1951, 1962, 1974, 1979, and 1983, the country has experienced little fundamental or enduring structural change. Even the transition from a Gairy, with his rural folk base, to a Bishop, with rule by brown, middle class intellectuals, was foreseen. And despite the New Jewel Movement's populist rhetoric and the increasingly strident Marxist-Leninist references to the masses, there is no evidence that the People's Revolutionary Government ever developed a genuine mass working class or rural base (aside from the very real personal popularity of Maurice Bishop).

On bureaucratic politics and elite cleavage, there is some evidence of coherently structured elite dissension prior to the active power struggle between Bernard Coard and Maurice Bishop. On the issue of private sector production, the regime apparently split into "scientific" and "pragmatic" wings, a not unusual fissure in radical or Marxist-Leninist Third World states.[38] Bishop was certainly taking a pragmatic approach toward Grenadian-U.S. relations in the months prior to his murder, a stance that alienated the hardliners within the leadership. A content analysis of Bishop's public statements revealed that he employed relatively little Marxist-Leninist rhetoric and class analysis terminology.[39] Others in the leadership, in contrast, were clearly hardline ideologues.

The struggle for power obviously accelerated in the several months prior to the coup and invasion.[40] As Bishop moved toward a possible rapprochement with the United States, his rival Coard began to call for tighter party control and an intensification of the "revolutionary process." Internal dissension within the elite could no longer be concealed after Bishop's arrest on October 13th.[41]

An alternative interpretation of the events leading to Bishop's ouster would emphasize a personal power struggle and personality clash between the popular prime minister and Coard, minimizing the significance and role of ideological and policy differences. While this is a plausible reconstruction--and probably is more valid than an ideological-policy interpretation-- it does not negate the fact that there were discernible hardliner- softliner policy tendencies on both domestic and foreign policy issues for some time before the blowup.

In a series of case studies on international crises between 1898 and 1973, Glenn Snyder and Paul Diesing discovered evidence of bureaucratic political processes in the form of internal differences of perspective for about half of the decisionmaking units involved.[42] Theoretically internal or intragovernmental and external decision processes should influence each other, and a government should be able to affect its opponent by exploiting its knowledge about hardliner versus softliner disagreements within the other regime.

This strategy does not generally work, however, and governments are not typically very accurate in assessing the other side's bureaucratic political configuration. But if the policymaker has some knowledge about the distribution of internal attitudes and influence, "he can explain and predict the outcome of bargaining episodes between states in greater detail and within narrower limits than would be possible with (purely interstate) bargaining theory alone."[43] For Grenada, information and analysis along these lines would have facilitated the bargaining (and signalling) process--at least prior to the events of October leading up to the invasion, when policy goals displaced intelligence as an input to what had been up to that point a noncoercive bargaining process.

Regarding the political intelligence issue of internal societal trends and processes, this kind of analysis is even more difficult than the admittedly analytically challenging task of foreign elite and bureaucratic politics assessment. Furthermore, unexamined policy premises can prevent this issue area from even being analyzed with any real rigor.

This apparently held for Grenada. The analytical and decision processes were locked into a framework which placed Grenada squarely within an East-West or Cold War conflict axis.[44] Further, the Grenada threat was anchored in the larger Caribbean policy arena, where the East-West struggle is assumed to be the primordial causal force behind stress and upheaval.

There is a sharply opposed viewpoint on this. As Wayne Smith points out, "A more realistic appraisal suggests that the conflict in Central America generally is essentially indigenous. It emerges from decades of fiercely repressive governments, grinding social injustices and economic underdevelopment."[45] Is insurgency in El Salvador, for example, fuelled by internal forces, by external factors, or by both--and, if both, to what extent do the two shape the conflict and how do they interact?

This central question is complex, and the answer to it has genuine and multiple policy ramifications. The Staff Report of the Subcommittee on Oversight and Evaluation of the Permanent Select Commitee on Intelligence (issued in September 1982) concluded that "most finished intelligence on Central America meets high standards."[46] However, some finished intelligence products on Central America have completely skirted the issue of the <u>extent to which</u> revolution there is the effect of factors indigenous to a country rather than outside actors. For example, a 1981 National Intelligence Estimate (NIE) described Nicaragua as "the hub of the revolutionary wheel" in Central America. But the estimate "shrank from seriously considering" the degree to which revolutionary processes in Central America flow from internal as opposed to external forces. Other intelligence products showed a similar failure to confront this central issue.

Given the fact that Grenada was viewed in the context of overall developments in Central America and the Caribbean and that both the Grenadian threat and the larger concerns were interpreted through a Cold War prism, it is reasonable to assume that policymakers maximized the role assigned to external Cuban, Soviet, and other influences. This made it easy to attribute whatever happened there to inputs from abroad. Simultaneously, of course, influences of a purely internal nature were given little or no causal weight in the analytical equation.

Yet extensive evidence (such as the academic works on Grenada referred to earlier) suggests clearly that the revolutionary process there unfolded in line with an exclusively domestic trajectory. In fact, the coup of March 1979 and the resulting revolution were not even reflections of a regional pattern, but constituted "a specific response to the particular political and economic circumstances of Grenada at the time."[47]

It could be argued that forces indigenous to Grenada continued to exert a profound impact after 1979 and that, at the least, U.S. policymakers overestimated the causal role of outside influences. Richard Betts has convincingly documented the central role of ultimately wrong strategic assumptions in accounting for and fooling the victims of military surprise attacks since 1940.[48] Analogously, other intelligence post mortems and academic research on psychology have shown that policy preconceptions and other mental sets or biases can shape analytical judgements and prevent people from perceiving reality accurately. The point here is not to argue that the U.S. policy community was necessarily wrong in its interpretation, but to underline the fact that premises drove analysis and that there was no indication that the theory underlying the conclusions was tested fairly and explicitly by developing and considering alternative hypotheses. This ultimate assessment is consistent with the policy without intelligence viewpoint.

CONCLUSIONS

Third World challenges, problems, and crises will continue to confront U.S. policymakers. Ellsworth and Adelman contend that the United States has traditionally viewed the Third World as a pawn between East and West, a passive player on the superpower stage, and that this is simply unwarranted.[49] To make policy on the Third World without intelligence--in the absence of reliable, valid, and complex information and analysis--is foolish and ultimately dangerous.

Grenada is not an isolated case. The Third World, a central arena for conflict, crisis, and war in the 1970s, will undoubtedly continue to be an even more dangerous environment in the 1980s.[50] We can expect an upsurge of both internal and external violence. Much of the growth of world military spending since 1968 can be attributed to developing states.[51]

No part of the Third World is free from endemic internal and external conflict. This impacts directly on U.S. concerns, both because it is a superpower with global interests and the developing world has been and will continue to be the primary surrogate arena of U.S.-Soviet competition. This does not mean that internal forces do not impinge on and, in some cases, drive the dynamics of change and stress within Third World societies. But the East-West dimension must be overlayed on the purely indigenous; maintaining an analytical balance between the two arenas and knowing when one is more influential than the other are particularly challenging tasks for the policymaker and the analyst.

At least until recently, the U.S. intelligence analytical bureaucracy lacked the resources necessary for studying developing societies in any real detail and with genuine sensitivity for the realities, complexities, and nuances of social, economic, political, and military trends and their interrelationships. Unfortunately, Grenada suggests an analytical performance level short of the optimum or even minimum. Wayne Smith notes that the U.S. intervention in Nicaragua in 1927 was justified on the basis of the need to suppress "Bolshevik guerrillas," sponsored, according to the official rationale, by communist Mexico. Smith concludes, "Our analysis is as bad now as it was then."[52]

This is an unfair judgment; there was clearly a threat from Grenada, although how it should have been dealt with (a policy question) and how serious it was (a policy judgment ideally based on high quality military and political intelligence) raise a whole host of concerns. Donald Zagoria clearly lays out the much larger analytical challenge:

> The challenge of dealing with communism in the Third World is as much a challenge to our understanding as it is to our policy. We need a much more sophisticated national understanding of radical movements and states than we presently have. Compared to the huge amounts of money and effort the government spends on collecting and evaluating military intelligence and "hardware," the amounts which it spends on political analysis is trivial. The problem is not merely a failure of gathering information or even a failure of proper evaluation. Even more serious, it is a failure to ask the right questions.[53]

Ray Cline contends that there is often an American imperative

to act--to do something--in response to a threat--sometimes before
it is fully understood. This pressure is coupled with the policy
without intelligence syndrome. In this sense, the invasion of
Grenada is very reminiscent of the 1973 alert.

NOTES

1. Barry B. Levine, Introduction to "The Alienation of Leninist
Group Therapy: Extraordinary General Meeting of Full Members of
the NJM New Jewel Movement," Caribbean Review 12(Fall 1983): 14.
We would like to thank Gene Gathright and Wendy Sheperd for their
invaluable assistance and Colonel Peter Dunn and Commander Bruce
Watson for their support in the preparation of this chapter. Any
errors are the responsibility of the authors.

2. Policy issues and implications of Grenada in the context of
the Caribbean crisis are illuminated in Gordon Connell-Smith,
"President Reagan and the Caribbean Crisis," Washington Quarterly,
7(Fall 1984): 13-9. A good background overview of the Grenada
revolution of 1979 and its aftermath is provided in Tony
Thorndike, "Grenada: The New Jewel Revolution," in Anthony Payne
and Paul Sutton, eds., Dependency Under Challenge: The Political
Economy of the Commonwealth Caribbean (Manchester: Manchester
University Press, 1984), pp. 105-25. On the invasion itself, see
Eldon Kenworthy, "Grenada as Theater," World Policy Journal
1(Spring 1984): 635-51.

3. The Rt. Hon. The Lord Franks, Falkland Islands Review:
Report of a Committee of Privy Counselors (London: H. M.
Stationery Office, January 1983). See also Gerald W. Hopple,
"Intelligence and Warning: Implications and Lessons of the
Falkland Islands War," World Politics 36(April 1984): 339-61.

4. Time (14 November 1983): 29.

5. "Pleased by Grenada Operation, Army Plans More Elite Forces,"
Baltimore Sun, 9 November 1983, p. 4.

6. Quoted in James B. Motley, "Grenada: Low-Intensity Conflict
and the Use of U.S. Military Power," World Affairs 146(Winter
1983-1984): 227.

7. "U.S. Now Puts the Strength of Cubans on Isle at 1,100," New
York Times, 29 October 1983, p. A6.

8. Ibid.

9. "Reports Cite Lack of Coordination During U.S. Invasion of
Grenada," New York Times, 4 December 1984.

10. "Senators Suggest Administration Exaggerated its Cuba
Assessment," New York Times, 30 October 1983, p. A22.

11. Robert A. Pastor, "U.S. Policy Toward the Caribbean: Recurring Problems and Promises," in Jack W. Hopkins ed., Latin America and Caribbean Contemporary Record, vol. I, 1981-1982 (New York and London: Holmes and Meier, 1983), pp. 79-89.

12. Nestor D. Sanchez, "What Was Uncovered in Grenada: The Weapons and Documents," Caribbean Review 12(Fall 1983): 21.

13. Cuba expressed anger, particularly about the murder of Castro's close friend Bishop. Moscow, in contrast, praised the newly installed Revolutionary Military Council under General Hudson Austin. See Tony Thorndike, "The Grenada Crisis," The World Today 39(December 1983): 474-5.

14. Kenworthy (p. 643) notes that, according to the State-Defense white paper (Grenada: A Preliminary Report, released on December 16, 1983), by 1986 the Grenadian Army would have totalled about 2,000 soldiers--twice its 1983 strength level but considerably lower than some other administration estimates.

15. For a useful discussion of political-military intentions and capabilities in the I&W analytical process, see Timothy M. Laur, "Principles of Warning Intelligence," in Gerald W. Hopple and Bruce Watson eds., The Military Intelligence Community (Boulder, CO: Westview, 1985).

16. Hopple, "Intelligence and Warning."

17. "Britain's Grenada Shut-Out," The Economist, 10 March 1984, p. 32. See also relevant articles in Newsweek (24 October 1983, and 31 October 1983) and the New York Times (27 October 1983, 28 October 1983, and 30 October 1983).

18. Newsweek (31 October 1983): 40.

19. "Joint Chiefs Supported U.S. Action as Feasible," New York Times, 27 October 1983, p. A23.

20. Robert F. Ellsworth and Kenneth L. Adelman, "Foolish Intelligence," Foreign Policy 36(Fall 1979): 147-77.

21. Ray S. Cline, "Policy Without Intelligence," Foreign Policy (1974): 121-35.

22. Ibid, p. 123.

23. Ibid, p. 129.

24. There was certainly evidence of "foolish intelligence," as is demonstrated in the preceding section of this chapter. However, it must be noted that the research reflected here did not include access to pre-invasion finished intelligence products; it is

certainly conceivable that the intelligence community may have produced assessments and estimates on the situation in Grenada that were more accurate than the evidence base which the policymakers employed. This was, for example, the case with the 1961 Bay of Pigs decision; intelligence analysts would have been able to tell the policymakers at that time that certain key assumptions which provided the foundation for the decision to invade Cuba were unwarranted, but the decision process was restricted to high level policymakers for reasons of security and lower level analysts were kept in the dark.

25. Time (14 November 1983): 29.

26. "Grenada: New Colony, New Myth," Baltimore Sun, 24 October 1984, p. 11.

27. "Reagan Aide Says U.S. Invasion Forestalled Cuban Arms Buildup," New York Times, 27 October 1983, p. A1.

28. "Grenada: New Colony, New Myth,", p. 11.

29. Kenworthy, p. 637; "School's Chancellor Says Invasion Was Not Necessary to Save Lives," New York Times, 26 October 1983, p. A20.

30. "Grenada: New Colony, New Myth," p. 11.

31. Connell-Smith, p. 14.

32. Ibid, p. 17.

33. For overviews of U.S. activity during the period from 1979 to the invasion, see: Kenworthy, pp. 644-5; and Thorndike, "The Grenada Crisis," pp. 468-9.

34. "Steps to the Invasion: No More 'Paper Tiger,'" New York Times, 30 October 1983, pp. A1, A20. See also: "Which Threat in Grenada?" New York Times, 26 October 1983, p. A26; "What Was He Hiding?" New York Times, 31 October 1983, p. A19; and "Licensed to Kill? " The Economist, 5 November 1983, pp. 11-13.

35. "An Invasion Prompted by Previous Debacles," New York Times, 26 October 1983, pp. A1, A17.

36. On divisions within the Cuban elite, see Robin S. Kent, Marilyn Blatnikoff, and Dewey Covington, "Divisions Within the Cuban Leadership: A Simulated Poll," pp. 179-208, in Gerald W. Hopple and James A. Kuhlman eds., Expert-Generated Data: Applications in International Affairs (Boulder, CO: Westview, 1981).

37. Aaron Segal, "Backgound to Grenada: When the Social Scientists Invaded," Caribbean Review 12(Fall 1983): 40-4.

70

38. Anthony P. Maingot, "Options for Grenada: The Need to be Cautious," _Caribbean Review_ 12(Fall 1983): 27.

39. Carl Henry Feuer, "Was Bishop a Social Democrat?" _Caribbean Review_ 12(Fall 1983): 39. Public articulations can of course be notoriously fallible. But elite statements can be useful diagnostically if analyzed carefully in relation to other signals and indicators.

40. For details, see; Thorndike, "The Grenada Crisis," pp. 473-4; Kenworthy, p. 645.

41. At this point, reliable and detailed intelligence evidence on the elite could have provided a key input to the decision process and would in fact have furnished impressive ammunition for the invasion rationale; the hardliners wanted to begin collectivization--ending the policy of tolerating a large private sector--and significantly advance the timetable for even closer relations with the Soviet Union. Instead, U.S. policymakers seemed to be confused about the views and characteristics of Bernard and Phyllis Coard, General Hudson Austin, and the other key participants in the crisis. At the first high level group discussion on October 20th, led by Vice President Bush, concern was voiced that the new military rulers on the island, particularly Austin, were the type of people who had held Americans hostage in Iran (_New York Times_, 30 October 1983), but there was apparently no detailed information on Austin and the other new rulers.

42. Glenn H. Snyder and Paul Diesing, _Conflict Among Nations: Bargaining, Decision Making, and System Structure in International Crises_ (Princeton, NJ: Princeton University Press, 1977).

43. Ibid., p. 523.

44. Pastor, p. 87; and Connell-Smith, p. 19.

45. Wayne S. Smith, "The Grenada Complex in Central America: Action and Negotiation in U.S. Foreign Policy," _Caribbean Review_ 12(Fall 1983): 36.

46. Staff Report, Subcommittee on Oversight and Evaluation, Permanent Select Committee on Intelligence, _U.S. Intelligence Performance on Central America: Achievement and Selected Instances of Concern_ (Washington, DC: U.S. Government Printing Office, September 22, 1982). All of the quotations in this paragraph are from this report.

47. Thorndike, "Grenada: The New Jewel Revolution," p. 105.

48. Richard K. Betts, _Surprise Attack: Lessons for Defense Planning_ (Washington, DC: Brookings Institution, 1982).

49. Ellsworth and Adelman, p. 155.

50. For a more detailed argument on the points raised here, see Hopple, "Intelligence and Warning." On the Third World in the context of the current international security environment, see Motley.

51. Edward A. Kolodziej and Robert Harkavy, "Developing States and the International Security System," in John J. Stremlau, ed., The Foreign Policy Priorities of Third World States (Boulder, CO: Westview, 1982), pp. 19-47.

52. Smith, p. 65.

53. Donald S. Zagoria, "Into the Breach: New Soviet Alliances in the Third World," in Erik P. Hoffman and Frederic J. Fleron eds., The Conduct of Soviet Foreign Policy (New York: Aldine, 1980), pp. 495-514.

7
A Decision Theoretic Analysis of the Reagan Administration's Decision to Invade Grenada

Stephen J. Andriole

INTRODUCTION

The U.S. invasion of Grenada on October 25, 1983 shook the international community. While there had been many indications of U.S. unhappiness with growing Cuban influence in the Caribbean, and the direction in which Maurice Bishop had moved the government since he seized power in a bloodless coup in 1979, very few anticipated an invasion.[1]

The invasion itself was unique for a variety of reasons. First, it was hastily conceived. Records of the decisionmaking process indicate that prior to the initial meetings regarding how to respond to the situation in Grenada, no contingency invasion plans existed. Second, the invasion was unique because it occurred in a relative great power vacuum. While there were certainly great power stakes involved, the U.S. moved against a disorganized regime whose ties to Cuba and, ultimately, the Soviet Union, were actually less developed than Bishop's. Third, the Reagan administration's decision to initially deny press access to Grenada was certainly not typical of U.S. military policy. Finally, the invasion was unique because it gave birth to a Caribbean policy that before the invasion was only vaguely developed; usually, military action results from policy, not the other way around.

This uniqueness is the subject of this chapter. The avenue into the uniqueness will be the decisionmaking process that was implemented at the highest level of the U.S. government just prior to the invasion. This chapter will reconstruct the decisionmaking process from what we know about the invasion; it will also retrofit some formal decision analytic techniques to the process in an effort to make the process explicit. This second step will be taken in order to convert what the narrative reconstruction tells us into some measurable equivalents. The retrofitting will also suggest how operations like URGENT FURY can be planned well in advance. The chapter concludes with some ideas for implementing and assessing high-level foreign policy decisions.

THE DECISIONMAKING BACKDROP

Maurice Bishop's bloodless coup in 1979 was met with mixed emotions by the Carter administration, though shortly after Bishop seized power there was no question about the direction in which he was taking Grenada. Soviet and Cuban influence began to grow dramatically, and within a few months it was clear that arms were to accompany the influence. When construction began on a major new airport on the south side of the island, all doubt was removed in Washington about adversary intentions.

While it is impossible to determine from open sources whether or not an invasion was contemplated prior to Bishop's overthrow on October 13, 1983, it is clear that the overthrow stimulated serious invasion discussions. The specific events and conditions that led up to the second coup, as well as the high level decisionmaking "style" of the Reagan administration, together comprise the decisionmaking backdrop to the October 25th invasion.

The decisionmaking style of the Reagan administration had already been well established by the time a decision was necessary in Grenada. Unlike many previous administrations, the Reagan administration's approach to domestic and foreign policymaking is highly decentralized. We know, for example, that the President is not always involved in the mechanics of every decision. Instead, he prefers to receive "minimemos" on even important issues and events. His immediate staff processes large quantities of information on his behalf; at the same time, there is evidence to suggest that the President's values, beliefs, and attitudes were not displaced during the Grenada filtering process.[2]

These values, beliefs, and attitudes became extremely important during the Grenada decisionmaking process which itself was characterized by a relatively high level of agreement among the participants. In fact, the National Security Decision Directives (NSDDs) clearly reflected Reagan's values and a group consensus.

THE DECISION PRECIPITANTS

On October 17, 1983, just four days after Bernard Coard overthrew Maurice Bishop, plans were in the works for a non-combatant evacuation of U.S. nationals from Grenada. This plan was not at all unlike the plans that are frequently made when U.S. citizens are threatened; there have been several evacuations from Lebanon over the years, and we are all familiar with the U.S. evacuation from Saigon. Typically, evacuation plans involve assessments about the likelihood of an evacuation becoming necessary coupled with assessments about the benefit of one evacuation plan versus another. In 1976, for example, the Ford administration had to decide whether or not an evacuation from Lebanon would be necessary and, if so, where the U.S. Sixth Fleet should be positioned in the eastern Mediterranean in order to minimize the fleet's exposure risks, how to send the "right" political signals to U.S. allies and adversaries, how to remain flexible, and how to minimize overall Mediterranean readiness costs.[3] After considerable discussion, the Sixth Fleet was moved to accommodate both the probability of an evacuation and the above four criteria.

Grenada evacuation plans were organized around 700 Americans who were students in an American medical school. On October 13th, President Reagan approved recommendations to begin the development of a specific set of plans for the evacuation.

In anticipation of the need for support during the evacuation, the carrier _Independence_ left Virginia on October 18th. The 22nd Marine Amphibious Unit left the United States on the same day, and while the carrier and the Marines were said to be on their way to the Mediterranean to relieve Marines in Lebanon, in retrospect it appears as though the key decisionmakers knew full well that the task force might be diverted to Grenada. As it turned out, it was--on October 20th--ordered to steam closer to Grenada. The day before, October 19th, Maurice Bishop had been killed and a twenty-four hour "shoot on sight" curfew imposed on the entire island.

By this time a crisis pre-planning group was already assembled.[4] After some deliberation the group decided that the events in Grenada should be analyzed directly by the special situation group of the National Security Council. One output from the special situation group was a first cut at a National Security Decision Directive (NSDD). Perhaps surprisingly, it was during the preparation of the initial NSDD that it was discovered that (a) there was no contingency plan on file for a possible invasion of Grenada, and (b) that maps and photographs of the island were inadequate.

It is interesting to study the decisionmaking process up to this point. During these initial days it was extremely procedural, dominated almost by organizational and bureaucratic procedures. From an intelligence perspective, the emphasis during this early phase was on the collection and assembly of information, not on its analysis. Up to this point no one had specified any courses of action, and no one had suggested any dimensions of value upon which the decision should be based. In terms of classic decisionmaking theory, the various Grenada groups were by the 21st of October engrossed in "problem definition" and "information gathering," though it is interesting that information gathering usually occurs _after_ the formulation of decision alternatives, not before, as was the case during the Grenada decisionmaking process (and many other government/intelligence/military decisionmaking processes).[5]

On October 22nd, things began to heat up, and the information gathering process began to transform itself into a bona fide decisionmaking process. For the first time, specific objectives were identified. They included the following:

      o   If at all possible, guarantee the safety of all the Americans;

o   Restore a democratic government in conjunction with friendly governments with the same interest; and

o   Eliminate and prevent Cuban activity on Grenada.

These objectives are extremely important to this diagnosis of the Grenada decisionmaking process because they yield a set of criteria that provide insight into how the decision was actually made.   For example, Vice President Bush is reported to have questioned the simultaneous pursuit of the objectives, and General Vessey, Chairman of the Joint Chiefs of Staff, felt that the risks were great to his special forces.[6] It is also interesting to note that Prime Minister Thatcher was not at all happy about the invasion, though Speaker O'Neill and Senator Baker were in complete agreement with the President's decision.[7]

There were of course a variety of discussions about the likelihood of success versus failure, and about the risks connected with the invasion.   Accounts of similar discussions suggest that while there is always an attempt to remain rigorous, the discussion often veers in many different directions.   There are also biases at work, and the influence of articulate and ranking members of the group.   Irving Janis' now famous work on the effects of "groupthink" deals with all of these issues; others, like De Rivera, have dwelled upon the impact of individual values, beliefs, and attitudes.[8]

Halperin's work on bureaucratic politics and foreign policy decisionmaking also helps us understand the Grenada decisionmaking process, as does Chan's work on the "intelligence of stupidity."[9] It is now clear, for example, that the Grenada decisionmaking group acted upon less than perfect intelligence about the number of armed Cubans on the island; geographic intelligence was also inadequate.   In spite of these problems, the decision was made to launch the invasion, apparently in response to judgements about the likelihood of success and the number of casualties that would be sustained.   While it is certainly possible to make a "bad" decision that results in a "good" outcome (just as it is possible to make a "good" decision that results in a "bad" outcome), there is not overwhelming reason to believe that the Grenada special situation group failed to execute any major steps of the decision-making process.

The invasion itself began on October 25th at approximately 5:30 a.m.   Though the United States and its Caribbean partners encountered much more resistance than anticipated, the island was taken and the American students were successfully evacuated.

The Grenada invasion decision was by no means a "textbook" decision.   At the same time, it was explicit enough to yield an assessment, which, no doubt, is already in the works. Unfortunately, however, because of the press blackout of the initial invasion there will always be at least a few questions left unanswered.

The purpose of this chapter is to reconstruct the Grenada decision first in narrative form and then graphically and quantitatively using decision analysis. We have completed the first major task; now it is time to retrofit a powerful analytical method to the decision in order to illuminate aspects of the process that may not be immediately apparent from the narrative. The retrofit will also enable us to determine the viability of "canning" certain decision problems on a contingency basis, problems (and solutions) ready to go at a moment's notice.

A DECISION ANALYTIC RETROFIT

What is decision analysis and what can it contribute to the analysis of the Grenada decisionmaking process? Decision analysis is a quantitative method which permits the evaluation of the costs and benefits associated with various courses of action. It involves the identification of alternative choices, the assignment of values for outcomes, and probabilities of those outcomes being considered. According to Barclay, et al:

> In the application of decision analysis, a problem is decomposed into clearly defined components in which all options, outcomes, values, and probabilities are depicted. Quantification in the form of the value for each possible outcome and the probability of those values (or costs) being realized can be in terms of objective information or in the form of quantitative expressions of the subjective judgments of experts. In the latter case, the quantitative expression serves to make explicit those subjective qualities which would otherwise be weighted in the decision process, albeit in a more elusive, intuitive way.

> Beyond its primary role of serving as a method for the logical solution of complex decision problems, decision analysis has additional advantages as well. The formal structure of decision analysis makes clear all the elements, their relationships, and their associated weights that have been considered in a decision problem. If only because the model is explicit, it can serve an important role in facilitating communication among those involved in the decision process. With a decision problem structured in a decision analytic framework, it is an easy matter to identify the location, extent, and importance of any areas of disagreement, and to determine whether such disagreements have any material impact on the indicated decision. In addition, should there be any change in the circumstances bearing upon a given decision problem, it is fairly straightforward to reenter the existing problem structure to change values or to add or remove problem dimensions as required.[10]

In order to accelerate the application of decision analysis to complex decisionmaking problems like the one faced by the special situation group, the Department of Defense (DoD) funded the development of a modeling technique for options screening and intelligence assessment, or "OPINT."[11] (In fact, OPINT resides on a microcomputer and can be implemented whenever and wherever a decisionmaking problem arises.)

Succinctly, OPINT is a decision-analytic, model-building system. Its general purpose is to aid decisionmakers by providing them a capability to construct, store, retrieve, exercise, and refine decision analytic models of complex decision problems. Each OPINT decision model has a unique label, and each is constructed by using the same general format shown graphically in Figure 7.1. The format always consists of all of the following elements.[12]

o   The decision - A short label, D, defining the decision problem;

o   Decision alternatives - A list of the decision alternatives (D_1, D_2, . . . D_n) available to the decisionmaker;

o   An uncertain future event - A key uncertain event, E, appropriately labeled, that will influence the eventual outcome of the decision;

o   Event outcomes - A list of event outcomes (E_1, E_2, . . . E_n) which together define the set of possibilities regarding the occurrence of the future event;

o   Event probabilities - A vector of probabilities (p_1, p_2, . . . p_n) associated with the event outcomes, such as p_i represents the probability that event E_i will occur; and

o   Decision outcomes - Paired combinations of one decision alternative with one event outcome.

The next three elements of the OPINT model specify the consequences associated with each decision outcome. The consequence of an outcome is in the form of relative "regret:"

o   Decision outcome criteria - Criteria (C_1, C_2, . . . C_g) by which the decisionmaker can judge the relative regret associated with each decision outcome;

o   Criteria weights - A vector of weights (w_1, w_2, . . . w_g) associated with the criteria, such that w_i represents the relative contribution of criterion c_i; and

FIGURE 7.1
An OPINT Decision Model

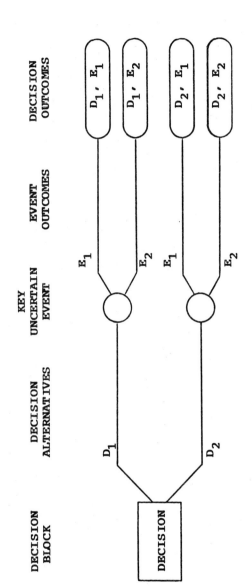

DECISION
BLOCK

DECISION
ALTERNATIVES

KEY
UNCERTAIN
EVENT

EVENT
OUTCOMES

DECISION
OUTCOMES

o   Regret - A measure of the consequence of an outcome.
     The total outcome regret is a weighted linear
     combination of the individual criteria regrets. For
     each criterion (c_i) and for each decision outcome
     (D_j, E_k), the user must specify a value of regret
     (r_{ijk}), all as suggested in Figure 7.2.

Let us reconstruct the Grenada decision with reference to
OPINT and its elements. First, the one key uncertainty concerned
the size of the Cuban-Grenadian resistance force. Estimates
regarding the size of this force were very soft prior to the
invasion. Nevertheless, a prudent decision analysis would have
included the possibility of encountering a very large, well-
equipped force, just as it would have included assessments
regarding the likelihood of encountering a very small force. In
fact, our decision analytic retrofit requires us to be very
explicit about the possible "outcomes" regarding likely
resistance, and recognize the following possibilities regarding
the size and nature of the resistance force:

o   Large, well trained, well equipped;

o   Medium size, well equipped, well trained;

o   Medium sized, adequately equipped and trained; and

o   Small, well or adequately equipped and trained.

This list is by no means comprehensive, but it does identify the
possibilities with the greatest implications for U.S. planning.
The special situation group determined that there was a high
probability that resistance would be small, almost insignificant.
This judgment was grounded in some (though far from complete) intelligence about force strength and assumptions about the value of
surprise. Apparently some relationship was assumed to exist
between adversary force strength and military surprise. Of
course, history suggests that often no such relationship exists.
How many options, or decision alternatives, were considered?
As suggested earlier, a military invasion was one option
considered after the coup in Grenada. But were there others? An
evacuation by peaceful means could have been considered, as could
a "hands-off" policy. Diplomatic intervention might also have
been considered. At least four options could thus have been
identified, and would have been required had a formal decision
analysis been conducted at the time. The four options are as
follows:

o   Do nothing;

o   Intervene diplomatically to affect change in Grenada
     and protect U.S. nationals in Grenada;

FIGURE 7.2
Decision Outcome Value/Regret Matrix

CRITERION: _____ WEIGHT: _____

		EVENT OUTCOMES			
		E_1	E_2	----	E_m
DECISION ALTERNATIVES	D_1	r_{111}	r_{112}	----	r_{11m}
	D_2	r_{121}	r_{122}	----	r_{12m}
	D_3	r_{131}	r_{132}	----	r_{133}
	┆	----	----	----	----
	D_n	r_{1n1}	r_{1n2}	----	r_{1nm}

o   Evacuate U.S. nationals by peaceful means; and

o   Invade militarily to affect events in Grenada and evacuate U.S. nationals.

The OPINT decision analytic model requires us to identify one additional set of factors: the criteria by which a decision option can be selected given the likelihoods of the uncertain event outcomes. Decision criteria are the most important drivers of the decisionmaking process. They provide the means by which values are translated into action, and by which tactical and strategic action evolves into policy.

What were the important criteria applied to the Grenada decision? We know from narrative accounts of the decisionmaking process that at least three objectives were identified, objectives that, in turn, can yield some specific criteria. The objectives included the (1) safety of U.S. nationals, the (2) restoration of democratic government in Grenada, and the (3) elimination of Cuban activity in Grenada. The criteria that can be gleaned from these objectives include the following:

o   Threat to U.S. citizens in Grenada;

o   Domestic political consequences of decision alternatives;

o   Military costs; and

o   International political consequences.

In a formal decision analysis each of these criteria (like each of the mission objectives) would be defined in detail. The threat to U.S. citizens in Grenada, for example, could be defined in terms of the number of citizens injured or killed; domestic political consequences could be measured by changes in the President's domestic popularity; military costs could be defined in terms of the number of soldiers injured or killed; and international consequences could be measured according to the number of nations that approved or condemned the invasion.

We now have all of the elements of the decision problem, save the ones that require the quantification and ranking of the elements. For example, how should the criteria be weighed? Should the lives of the citizens be weighed more heavily than political consequences? What about probabilities? Is it more (.9) or less (.3) likely that U.S. troops will be confronted by a large, well trained force?

If the decisionmakers in the Reagan administration had quantified the probabilities and utilities of the Grenada decision they would have generated a matrix similar to Figure 7.3 for each of the decision criteria.

Formal decision analysis would require the decisionmakers to estimate quantitatively the likelihood or probability of each of

FIGURE 7.3
Grenada Decision Criterion Value/Regret Matrix

CRITERION: Hostage Lives   WEIGHT: 40%

		PROBABILITY OF RESISTANCE			
		Level 1	Level 2	Level 3	Level 4
DECISION OPTIONS	#1				
	#2				
	#3				
	#4				
	#5				

the possible levels of resistance likely to be encountered by U.S. troops. These probabilities would then be integrated with the options and the weighed criteria. Through some calculations beyond the scope of this article a value/regret matrix for each of the criteria would emerge. This matrix would make it possible for decisionmakers to look at each of the options vis-a-vis each of the possible levels of resistance for each of the criteria and determine which option would be likely to yield the highest value or least regret. Following the analysis of each criterion, option, and probability, the decisionmakers would then combine all of the criteria to produce what is referred to as a combined value matrix. This matrix would yield quantitative measures of the "value" that the decisionmakers could expect to gain by implementing each of the options.

The decision analytic retrofit thus far has involved the identification of four decision options, four possible outcomes regarding the size of the resistance force on Grenada, and four criteria for assessing the options in the light of the possible resistance outcomes. The first option calls for the United States to do nothing. The second option calls for the United States to intervene diplomatically, while the third suggests that the United States ought to evacuate U.S. nationals by peaceful means. The last option involves a military invasion of Grenada. The four possibilities regarding the size and nature of the resistance force on Grenada include the likelihood of encountering a (1) large, well trained, and well equipped resistance force; a (2) medium sized well equipped, and well trained resistance force; a (3) medium sized, adequately equipped and trained resistance force; and a (4) small, well or adequately equipped, and only adequately trained resistance force. Finally, the four criteria used to determine the "payoff" connected with the implementation of each option given the resistance probabilities include (1) threats to U.S. citizens in Grenada; (2) domestic political consequences connected with the implementation of each decision alternative; (3) military costs; and (4) any international political repercussions. Once all of these elements have been specified then a formal decision analysis can take place. All of the probabilities and utilities should be quantified using subjective or expert-generated data. Some simple decision analytic calculations would be made on the quantitative data in order to determine which option is most likely to yield the largest payoff.

The keys to any formal decision analysis lie in the uncertainty that confronts the decisionmakers and the evaluative criteria that they establish for themselves. The uncertainties and criteria "drive" the decision process by way of probabilities and utilities elicited from the expert decisionmakers. After probabilities and utilities have been elicited, then it is a relatively simple matter to determine which option should be implemented.

A GRENADA RETROSPECTIVE

It is clear from published reports about the Grenada invasion, and the decision analytic retrofit developed here, that the Reagan administration believed that a military invasion of Grenada (option 4) was perceived as likely to produce little threat to U.S. citizens in Grenada, result in manageable if not favorable domestic political consequences, produce a small military cost, and trigger short-term international political repercussions. In other words, based on what we know about what actually happened and how decision analytic methodology works, the invasion option scored very highly across the four criteria.

We also know that there were expectations about the size and nature of the resistance force on Grenada. Published accounts suggest that there was a consensus that the resistance force would be very small and relatively ill-equipped. In fact, there was evidence to suggest that the resistance force would be comprised of workers who had been sent to Grenada from Cuba as well as indigenous Grenadians. Interestingly, many of the same published reports suggest that the resistance was larger, better equipped, and better trained than anticipated.

The difference between the anticipated and real resistance force is important because it suggests how options fall in and out of favor depending upon the likelihood of various uncertainties. Would the invasion option have been as popular if the probabilities of a large, well trained, and well equipped resistance force were very high? Perhaps if a consensus had been reached regarding the existence of such a force, then another decision option would have been implemented. At the same time, large swings in one's criteria weights or scores can also affect the selection and rejection of decision alternatives. For example, had domestic and international political consequences been expected to be severe, then perhaps the Reagan administration would have attempted to evacuate U.S. nationals by peaceful means instead of a military invasion. Similarly, had military costs been expected to be high, then another alternative might have been implemented.

Assuming rationality, the decision analytic retrofit suggests quite clearly that the Reagan administration did not expect to encounter a large resistance force on Grenada and it did not believe that any of the four criteria would be violated by the invasion option. Remember, however, that the decision option with the highest likely payoff is not always the option implemented. Often decisionmakers will select an option because it scores well on one or two heavily weighed criteria, even though it "loses" the overall decision analysis. If, on the other hand, there was evidence to suggest that the Reagan administration expected to encounter a large, well trained, and well equipped resistance force, and it also believed that political and military costs would be high, then we can safely assume "irrationality," or an inclination to implement an option based on a series of preconceived notions about the value of that option.

WHY DECISION ANALYSIS?

Decision analysis can improve decisionmaking before, during, and after the decisionmaking process. Strategic and tactical crisis management, for example, always involves contingency planning for classes of crises, planning which enables crisis managers to approach critical decisionmaking problems from positions of analytical strength rather than weakness. Contingency planning based upon decision theoretical principles involves the identification of the likely key decisionmakers, the listing and modeling of decision options, and the specifications of the criteria which will facilitate cost/benefit and trade-off analyses of the options. It also involves the development of tools for assessing the probability of the key uncertain events likely to drive the decision. In the case of an OPINT-like problem, strategic contingency planning might involve the structuring of OPINT models for specific kinds of high order crises, such as hostage situations, political and military coups, and military invasions. Such planning would permit decisionmakers to deal with crises much more rationally and effectively. "Pre-canned" OPINT models would reduce the danger of bias, irrationality, groupthink, and other threats to decisionmaking.

During the decisionmaking process, decision analytic tools like OPINT can help make the process explicit. As suggested above, decision analysis is a technique which requires decisionmakers to divide and conquer decision problems by breaking them down into ever smaller pieces for subsequent analysis. But more importantly, decision analysis requires decisionmakers to expose their estimates and values in a way which subjects them to systematic analysis. If a decisionmaker, for example, favors an option which flies in the face of relevant probabilities and utilities, then he or she had better be very persuasive. In fact, well-done decision analyses require decisionmakers to offer rationale for each of their probability and utility estimates. Explicit rationale, along with quantified probabilities and utilities, render the decisionmaking process completely transparent. The methodology prevents a single individual from dominating the decisionmaking process, or making judgements based upon pre-conceived notions or inherent biases. Perhaps most importantly, decision analysis renders a ranking of decision options according to their likely payoff.

Following the implementation of a decision option, decision analysis can help with the proverbial postmortems. Decision analytic retrofits such as attempted here, enable us to understand the values and probabilities of those who made a particular decision. It structures after-the-fact evaluations of previous successful and unsuccessful decisionmaking processes. Retrofits can also expose the use or neglect of criteria, or the obvious weighing of preferred criteria. Finally, retrofits permit an integrated analysis of the role of intelligence vis-a-vis operations. Perhaps not surprisingly, decision analysis has been used very successfully as a way to bridge the gap between intelligence and operations personnel; consequently, decision analysis can bridge the intel-ops gap before, during, and after the decisionmaking process.

One last point deserves special attention. Frequently decision analysis is perceived to be a tedious, difficult process. Many decisionmakers are reluctant to convert their probabilities and utilities into quantitative estimates, just as many are unwilling to publicly express their rationale for alternative options. Over the past few years, however, the decision analytic process has been greatly simplified via the development of some friendly computer programs that enable decisionmakers to run through the process relatively painlessly. In fact, some imaginative applications of decision analysis involve the development of decisionmaking "templates" which include everything but the numbers. When a decision must be made, all the decisionmakers need do is make the necessary probability and utility estimates and the computer program does all the rest. The OPINT decision model discussed in this chapter has been computerized in a computer program of the same name, just as many others have been implemented on minicomputers and desk-top microcomputers.[13] The suggestion here is obviously not to require high-level decision-makers to convert their probabilities and utilities into quantitative form; rather, it is proposed that the methodology be studied by those responsible for the formulation of contingency plans as well as the development of decision options. Certainly members of the National Security Council would benefit from the use of a methodology which made explicity a process which is so very often vague and erratic. Joint Chiefs of Staff (JCS) level intelligence and operations officers might also benefit from the use of this structured methodology. In any case, there is now a formidable track record of successful applications of decision analysis to complicated strategic and tactical problems. Hopefully the Grenada concept application developed here will stimulate additional ideas.

NOTES

1. At least not in the immediate future, though some published accounts suggest that long-term goals would not necessarily preclude such aggression.

2. For more on this topic see "How Reagan Decides," Time (13 December 1982): 12-18; and Meg Greenfield, "How Does Reagan Decide," Newsweek (20 February 1984): 80.

3. See Clinton W. Kelley, et al., "Computer-Based Decision Analysis: An Application to a Middle East Evacuation Problem," Jerusalem Journal of International Relations 2(1981): 62-84.

4. See Department of State, Grenada: A Preliminary Report (Washington, DC, December 16, 1983); and Ralph Kinney Bennett,

"Grenada: Anatomy of a 'Go' Decision," Reader's Digest (February 1984): 72-8.

5. See, e.g., Thomas L. Saaty, et al., "Concepts, Theory, and Techniques: High-Level Decisions--A Lesson from the Iran Hostage Rescue Operation," Decision Sciences 13(April 1982): 185-206.

6. See Department of State, "Grenada;" Bennett, pp. 72-8; Newsweek (7 November 1983); and U.S. News and World Report (7 November 1983).

7. U.S. News and World Report (7 November 1983).

8. It is difficult to overestimate the impact of such phenomena; it is also very difficult to measure them.

9. See Steve Chan, "The Intelligence of Stupidity: Understanding Failures in Strategic Warning," American Political Science Review 73(1979): 171-80.

10. Scott Barclay, Rex V. Brown, Clinton W. Kelly III, Cameron R. Peterson, Lawrence D. Phillips, and Judith Selvidge, Handbook for Decision Analysis (McLean, VA: Decisions and Designs, Inc., September 1977), pp. vi-vii.

11. See Dorothy M. Amey, Phillip H. Feuerwerger, and Roy M. Gulick, Documentation of Decision-Aiding Software: OPINT Functional Description (McLean, VA: Decisions and Designs, Inc., April 1979), for a more complete look at OPINT's capabilities.

12. Ibid.

13. Ibid.

8
Amphibious Aspects
of the Grenada Episode

Frank Uhlig, Jr.

The amphibious assault ship USS <u>Guam</u> (LPH 9), flying the broad command pennant of Captain Carl R. Erie, Commander, Amphibious Squadron FOUR, was sailing eastward at an easy fourteen knots. Now, several days after leaving Norfolk, Bermuda too was astern and she was headed for the Strait of Gibraltar. In company with the <u>Guam</u> were four other amphibious ships, the <u>Trenton</u> (LPD 14), <u>Fort Snelling</u> (LSD 30), <u>Manitowoc</u> (LST 1180), and <u>Barnstable County (LST 1197)</u>. Distributed among Commodore Erie's five ships were the 2,000 Marines of Colonel James Faulkner's 22nd Marine Amphibious Unit.

That unit consisted of a battalion landing team (the 800 men of the Second Battalion, Eighth Marines, who were formed, in the main, into three companies, E, F, and G), a six-gun battery of field artillery, five M-60 tanks, a large squadron of helicopters (HMM-261, with twenty-two aircraft of assorted sizes), and all the communicators, Navy hospital corpsmen, intelligence interpreters, aviation maintenancemen, and other specialists necessary to make effective even a small combat unit.

All, ships and Marines alike, formed Mediterranean Amphibious Ready Group 1-84 under the command of Commodore Erie. They were destined for Beirut, Lebanon, where they were to relieve on station those Marines and amphibious ships which had long been there. But first they had to take part in an exercise off the Spanish coast in company with the ships and aircraft of Rear Admiral Richard C. Berry's USS <u>Independence</u> battle group.

Carrier battle groups and amphibious ready groups seldom steam in company, and they certainly were not doing so now. The <u>Independence</u> (CV 62) and her consorts (a cruiser, three destroyers, and a frigate) were also heading eastward, but they were about 150 miles to the north.

It was after midnight on October 21, 1983, when orders came in to Erie to change his course. In electronic silence his ships were to proceed southward toward a position on the ocean not far from the island of Grenada. If no further word came by the time they reached that point, the ships were to head once more for Spain. To make this long detour and still reach the Spanish coast on time, the ships obviously could no longer steam at their most economical speeds, and they did not. The slowest of them was

89

designed for twenty knots and the squadron's speed was not far short of that. Admiral Berry's carrier group also turned south and speeded up.

It was no secret that Grenada was in deep domestic trouble. So, though they had been given no specific tasking, Erie, Faulkner, and the officers of their staffs and subordinate units began to plan a noncombatant evacuation of the Americans on that island. They had no idea how many such Americans there were. They had neither maps of Grenada nor detailed nautical charts of the surrounding waters. Fortunately, a few years earlier the squadron's chief staff officer, Commander Rick Butler, had sailed in those waters in a small boat and had become familar with the island. One of the Marines had also been on the island.

Grenada is an oval about twenty miles north and south by twelve miles east and west, with a stem at the southwestern corner. Most of it consists of mountainous jungles, but there is a coastal plain, wide at the south, narrow elsewhere. The stem is deeply indented with bays and inlets, but it is flatter than most of the island and, because there the rains seldom come, there is no jungle growth. It is on that stem that the well known Point Salines airfield with its 9,000-foot runway was being built by Cubans. Just to the north, on the west coast, lies the capital, St. George's.

St. George's is not only the capital; with a population of about 35,000, it is the only sizable city on the island. It consists of tile-roofed buildings clustered around a small harbor. Several eighteenth-century forts guard the city, some of them at the harbor's mouth and others on the hills which rise steeply around the harbor. The spiny island has a total population of 110,000 people--most of them poor. Roads, some of them built by the French when briefly they were in possession two centuries ago, are scarce and not much better now than they were when they were new.

Until the jet-capable field was ready for business, people who wished to fly to or from the island had to use Pearls airfield, a narrow, 3,000-foot strip more than halfway up the island's windward, or eastern, coast. One end of Pearls faces the mountains and the other is at the water's edge. Though small, it is adequate for the propeller-driven commuter planes which fly the 130 miles between there and Barbados. The nearest town is the village of Grenville, about eighteen miles from St. George's.

Two days passed while the amphibious and carrier groups sailed south. Little information came their way, and they, under radio silence, could not ask for more. On the 23rd the _Guam_ was ordered to close within helicopter flying distance of the island of Antigua. She was to dispatch a helo which would pick up representatives of the Atlantic command's headquarters who had come from Norfolk.

The representatives, one lieutenant colonel from the Army and one from the Marines, with a brief case, a map, and not much else, arrived on the deck at 11 p.m. that night. What they had to say was a stunning surprise to their hosts.

The Navy and Marines were to make no noncombatant evacuation of Americans from St. George's. They were not even to go there. Instead, they were to make an assault landing at daybreak on the 25th upon the airstrip at Pearls and the village of Grenville. Then they were to secure the northern half of the island. Simultaneously, Army Rangers would parachute in to seize the incomplete Point Salines airfield. Thereupon Air Force C-141 troop transports would land and discharge elements of the 82nd Airborne Division. These forces would move on St. George's. Meanwhile, some Rangers and Navy SEALs would have been inserted secretly before the main assault, would capture the murderous band under General Hudson Austin which had just seized power, rescue Governor General Sir Paul Scoon from house arrest, and free the still-living political prisoners from Richmond Prison. Then, or along the way, the Americans would also be rescued. Reportedly, there were 600 of the latter, mostly students at a medical school. Still under electronic silence, there was no way for the officers in the Guam to verify this astonishing news. With the lone map the emissaries had brought with them, the officers began to plan for their share in the forthcoming events.

Continuing south, on the 24th the Guam once again closed to within helicopter distance of an island, this time Barbados. That night several helicopters flew off to Barbados and brought back to the ship the commander of the just-formed Joint Task Force 120, Vice Admiral Joseph Metcalf, and thirty-seven members of his staff. Metcalf's normal billet was Commander, Second Fleet, the operational part of the U.S. Atlantic Fleet, and when he was not at sea he would usually have been in Norfolk.

With Metcalf on board, plans were completed for an air- and surface-borne amphibious assault on Pearls airfield. The time for both parts of the assault to touch down was at first light, or 5 a.m., only a few hours distant. The Guam's flag spaces and communications equipment are built to serve the needs of the ten or a dozen officers normally on the staff of an amphibious squadron commodore. The Joint Task Force staff raised the number, trying to jam themselves in and do work, to about fifty. It was a crowded place from which to command a complex, fast moving, multiservice operation. Fortunately, the admiral's voice was ample enough to be heard above the din.

The Guam and three of her consorts steamed in company. All were darkened and the men were at Condition 3, with about one-third of them at their battle stations. The fifth ship, the Fort Snelling, had already gone ahead. Arriving off Pearls airfield about 11 p.m. that night, six hours before the main landing was scheduled, she placed in the water a small, quiet Sea Fox raiding boat. Men from SEAL Team Four were in the boat. Their task was, without being discovered, to go ashore, survey the beach, judge the state of the surf, and then deliver an informed opinion on the condition of defenses if, indeed, there were any.

There were some. A pair of 12.7mm antiaircraft guns commanded the airstrip from a hill just to the north. The gunners, members of the Grenadian army, were asleep nearby. Other

Grenadian soldiers were supposed to be busy digging foxholes near the beach, so obviously someone expected the Americans to come. But it was the rainy season, the men were drenched, and they said plainly that they did not expect the Americans to visit their island. The SEALs, who heard the conversation, had just come out of the surf which was pounding away at the beach. The problem those particular SEALs had was to get away without being noticed by the neighboring military skeptics. The latter solved the problem by moving off to a drier spot. The SEALs found and reported back that the surf was too high for the planned seaborne assault. The entire attack would have to be made by helicopter.

While the SEALs were on the beach the Trenton and the two LSTs arrived and, still blacked out, anchored a few miles offshore. The Guam, with her helicopters, stayed underway about ten miles out. The guided missile destroyer Coontz (DDG 40), which Admiral Berry had detached from the carrier group, was also on hand. The Coontz was able, if such an unlikely need were to develop, to provide the amphibious force with protection from air, submarine, or surface attack. She also could provide gunfire support to the troops ashore if it were needed. She had only one 5-inch gun for this purpose, but none of the other ships present had any such weapon.

Berry detached most of his other screening ships, too. The frigate Clifton Sprague (FFG 16) and the destroyers Caron (DD 970) and Moosebrugger (DD 980) were sent to work in support of the Rangers. With two 5-inch guns each, those modern destroyers were the best ships available for gunfire support. The carrier, which needs a lot of sea room to launch and recover her aircraft, operated between twenty and sixty miles from the island. Throughout the operation the Independence provided continuous air support to elements of the joint task force. Altogether she launched over 700 sorties. Initial control of these aircraft was provided by the tactical control squadron embarked in the Guam. During this period the carrier was screened solely by the cruiser Richmond K. Turner (CG 20).

At 4:00 a.m. the Guam launched the first wave of helos. This was to get those aircraft off the flight deck while the second wave was brought up on elevators from the hanger deck. After the second wave was fueled and filled with Marines, it was launched. Then the aircraft from the first wave returned to the ship, topped off on fuel, loaded their Marines, and were airborne again. A thunderstorm passed through at this time, delaying the assault. But both groups of helos, flying behind the storm, hid the sound of their approach from the defenders until almost the last moment.

Finally awakened by the helos' clatter, the Grenadian gunners raced to their weapons and opened fire. The 230 Marines of E Company, however, foiled them for at 5:20 a.m. they landed, not on the airstrip where they could have been mown down, but on a field just to the south of it, where the guns could not reach. A couple of Marine AH-1T gunship helicopters soon opened fire on the antiaircraft guns and the weapon's crews took off into the jungle. Meanwhile, F Company landed near Grenville and took the village without encountering any resistance. By 7:30 a.m. both objectives were declared secured.

That morning a tracked landing vehicle was sent in from the Manitowoc to test the surf. It got ashore, but barely, and the decision was made to leave well enough alone.

Except in the Guam's flag plot, the rest of the morning was quiet both ashore and afloat. In flag plot Admiral Metcalf was trying to get a picture of events at the southern end of the island. Those events, at Point Salines airport, were not moving as fast as he had hoped, for the 784 Cubans on the island--most of whom were at the airport--were putting up a strong fight.

In St. George's, twenty-two Navy SEALs had landed clandestinely during the night and gained control of the governor-general's residence. The governor-general and ten other people with him were safe for the moment, as were the men who had come to rescue them. But, equipped with both of their army's Soviet-built armored personnel carriers, Grenadian troops had surrounded the house and were firing into it. Since the main body of Rangers and the 82nd Airborne Division were tied up at Point Salines, there was no hope of early relief from that quarter.

During the afternoon Metcalf and his Army advisors decided that the fastest way to save the situation in St. George's was to get the Marines in there, so they shifted to the south the boundary separating the Marine's and the Army's tactical areas of responsibility--thus placing the city inside the Marine-Navy umbrella.

The ships still bore over 200 riflemen, those of G Company, and most of the Marine amphibious unit's combat support elements. All ships off Pearls except for the Trenton and the Coontz were ordered to steam southward towards St. George's. The two left behind would continue to support the men at Pearls and Grenville.

As the ships steered toward St. George's, the commanders and their staffs had to decide where, exactly, they would land. Though they lacked suitable charts, it was clear that no beach on the western, or leeward, side of the island would be subject to the sea conditions which had led them to cancel the surface landing at Pearls. But what else? What other hazards, what other opportunities, lay on the leeward side? There was no time to send SEALs ashore to find out. Fortunately, when he was vacationing on the island, the chief staff officer had sailed a dinghy right onto the beach at the forbidingly-named Grand Mal and found it clear of coral reefs. So it was at Grand Mal, about three "clicks," or two miles, north of St. George's harbor, that the Marines would make their next landing. The timing was set for dusk.

At about 7 p.m. the Manitowoc anchored half a mile off the chosen beach. Then, maneuvering so that her stern pointed directly at the beach, she opened her stern ramp. Once every ten seconds, for just over two minutes, thirteen camouflaged amtracs, or LVTPs, roared out of her tank deck and plunged into the sea. Inside those armored, barely floatable machines sat the men of G Company. Even at seven knots, it did not take the amtracs long to go half a mile. Then they climbed out of the sea, onto the beach, and moved inland. Next, it was the turn of the M-60 tanks from the <u>Fort Snelling</u>, which went ashore by LCU and LCM-8 landing craft. By the time they arrived on the beach it was 8 p.m. and dark. When General Austin's People's Revolutionary Army saw the armored troop carriers and tanks coming ashore, they knew that their moment of rule was over. Even though the tanks got stuck for a while in soft sand just inland from the beach, the word went out that the adventure was over. Most of Austin's soldiers discarded their weapons, slipped out of their uniforms, and faded into the population from whence they had sprung. They caused no more trouble.

Even so, the Marines had difficulties. They were in a strange city, without knowledge of where their objective--the governor-general's house--was, without even a map, and not at all sure what they might face at the next street corner.

Meanwhile, well before dawn on the 26th, the <u>Guam</u>'s helicopters met the men of F Company at Pearls and carried them to a landing zone near Grand Mal beach. While F Company secured the beachhead, G Company, with the platoon of tanks, found the house they were looking for at about 7:30 a.m. The appearance of the amtracs and tanks, and a few menacing noises from their guns, sufficed to disperse the besiegers. Scoon, his party, and the Navy SEALs were safe.

Because more infantry were needed ashore, the artillerymen of H Battery, 3d Battalion, Tenth Marines, were formed into a provisional infantry unit, H Company. Their main tasks were to protect the command post ashore and to guard the prisoners of war, a group whose number was growing. On D+4 it was H Company which, on a tip, captured the number two revolutionary, Bernard Coard, and the men and women of the little junta. General Austin was captured later by the Army.

On D+1 a second campus of the medical school was discovered, at Grand Anse Beach to the south of St. George's. The Marine ground forces were all busy and could not be employed for the rescue of students at Grand Anse. But for the moment six helicopters of HMM-261 were free and so were a battalion of the Army's Rangers. So the helos left their ship, picked up the Rangers at Point Salines, and carried them to Grand Anse. There, under fire, they made a vertical assault. The fire killed no one but did destroy a CH-46 helicopter after it had landed. The other helos took all the students at Grand Anse to Point Salines before returning to the ship. (The CH-46 was the third of three Marine helos lost at Grenada. Two AH-1 Cobra gunships were downed earlier while supporting some Rangers in St. George's.)

Meanwhile, on D+1 and D+2 the Marines at St. George's took the harbor works and the hilltop forts--not much fighting was involved, but no one was to know that until it was over--and on the 28th, with St. George's declared secure, they linked up with the elements of the 82nd Airborne Division.

A couple of days later, on the 30th, or D+5, E Company, starting by jeep from Pearls, reached the village of Sauteurs at the northern end of Grenada and found no foes. The same day G

Company, riding in the thirteen LVTPs, took the west coastal road in the same direction toward the towns of Gouyave and Victoria. In case the little expedition ran into trouble, the Navy paced it to seaward with an LCM-8 (in which a tank was embarked), an LCU, an LST, and a destroyer. A couple of HMM-261 Cobra helicopter gunships went along, too. The episode resembled a similar operation by the U.S. Army and Navy along the coast of Morocco in November 1942. Just as on the earlier occasion, everything went peacefully and in a couple of hours the Marines had reached both their objectives.

The next day responsibility for affairs in Grenada was turned over to the Army and to the small multinational Caribbean Peace Force. The latter consisted of lightly armed units from neighboring island states.

While all these events were going on, the _Guam_ transformed herself into a hospital. Over a fifty-hour period some seventy-eight battle casualties were brought to that ship for help. They got it. No one who reached the _Guam_ died of his wounds.

During their brief visit ashore the Marines took the one city and all the important villages in Grenada. By 4:30 p.m. on the 31st all the Marines were back in their ships. The next morning, November 1st, by both air and surface they landed on Carriocou, a small island dependency just to the north of Grenada. There, as elsewhere, they found a considerable stock of small arms. But they met no resistance. The following day, as soon as they once more were back in their ships, they resumed their interrupted voyage to Beirut. That transit, which had begun routinely, had become urgent for, while the men of the 22nd MAU had been approaching the beaches at Grenada, those they were to relieve at Beirut had been devastated by the suicide bombing of their quarters which killed 241 of their number.

In summary, while the Army used close air support from the _Independence_, the Marines used only the carrier's aerial reconnaissance capability. Gunfire support was called for only once, again by the Army. The _Moosebrugger_ fired a single shot, before a heliborne assault. The target, at the Calvigney Barracks, was hit and that was that. Those Marines making a night approach on the hilltop forts once asked a destroyer to fire a star shell for illumination. After a long wait while communications worked their way back and forth, a shell was fired. It failed to illuminate. Another long wait, another star shell, another dud. Finally, the third shell did its job, half an hour after the illumination had been requested.

What should we make of the amphibious aspects of the little Grenadian episode? Commodore Erie pointed out three important items:

o "The use of armor, i.e., tanks and LVTs, in a Grenada-type scenario proved to be very effective. The 'shock effect' of these mechanized forces was tremendous. Once the Grenadian forces realized the Marines were ashore with armor they quickly broadcast this to these units and basically told them it was all over."

o "Conducting amphibious assaults in the dark was very effective. Night assaults should be the desired option whenever feasible."

o "Grenada demonstrated that a Navy-Marine ATF is capable of fast, flexible combat operations in support of joint task force operations."

There were other lessons. One, perhaps, was how fortunate the United States was that an amphibious ready group was available when it was needed. Indeed, this force, supported by the ships and aircraft of the Independence battle group, could have done the job alone. But it would have taken longer; probably more Americans, Cubans, and Grenadians would have been killed and wounded; probably more damage would have been done; and perhaps those very people the Americans were trying to rescue would have perished before help could reach them. Much the same thing, of course, might be said about leaving the whole task to the Army. Because they came by air, the soldiers, though numerous, were more lightly armed than the Marines. So, while fewer or less well equipped forces than were sent might have done the job adequately, true economy of force was served by sending all that could reasonably expect to be used.

A point worth thinking about is how difficult it is to run a multiservice operation without either a plan, a staff appropriate to the task, or a command center adequate to the need. Without any of those things, Admiral Metcalf and his people about him did well. Perhaps they, and we, should be grateful that the problem they were called on to solve was no more difficult than it was.

Should we let it lie there? Or should we see what can be done about providing plans for such actions; communications equipment which can link the units of one service with those of another; staffs experienced in overcoming the complexities of multiservice combat; and flagships, or other command vehicles, up to the need? It may be that we would prefer to wait until, in another pick-up operation, the effort fails. Surely, then, we could blame those on the spot for whatever their shortcomings proved to be. DESERT ONE certainly provides an example of that.

But blaming those who failed is not nearly so satisfactory as knowing that we--Congress, taxpayers, defense officials, and the Armed Services alike--had provided those whom we sent to fight with the organizational and material instruments which helped them win their victory.

NOTES

A note on sources:

Newspapers and news magazines were filled with accounts of the fighting and associated events during and just after the military activities at Grenada. Even in the best of circumstances it is almost impossible for such reports to be accurate in more than the most general sense. At Grenada not only were reporters not present during the early days when most of the events herein discussed took place, but those who did get there later were not all that well equipped with an understanding of military matters. For these reasons, their reports, while good enough for the moment, were not good for much more.

The sources upon which this account depended are these:

1. A letter from Captain Carl R. Erie, U.S. Navy, 5 July 1984.

2. Discussions with Commander Richard Butler, U.S. Navy, in mid-July 1984.

3. COMPHIBRON FOUR Staff. "Grenada: Navy's Urgent Fury." Surface Warfare (March-April 1984): 16-20.

4. Lieutenant Colonel Michael J. Bryon, U.S. Marine Corps, "Fury from the Sea: Marines in Grenada," Naval Review 1984 (May 1984, U.S. Naval Institute Proceedings): 118-131.

5. Second Lieutenant James B. Seaton, "NGF Procedures Rusty," Marine Corps Gazette (June 1984): 35-36.

Additionally, I am indebted to Rear Admiral Robert B. Rogers, U.S. Navy, Commander, Amphibious Group TWO, Atlantic Fleet, for his assistance.

9
Urgent Fury: The U.S. Army in Grenada

Dorothea Cypher

> Sergeant Tom Wilburn was hanging in his parachute, 400 feet above the island of Grenada, when he concluded that the United States invasion of that small, lush dot in the Caribbean was not going to be the pushover that he had expected.[1]

Before Operation URGENT FURY ended many would share Ranger Wilburn's sentiments. His unit, the 1st Battalion (Ranger), 75th Infantry, Hunter Army Airfield, Georgia, and the Rangers of their sister unit, the 2d Battalion, Ft. Lewis, Washington, were the first soldiers to arrive in Grenada that Tuesday morning, October 25, 1983. The Army committed many other units to the operation as well: several elements of the 18th Airborne Corps, including a good portion of the 82d Airborne Division and the 101st Air Assault Division aviation assets, some Army Special Forces, and various Army Reserve units. By October 28th, nearly 6,000 Army troops were on the island. The Rangers, their missions completed, departed Grenada by October 30th, followed by all U.S. combat forces by mid-December. Two to three hundred specialists remained, however, as the first anniversary of URGENT FURY passed.

At the one year mark the "fog of battle" had not completely lifted from the U.S. action in Grenada. U.S. government claims of extensive Cuban involvement and a potentially threatening situation for American citizens in Grenada were supported by the capture of large caches of weapons and People's Revolutionary Government (PRG) documents. A congressional fact-finding committee visited the "Isle of Spice" the first week of November 1983 to investigate these claims. The military's handling of the operation also came under fire. Pentagon spokesmen were required to testify before a hearing held on January 24, 1984, by the House Armed Services Committee (HASC). In April 1984, Representative James Courter (R-NJ), a member of the HASC and head of the Congressional Military Reform Caucus, released a study (prepared for the caucus by William S. Lind) that was very critical of the Grenada operation. General Vessey, Chairman of the Joint Chiefs of Staff (JCS), issued a rebuttal in response to Lind's charges. The debate on Grenada persisted in the media as well.

Part of this troubled debate relates directly to the restrictions on and the role of the press during the early phase of URGENT FURY. Another is the military's understandable unwillingness to release information which might compromise any future similar mission or be taken out of context. Additionally, a few of the incidents that occurred in Grenada, though hardly remarkable in a combat mission, appear embarassing in the context of a rescue operation where the advantage so clearly lay with the United States. Finally, some officials were somewhat reluctant to discuss a situation in which the United States had been portrayed as the aggressor, especially in an election year.

While the debate has not ended, this chapter presents a factual account of U.S. Army involvement in Grenada. It is based on information provided by the participants, defense officials, unclassified military documents, and media coverage. No attempt is made to evaluate the participation or identify "lessons learned." Rather, this treatment simply describes Army involvement and related issues in what was originally only a "noncombatant evacuation operation" (NEO). It describes the role the Army played throughout the rescue, restoration of law and order, and peacekeeping operation.

The events which triggered Operation URGENT FURY began long before October 25, 1983. A rift developed in the New Jewel Movement (NJM), Grenada's ruling party, when a dispute broke out between Prime Minister Maurice Bishop and his deputy, Bernard Coard. As a result, Coard resigned on October 13th. A state of chaos developed when Bishop was placed under house arrest on October 14th. This lack of leadership fomented confusion and panic. Five cabinet members resigned on October 15th. Three were arrested while a fourth organized a demonstration calling for Bishop's reinstatement. Grenada's neighbors, monitoring the situation, expressed alarm over the state of affairs. The situation also generated concern about the safety of the large number of American citizens on Grenada. These events led to official consideration of U.S. political options on Monday, October 17th.[2]

On Wednesday, October 19th, thousands of Bishop's supporters stormed the charismatic leader's house, setting him and his companions free, and escorted him to Fort Rupert. His release was shortlived. Troops loyal to the Central Committee fired on the crowd, killing a number of Grenadians, including women and children. Maurice Bishop and three of his cabinet members were taken inside the fort and summarily executed. General Hudson Austin, Commander of Grenada's military forces, subsequently announced the formation of a Revolutionary Military Council headed by himself. He immediately imposed a twenty-four hour, shoot-on-sight curfew.[3]

The total disintegration of the Grenadian government prompted activation of U.S. National Security Council (NSC) crisis management mechanisms. On Wednesday evening a JCS warning order for a noncombatant evacuation was sent to the Commander-in-Chief Atlantic (CINCLANT), Admiral Wesley McDonald. On Thursday morning the NSC Crisis Pre-Planning Group (CPPG) met to consider the deteriorating situation. As a precaution, the USS Independence battle group and Amphibious Squadron Four, en route across the Atlantic to the Mediterranean, were diverted toward Grenada. On the CPPG's recommendation Vice President George Bush convened the NSC Special Situation Group (SSG) to consider U.S. options for President Reagan's consideration. After being apprised of the situation, President Reagan directed the NEO planning to continue.

The United States was not the only nation concerned about the upheaval in Grenada. Neighboring island states met on Friday, October 21st, under the auspices of the Organization of Eastern Caribbean States (OECS), to discuss their concerns. Two non-members, Jamaica and Barbados, also joined the emergency meeting. The OECS (less Grenada) voted unanimously to intervene in Grenada, by force if necessary, to protect the region. They sought the assistance of Jamaica, Barbados, and the United States in the venture. The SSG factored the OECS request into their deliberations on Saturday and prepared a revised plan expanded beyond the scope of a noncombatant evacuation. The President eventually approved the plan and appropriate guidance was passed to CINCLANT.[4]

Initially CINCLANT developed several courses of action to evacuate U.S. citizens and other foreign nationals from Grenada, including a unilateral Navy-Marine effort. This option was discarded because of the importance of simultaneously seizing Pearls airport on the east coast and multiple targets in the southern portion of the island. The number, size, and location of the various objectives exceeded the capability of a single Marine battalion.[5] Taking this into consideration, the plan briefed by CINCLANT on Saturday, October 22nd, called for a combined service organization, designated Joint Task Force (JTF) 120, commanded by Vice Admiral Metcalf. The island was divided roughly in half with the Marines responsible for the northern part and the Army for the southern. Marines and Rangers, reinforced by the 82nd Airborne Division, were to seize the airheads and key objectives. Forces were ordered to secure the island with minimum casualities and destruction.[6]

URGENT FURY planning and troop selection subsequently became an object of controversy. Months after the operation, in response to the "Lind Report," General Vessey explained:

Forces used in URGENT FURY were chosen based on their capability to fulfill the mission. ...The Marine Amphibious Unit (MAU) was used because of its proximity to the area. ...The Rangers and other Special Forces were chosen because of their unique capability to secure airfields, rescue hostages, and attack selected point targets. Based on the enemy situation...the 82d Airborne was included to ensure an adequate combat power ratio and permit early redeployment of the Special Forces and the MAU to fulfill pending commitments.

The size of the U.S. force used in Grenada was determined based on an analysis of the military mission, enemy forces, U.S. forces available, and the terrain. The principal military mission was to rescue U.S. citizens and other foreign nationals. In order to achieve this objective, it was determined that Cuban and Grenadian forces would have to be neutralized and a stable situation on the island achieved. U.S. intelligence sources identified the Cuban strength on Grenada to be approximately 700. Grenadian forces included 1,200-1,500 members of the People's Revolutionary Army and 2,000-5,000 members of the Territorial Militia. During the planning period... there was no way of determining how much of the enemy force would fight. Therefore, U.S. forces had to be sized to meet worst case conditions.[7]

Intelligence gathering and planning for Operation URGENT FURY continued at all levels throughout the weekend. Although the bombing of the Marine barracks in Beirut occurred on Sunday, October 23rd, additional considerations prompted the President to give his final approval to the Grenada rescue mission that evening. The official objectives were to protect and evacuate U.S. and designated foreign nationals, neutralize Grenadian forces, stabilize the internal situation to maintain peace and order, and in conjunction with OECS/friendly participants, assist in the restoration of democratic government on Grenada.[8] The President's approval gave impetus to the final stages of planning on Monday, October 24th. Some units began pre-deployment to staging areas in Barbados. The 82d began full-swing participation by activating their twenty-hour emergency deployment sequence. Command and control organizations continued feverish planning and coordination.

These events resulted in Sergeant Wilburn parachuting to the unfinished Point Salines airfield about dawn on October 25, 1983. The Rangers flew nonstop from Savannah, Georgia, contending with a storm and navigation equipment problems on the lead C-130 aircraft. Their arrival over the Point Salines drop zone at 5:30 a.m. was a half-hour behind schedule and a short time after the Marine landing at Pearls airport on the east coast.

Heavy resistance greeted the Rangers at the Point Salines airfield. Two wing aircraft were turned back by the unexpectedly intense antiaircraft fire and bright search lights which blinded the pilots. Lieutenant Colonel Wesley B. Taylor, Commander, 1-75th Rangers, decided that the situation, further complicated by wind and a drop zone with water on three sides, required a change in normal procedures. He ordered his paratroopers to jump at 500 feet, less than half the usual 1,100 feet. This limited the exposure and vulnerability of his men. Despite this change, and probably because of it, only one soldier was injured during the jump.[9]

Once on the ground the Rangers called in AC-130 gunships to suppress the air defense emplacements along the ridge above the runway. Meanwhile the men rapidly organized and pressed on with their dual mission: securing the airfield for the follow-on elements of the 82d Airborne Division and ensuring the safety of U.S. citizens in the area, the majority of whom were medical students at the St. George's Medical School. To clear the construction equipment, wire barriers, and metal spikes emplaced by workers to impede use of the runway, several innovative soldiers hot-wired nearby bulldozers. Despite the fact that they were receiving fire from snipers, automatic weapons, and antiaircraft guns, the runway was cleared by 6:30 a.m. and declared secure by 7:15 a.m.

By 7:00 a.m., B Company, 1-75th Rangers, positioned on the west end of the runway, began fighting their way through defensive positions en route to the main Cuban construction workers' camp. A Company, 1-75th Rangers, began a similar move from the east. Once at the camp an air strike was considered but discarded since it could not be determined if there were civilians inside. Instead, B Company snipers were able to destroy a number of Cuban mortar positions while A Company captured a ZPU 23-mm antiaircraft weapon and turned it against the camp. By midday the B Company first sergeant sent a Cuban worker into the camp with instructions to surrender in fifteen minutes "or else." Approximately 175 Cubans surrendered.[10] At the same time, another group of Rangers moved east toward the True Blue campus of the medical school, approximately a mile and a half away. When the Rangers arrived, they found 138 scared but unharmed students. The campus was secured by 8:50 a.m. During these first hours the Rangers had neutralized a number of strong points and taken hundreds of prisoners. While at True Blue the Rangers learned that another 224 students were located at a second campus at Grande Anse, halfway to the capital city of St. George's. The Rangers contacted the Grande Anse campus by phone and determined that the students, while safe, were nearly surrounded.

While the Rangers were busy on Grenada, the 82d Airborne Division was making frenzied last minute preparations to relieve and reinforce them from Ft. Bragg, North Carolina. "Wheels up" on the first C-141 transport aircraft was at 10:07 a.m. Some 1,600 troops of the 2d and 3d Battalions of the 325th Infantry, 2d Brigade, 82d Airborne Division began landing at Point Salines at 2:05 p.m., under fire. The Commanding General of the 82d Airborne Division, Major General Edward Trobaugh, accompanied his soldiers on the first aircraft. His missions were to: conduct airborne/airland operations to secure the island of Grenada; establish military control; perform peacekeeping duties as part of the Caribbean Peacekeeping Force; evacuate U.S. nationals; and provide refugee control.[11]

Point Salines was not the only scene of intense action. Navy SEALS were pinned down in the Governor General's residence on a hilltop just north of St. George's, within the Army's sector of responsibility, and Vice Admiral Metcalf authorized Marine Corps AH-1T Cobra gunships to provide air support to them. Two of these helicopters were shot down by Grenadian People's Revolutionary Army (PRA) antiaircraft weapons. Three pilots were killed and the fourth wounded. Still needing relief, the SEALS called an air strike on Fort Frederick, an installation in the hills from which much of the fire was coming. An A-7 from the USS Independence roared in and silenced the fire. U.S. forces, not occupying the site, did not realize that a wing of a mental hospital contiguous with Fort Frederick had also been destroyed.

Several days later CINCLANT initiated an investigation into the unfortunate incident at the mental hospital. The facility's director reported that eighteen patients had perished or were missing after the attack. He also stated that at the time of the air strike, PRA troops were not only in the building firing at U.S. forces but had armed both patients and staff to resist as well. Additionally, the building was not marked as a hospital. Rather, the PRA had raised a flag in front of the building as a rallying point for their forces.[12]

Enemy resistance continued in the vicinity of St George's. To relieve pressure on the SEALS Admiral Metcalf decided to move Marines and tanks into the city. This decision shifted the north-south boundary of responsibility between the services and reassigned some Army objectives to the Marines. The Marines, standing off Pearls airport on the east coast, subsequently sailed to Grand Mal Bay on the west coast, just north of St. George's. They prepared for a landing early the next day in order to effect a pincer movement on St. George's with Army forces moving up from the south.

The Army continued to consolidate in the southern zone. At 7:00 p.m., the 82d assumed operational control of the Rangers and responsibility for airfield security. The buildup of 82d troop strength at Point Salines was slowed because of difficulties in operating aircraft on the uncompleted runway with limited useable ramp space. The second battalion did not arrive until 2:45 a.m. on October 26th. On Wednesday morning, the 82d received JCS authorization to deploy two additional battalions in response to indications of greater enemy strength than anticipated. The remainder of the 2d Brigade arrived at 9:17 p.m. on Wednesday, October 26th. Part of the division's 3d Brigade, the 1-505th Infantry, completed its air move by 9:30 a.m. on Thursday, while the remainder of the Brigade, the 2-505th Infantry and the 2-508 Infantry arrived on Friday. These were the final rifle battalions to deploy.[13]

At 6:30 a.m. on Wednesday, October 26th, the 2d Brigade attacked eastward and seized the Calliste village complex, killing sixteen Cuban personnel and capturing eighty-six others. At 11:00 a.m., the 82d was ordered to rescue the 224 students at the Grande Anse campus. The Division assigned this mission to the Rangers. Since Army airmobile units had not arrived, a mixed force of Marine CH-46s and CH-53s were assigned the task of lifting the Rangers over Cuban positions into Grande Anse. The air assault took place at 4:15 p.m. and lasted only twenty-six minutes. When one CH-46 was damaged by enemy fire, twelve Rangers remained behind so that the students could be immediately evacuated to

Point Salines. These Rangers conducted escape and evasion tactics using a captured boat to escape under cover of darkness.[14]

While the Rangers were executing the Grande Anse student rescue, the 2d Brigade captured the Frequente military supply depot. Reportedly, they found enough weapons to equip five infantry battalions. During the day the 2d Brigade also evacuated the True Blue campus students from Point Salines. They continued to provide airhead security as well as process over 600 Cuban prisoners and many Grenadian detainees and refugees.

Since the 82d had been unable to link-up with the Marines on Wednesday, the 2d Brigade advanced to clear the area between Point Salines and St. George's at 6:30 a.m. on Thursday, October 27th. The pincer movement around St. George's was anticlimactic, as the opposition had melted away. Likewise Marines found Richmond Hill prison abandoned, although earlier an Army Special Forces helicopter assault had been repelled there.[15]

At 12:20 p.m. on October 26th, the 82d was ordered to secure the last remaining strong point at Calivigny Barracks before dark. U.S. troops met resistance at the barracks complex, six miles south of St. George's. Meanwhile, other 82d soldiers were pinned down nearby at Frequente. Prior to the assault on Calivigny, artillery and close air support were called in. One of the four Navy A-7s responding to the call was directed to support the Frequente operation and raked an unmarked target with 20-mm cannon fire, wounding sixteen 82d paratroopers. One soldier died of these wounds on June 30, 1984. The mistake was originally attributed to a "hung" bomb, a mechanical error. Later, a CINCLANT investigation cited human error: "misidentification of the target by the A-7, based on information passed by Air and Naval Gunfire Liaison Company (ANGLICO) on the ground."[16] The small ANGLICO team detachment itself was under hostile fire when it directed the attack. The situation was further complicated by the fact that the 82d's position was not marked with colored smoke as were most of the other friendly positions. When an ANGLICO team member saw that the wrong target had been hit, he radioed a cease fire immediately.

The air assault into the Calivigny Barracks was assigned to the Rangers, who had been resting at Point Salines. At 4:30 p.m. an air assault of eight Blackhawk (UH-60) helicopters from the 82d Combat Aviation Battalion flew into the barracks compound in two flights of four, staying below the line of fire of the ZSU-23mm anti-aircraft guns positioned on the cliffs above the camp. The first two helicopters landed and began discharging their troops. Ground fire struck the tail rotor of the third Blackhawk while it was still about six feet off the ground, causing it to spin into the second helicopter already on the ground. Four Rangers were killed in the collision. The fourth helicopter veered left to avoid the mishap, came down hard and chopped off its own tail. However, the second flight of four UH-60's landed without incident and by 9:00 p.m., the barracks were reported secure.[17]

Helicopter survivability was singled out for criticism after the operation. Official sources stated that one Army and three Marine helicopters were destroyed during the operation, but unofficial reports put the total at nine or ten aircraft.[18] The Lind report alleged that "a loss rate of 9% in three days against an opponent with no anti-aircraft missiles, only guns (which can be highly effective), is not easy to pass over."[19] In response, the JCS expressed satisfaction with the loss of only four aircraft which could not be repaired and with the Army's new Blackhawk helicopters. One Blackhawk had sustained forty-five bullet holes and other extensive damage, yet still completed its mission. They also noted that one of the primary concerns in Grenada was to minimize casualties to the civilian population. Given a different scenario, the Marine AH-1s would probably not have been used for supporting fire and some of the other helicopter losses may have been avoided by greater use of suppressing fire.

The capture of the Calivigny complex marked the end of significant military activity and enemy resistance on Grenada. Friday, October 28th was basically a day for consolidation. Elements of the 82d swept through the Lance aux Epines peninsula and evacuated another 202 American students.

The 82d Division relieved all Marine positions on Grenada and assumed responsibility for Pearls airfield on Monday, October 31st. They continued to clear the island, uncovering multiple arms caches. After withdrawing from the main island of Grenada, the Marines deployed to Carriacou, the northernmost of the islands that make up Grenada. The small island reportedly harbored a significant PRA force. However, the Marines encountered no resistance when they assaulted Carriacou on the morning of November 1st. The amphibious force was relieved in place by Company B, 2-505th Infantry at 10:05 a.m. The 22nd MAU embarked for Beirut once again.

The URGENT FURY redeployment phase and peacekeeping operation began on November 2nd. Hostilities ceased officially at 11:00 a.m. On November 3rd, Vice Admiral Metcalf, Commander of the Joint Task Force, transferred his responsibilities to Major General Trobaugh, Commander, U.S. Forces Grenada, and Brigadier General Rudyard E.C. Lewis, Commander of the OECS established Caribbean Peace Force. The initial elements of the 82d began to depart on November 4th. The 1-508th Infantry left on November 12th; and the 1-505th Infantry and 3d Brigade headquarters left on November 22nd, leaving only their 2-505th Infantry as a major division combat unit. This unit left on December 12th, and by December 15th, the U.S. presence on Grenada consisted of only about 300 U.S. military police, technicians, and support troops as part of the multi-national peacekeeping force. No exact timetable for their departure was published.

Nineteen U.S. servicemen lost their lives during Operation URGENT FURY; twelve of them were soldiers. Another 116 were wounded, 108 of them from the Army. Almost 10,000 Army decorations were awarded. Seven hundred and forty U.S. citizens

were evacuated from Grenada; medical students accounted for 595 of them. On the other side, twenty-five Cubans were killed, fifty-nine were wounded, and 634 were taken prisoner. Additionally, forty-five PRA were killed, 337 were wounded, and sixty-eight were captured.[20]
Official casualty lists do not close the chapter on U.S. Army participation in the operation. Psychological operations, civil affairs activities, local militia member training, and document and equipment exploitation are a few examples of portions of URGENT FURY which continued long after December 1983. As noted earlier, the debate over many aspects of the U.S. action also continued. Questions concerning such issues as force utilization, helicopter survivability, decorations awarded, the role of the press, and others have not been answered to everyone's satisfaction, despite the explanations offered here. Official reports and evaluations continue to dissect URGENT FURY, but some of the issues are likely to remain for some time to come.

NOTES

1. B. Drummond Ayres, Jr., "Grenada Invasion: A Series of Surprises," New York Times, 13 November 1983, p. 1.

2. U.S. Department of Defense, Grenada: October 25 to November 2, 1983 (Washington, DC: Department of Defense, 1983), pp. 5-7.

3. Ibid.

4. Ralph Kinney Bennett, "Grenada: Anatomy of a 'Go' Decision," Reader's Digest (February 1984): 72-5.

5. Benjamin F. Schemmer, "JCS Reply to Congressional Reform Caucus' Critique of the Grenada Rescue Operation," Armed Forces Journal International (July 1984): 13.

6. U.S. Joint Chiefs of Staff, "Urgent Fury Chronology of Events," Working Paper, no date, p. 2. (Hereafter referred to as JCS.)

7. Schemmer, pp. 12-3.

8. JCS, p. 2.

9. Schemmer, p. 14.

10. Ibid, p. 18.

11. 82d Airborne Division Public Affairs Office, Untitled Briefing Slides.

12. US Army Public Affairs Office, Press Advisory, 31 October 1983.

108

13. 82d Airborne Division Briefing Slides.

14. Frank Colucci, "Grenada: An Exercise in Helicopter Power," Defense Helicopter World, 2(June-August 1984): 15.

15. Schemmer, p. 14.

16. Tom Burgess, "Target Confusion Blamed in Air Attack Against Soldiers," Army Times, 23 July 1984, p. 2.

17. Colucci, p. 16.

18. Ibid.

19. Schemmer, pp. 18-9.

20. US Army Public Affairs Office, Consolidated List, June 1984.

10
Grenada and the News Media

George H. Quester

The October 1983 intervention in Grenada might just illustrate the deepest and most explicit tension between the press media and the U.S. government for all of our history. U.S. reporters seeking to accompany the Marines and Airborne troops in the landings on the island were denied permission to do so, and were given no assistance in getting to the island. Reporters arranging to get to Grenada on boats they had chartered were warned away, or were arrested if they had reached the island. As the U.S. military leadership claimed that these barriers were intended for the safety of the reporters themselves, the media representatives could be excused for crying foul when some of them heard shots fired over their heads as their boats approached Grenada, shots fired by U.S. Navy aircraft.[1]

What do the events in Grenada show about the role of the press in U.S. political life, about the needs for (and limits on) press coverage where military combat operations are involved? What do the particular episodes in Grenada say about the larger relationship of the press to our government for the framing and consideration of all of our foreign policy?[2] If Americans are now far less united on foreign policy than they used to be, does this thrust the press automatically into a much more bitterly adversary role, taxing and straining our First Amendment guarantees of freedom of the press?

The Grenadian episode may illustrate the Reagan Administration at its worst in terms of low sensitivity for liberal considerations of freedom of information. It may show the worst of our military, chafing about the burdens of having to deal with an enquiring press establishment. Yet the episode may also illustrate some recent failings of U.S. newspaper and television reporting in showing the media at their worst; after Vietnam the media instinctively assumed that any foreign policy venture was automatically bound to be wrong-headed in its conception, and sure to be an ultimate failure. Only somewhat belatedly have the news columns of the New York Times or the Washington Post begun to confirm what many Americans might once have assumed, that the island's population indeed preferred to be rescued by U.S. military forces rather than continuing to be governed by one form or another of Marxist dictatorship.[3]

SOME BAD REASONS FOR EXCLUSION

Why did the U.S. military work so hard to keep the press away from the first days of combat?

One argument might impute a very nefarious and self-serving motive to the U.S. military commanders in the Grenadian operation, and to their civilian superiors, namely that the press was to be excluded simply to keep the U.S. public from knowing more of the facts, facts which would have shown the operation to be bad service of the U.S. public interest, facts which would have then endangered the jobs of all involved, threatening the re-election prospects of President Reagan.[4]   This is what the press instinctively suspects at the onset of virtually any executive branch attempt at a news blackout.   It is what our founding fathers, in essence, anticipated when they decided to enshrine the press with such a specially protected status in the First' Amendment.   Free elections do not amount to very much if the electorate cannot get at the information needed to judge whether the incumbents deserve to be re-elected, or whether their opponents have a better claim to be executives and legislators.

As admitted in an unguarded moment by Admiral Joseph Metcalf, the overall commander of the Grenada operation, a baser part of the hostile relationship between military and the press may have stemmed also from a more general simple dislike.[5] A great number of the U.S. military officers who had seen duty as Colonels and Navy Commanders in the Vietnam War blamed the press, in part, for their defeat in that war. They regarded the Tet offensive of 1968 as a defeat for the Viet Cong--converted into a victory for the Communists by the tendentious reporting of the U.S. press.   In general, they also saw the television and newspaper coverage of the war as emphasizing U.S. failings and mistakes while ignoring the moral failings of the Communist side.[6]

Some competition between professions is to be regarded as normal.   Academics, for example, normally have disparaging comments to make about journalists, just as journalists have disparaging comments about ivory-towered academics. Yet, the tone to be heard during the Grenada operation became several notches nastier, with military men accusing journalists of everything from pampered cowardice to publication-enhancing irresponsibility, and the military being virtually accused of launching a police state, in a trampling on freedom of the press and the First Amendment.[7]

GOOD REASONS FOR EXCLUSION

A very different interpretation of the media's role in the Grenada operation would begin at the opposite extreme, assuming that secrecy and press restraint are indeed necessary by the most high-minded and public spirited of motives. A standard argument against total press access to the scene of military operations is straightforward enough, namely that of classical military secrecy. The enemy can read our newspapers. Some of the information he derives therefrom might be what he could not have obtained in any other fashion, information which will allow him to surprise us, and which will keep us from surprising him. This is an argument which would, in any war of the past, have excused some censorship, and some limiting of military cooperation with the press. Conversely, it is an argument which would have persuaded the press to submit to some forms of censorship, even to join in with self-censorship, and to accept limits of access to the battlefield.

But defenders of the press would counter that such a justification for secrecy can only apply to facts that the adversary does not itself know. Can there be any point to concealing information on exactly how many Cuban personnel seem to be on the island of Grenada, when Havana will know how many are there? Can there be any point in concealing the nature and quantities of Soviet-produced weapons stockpiled at the Grenada airport, or the nature of documents on communications between Moscow and the Marxist regime on the island, when our enemies delivered those arms and wrote those documents in the first place?

Alas, for those who would have wished to make the issues on a legitimacy of secrecy simple, there are indeed some other good public-spirited grounds for such secrecy beyond the simple and basic category of "what the enemy does not know." There will be times when it is important for us to conceal how much we know, lest our sources of information and mode of obtaining information become too obvious to the enemy, lest he then be able to counter and close off such avenues of information. There will be times when the enemy is counting on us being surprised, where we can instead tactically succeed in surprising him, if this impression is not prematurely dispelled.[8]

As a result, such categories indeed are justified as "things he knows, but he does not know that we know", or "things he knows, but things he does not know that we know he knows", etc. The press owes it to the public to defend its rights to gather information with maximum vigor. Yet this should not mislead us into taking as convincing all its claims as to the alleged follies and conspiracies in each and every denial of information, for some of the arguments which may seem so mind-numbingly foolish are indeed strategically appropriate.

A DEBATABLE LINE OF REASONING

There is yet another category of secrecy which is neither quite fish nor fowl by the above distinctions, but which, after the experience of Vietnam, may have seemed powerfully persuasive for the U.S. commanders in Grenada just as they were for the British commanders in the recovery of the Falklands.[9]

Some wars are not won or lost on the basis of reciprocal surprises and sneak attacks, but rather on the basis of the comparative endurances of the two sides, the comparative willingnesses of the home fronts to put up with sacrifices and setbacks in the short run, while imposing similar sacrifices and setbacks on the opposing side. The side which holds out the longest wins the victory in the end. This was very much the pattern in Vietnam, with the Communists winning the war because the United States became tired of its costs. This was also very much the pattern in World War I after its outbreak, with the

Allies winning in the end because the German population crumbled first.

Here the public-spirited military officer might not have to feel that he has any malfeasance to hide from the public, but only the news and views that would have prematurely led to a cancellation of the operation under way, operations which might look pointlessly costly in a too-early taking of stock, but which would eventually pay off nicely in the recovery of the Falklands or the liberation of Grenada. The public will get all the facts in the end, and the public may reach the conclusion then that the entire project was indeed worthwhile. Clemenceau concealed the news of the 1917 French Army mutinies as much as he could, not just from the Germans, but also from the French public and the rest of the French Army. Did not the French public regard this as a most useful service on his part, when they had all the news in front of them after the Allied victory in 1918?

This kind of argument is of course fraught with peril. The military commanders, their civilian Secretary of Defense, and their President can claim that they were guarding the nation against panic, knowing that the total picture of facts at the end would vindicate their holding back some of the facts at the earlier stages. Yet there is no easy stopping place in this kind of paternalistic premise by which the government was empowered to judge what was safe for its public to know.

The self-serving goal of guarding one's re-election prospects would always lie suspiciously close to the information-denial policy being imposed. Memory has a tendency to grow nostalgic and forgive. If the public learns of the costs of an operation only very late in the day, when some kind of meager victory had partially compensated for such costs, the public might be of a mood to forget, indulging in the euphoria of toasting whatever victory had been achieved.

Similar tricks get played all the time on the investment side of military procurement, or in civilian-sector investments, as the true costs of a new bomber or a domed football stadium are concealed at the outset; they then are somewhat forgotten and forgiven as the bombers or stadiums look impressive enough at the end, being something in any event for which one cannot reverse the sunken cost commitments. Can it be that the mentality of cost overruns, and "buying in" to defense contracts, has now become central to the winning of wars, the wars of endurance which compromise so much of the armed conflict we may have to anticipate for the future?

SOME SPURIOUS REASONS

The excuse that reporters were being barred from Grenada out of governmental concern for their physical safety was surely among the more flimsy of the arguments. The U.S. press has proved its physical courage on enough occasions in the past, wading ashore at Normandy and Iwo Jima, losing people out and away from the protection of U.S. troops in the 1970s in Cambodia, and today in El Salvador.[10]

During the Grenadian operation, one could hear professional military officers questioning the personal bravery of reporters, remembering some of their harsher critics in Vietnam who may never have left the comparative safety of Saigon, suggesting that a leftist outlook on military matters was correlated with an unwillingness to risk one's life on behalf of one's country. Yet a reasonable generalization about the press would have to resemble a similar generalization about the military itself. Each will include instances of bravery, and instances of prudence, even instances of cowardice, and cowardice disguised as bravery, as it becomes possible to have been close to a combat zone without being very much endangered by combat. Within each group one will also see some reckless bravery, often associated with the stamina and zeal of youth, in acts of daring which the survivors would not choose to repeat some ten years later. Young reporters and cameramen out to get a story may irritate local U.S. military advisors by moving into the bush to try to talk to Communist guerrillas in Southeast Asia or El Salvador, and might then have judgements raised about their objectivity as reporters, or about their perceptions of what is in the U.S. national interest. But it would seem a slander to impugn their personal bravery.

One suspects that the raising of the personal safety issue in the Grenada case was almost a double-edged propaganda ploy, offered as an excuse, offered also to try to induce the average American to distrust the press even more, on the inference that newpapermen normally needed to be coddled and shielded and protected, and that their judgement as Americans should be questioned because their manly heroism was in question.

In the Grenada case, the suggestion was also offered that the press was demanding material support and physical arrangements which the fighting soldiers and the taxpayers could not afford to give. Again, if the press was prepared to pay its own costs in getting to an island in the Caribbean (which it was), then this kind of objection also lost its punch. The ingenuity demonstrated by the press in chartering transportation to approach Grenada surely taxed the U.S. Navy's resources in keeping them away; but a U.S. taxpayer might then argue that the navy had no business in wasting its resources on precluding such press access in the first place.

SIMPLE UNTRUTH IN GOVERNMENT

Compared to the systematic exclusion of the press from a combat zone and the physical arrest and incarceration of some U.S. reporters, most of us might be somewhat less seriously abashed by another form of abuse of the press practiced in this operation, one which has been practiced many times before, a simple lying to the press, and to the public, about the facts as they were happening.[11]

Governments have to keep secrets sometimes, and have to tell lies sometimes, and we should hardly collapse into a state of shock when this occurs. If a government becomes too secretive, or becomes inclined to disseminate untruths as a matter of normal practice, it suffers after a time for the reputation it has established, and the nation it governs will also suffer. As long as democracy has not otherwise been compromised, however, and as long as the press has not had its editors arrested and its printing presses smashed, the voters will soon enough be able to divest themselves of an administration which dishes out so much less than the optimal amount of the truth.

We would expect the government of the Soviet Union to tell a great number of lies, just as we would expect the government of President Marcos in the Phillipines to be totally callous about rendering the truth. Yet the crucial distinction between those governments and ours is not in that they are in the habit of lying and concealment, but that they have eliminated any possibility of their being ousted by opponents in a free election process.

Yet even this much lying had its costs. To begin, any extensive pattern of disseminating false information is worrisomely consistent with a greater general contempt for the press, a kind of contempt which would then lead to some of the other steps noted, in a quantum jump more menacing to American freedom. Short of such a jump, the practice of outright lying also erodes the impact of one's own press influencing the outside world. When the British command in the Falklands operation thus misled the British press, this had the bizarre impact of making the Argentine press look a bit more credible, and British newspapers a little bit less credible, in the contest for the sympathies of world opinion. Misleading the American press--this occurred most dramatically on the prior initial question of whether any U.S. intervention was possible, or whether this was merely the normal Cuban and Soviet propaganda--thus similarly had the unfortunate cost of making what the New York Times prints a little less persuasive for foreign readers in the future, and of somehow making Cuban news services something that an information-hungry person might be more ready to read seriously.

How does one draw any firebreaks on this particular issue, on how much the government can tell lies in its statements to the press? We are not dealing here with legal or constitutional questions of perjury, or testimony under oath, as before Congressional committees. Nothing in the First Amendment precludes the government from hiding something from the press, or from lying to the press.

Common sense dictates that a government which lies all the time will no longer be able to fool the press, but--simply for outlining the prerequisites of effective government--surely we would want to draw the line further back than that. One technique that has been used effectively for the drawing of boundaries here is an old one, namely that any administration press spokesman stuck with disseminating more than the normal maximum of untruths has to resign, as a sacrificial lamb, when the lying is exposed, as his personal honor has been compromised. Les Janka, the Deputy White House Press Secretary for Foreign Affairs, thus turned in his resignation on October 28, 1983, after having been left in the situation of disseminating information to the press which his superiors knew to be untrue. While this might seem to impose the penalty exclusively on the innocent middle man (who typically goes on to a much better paying job in the private sector), it imposes a penalty and check on the administration itself; one cannot have press secretaries resigning on principle month after month without very totally mortgaging one's credibility, and without a general loss of effectiveness in the administration as well.[12]

THE PEOPLE'S RESPONSE

If Americans are to become upset about the Grenada operation, the more serious grievance is thus not the Reagan Administration's failure at times to tell the truth, as on the number of Cubans found on the island, or the number of battles still underway at various locations, but rather the administration's failure to allow the press in to hunt for the truth, and its imposition of physical barriers to hold the reporters out.

One of the most interesting and important "bottom lines" on our issue comes then in the reaction of the general public to the exclusion of the press. As the readers who had been denied access through the manhandling of the media, Americans as a whole might presumably have been expected to share in the indignation of the press, and most editors seem to have assumed and counted upon such a constituency being there to back them.

Instead, however measured, by letters and phone calls, or by more scientific survey research, the reaction of the general public shows a surprisingly strong endorsement of the exclusion of the press, as well as of the Grenada intervention in general.[13] Dismaying the newspaper and television news editors of this country, this public reaction remains to be more fully explained.

A part of it is probably due to the afterglow of an easy "victory"; the public had been starved for victories, and thus-- since the affair over the "Mayaguez"--was ready to make a great deal out of minor triumphs. Related to this, we probably have some subtle and low-key endorsement of the alleged lesson of Vietnam, whereby it is better for the public not to be too much exposed to the grim details of the investment in force too early, lest this keep the investment from being carried through to fulfillment, and lest the ultimate project not be completed.

Another part of the reaction is probably directed at what the public may now perceive as an instinctive left-of-center reaction from the media, both from the newspaper and television networks, where operations in a place like Grenada are condemned by word and nuance before anyone has had a chance to weigh them at any length. The U.S. press has probably moved somewhat leftward in reaction to the Reagan Administration, and earlier even more in reaction to the Vietnam War, but it may have moved more than the public it means to be serving, such that the public does not so fully trust it. Inclined to be in step with an eastern seaboard academic establishment, with its news operations run mainly out of cities like New York and Washington, the press may have exposed itself to a kind of caricature painted by professional military officers, and by ordinary Americans across the center of the country and center of the political spectrum.[14]

Can it thus be that the general public no longer sees its press as a reflection of itself, as a surrogate and agent for its own interests, as a check on nefarious government, policed by the free choices of the marketplace, as we purchase newspapers or turn our television dials? What if we now instead see the press as taken over by a liberal establishment, or as monopolized by economies of scale which give a few networks and newspaper chains too much of an advantage; or what if the press is too intent on selling us a product--announcing crises and scandals that are not really there? A very dangerous kind of alienation may have settled in, reflecting and amplifying some other major breaks in the consensus Americans used to feel about both domestic and foreign policy.

As with any complicated issue, the question of press access here is not without its ironies. Patrick Buchanan, a columnist of presumably good conservative credentials, spoke out to attack the complaints of the press in the case of Grenada, in the following terms: "If the people who exhibited such arrogant and infantile behavior are 'representatives of the American public' when exactly did we elect them--and how do we go about canning them?"[15] Yet, since when have conservative Republicans in the United States respected the credentials of those who had proven their merits in the competition of the private sector? A real believer in the processes of free choice should have had an easy enough time answering Buchanan's questions. No one appoints or elects press critics of government, except by buying their newspapers or by tuning television sets to their programming. Anyone wishing to "can" such new authorities might do so easily enough by buying something else to read. Buchanan's citing of state authority, in the validation of news, over pluralistic private sector authority, is hardly the stuff of what John Locke, Thomas Jefferson, or Milton Friedman have donated to an American tradition of distrusting government. Thomas Jefferson, always the master of the memorable quotation, once said that if forced to choose between a government with no newspapers, and newspapers with no government, he would surely opt for the latter.[16]

Power politics realists might dismiss this as a preference which could be indulged only where foreign governments are not threatening us with invasion or harm. The threat of a foreign enemy is thus always one plausible justification here for trusting in governments at the expense of newspapers. More disturbing for any U.S. liberal, however, are the cases where other considerations would be tipping the scales toward governments rather than the press, such as the insecurity of incumbents in governments, or the distrust some people in power feel for the attitudes and intentions of the public at large.

CHANGES IN THE CHARACTER OF THE MEDIA

The U.S. public may thus no longer trust itself, seeing itself as having prematurely panicked in recent contests of will-- as having been led to a too pessimistic picture of Vietnam by a one-sided press coverage. We have seen the flow of "boat people" from Vietnam, risking their lives to escape Communist domination, amid other tangible signs that this Vietnamese regime could be every bit as brutal as the regime we had once supported; some of the U.S. guilt at the costs we imposed on Vietnam--costs so graphically and extensively reported in the press--has thus been replaced by a different kind of guilt at having abandoned millions of people to a politically grim existence.

The Vietnam memory affects each of us in different ways, of course, with only a fraction of the public now coming to blame a liberal press establishment (or "media hype") for having lost that war. Yet we surely now have fewer Americans trusting the media than at the peak of that war.

As the Vietnam War ground on, Americans lost faith in their own government, and in the goals of their post-World War II foreign policy. With that war behind us, we have moved in different directions, hardly reestablishing any kind of clear consensus about out goals. The respect and trust we feel for the printed press, and especially for the electronic media, has thus definitely declined in the years since the end of the Vietnam War. If the press served the public by being skeptical and quizzical, by being a muckraker and a naysayer, the press may now have been type-cast in the recesses of the public mind as overly much inclined to this role. We are surely not ready to have Richard Nixon come out of retirement and campaign for the Presidency, yet the public probably would be less inclined to worship Woodward and Bernstein as heroes today than ten years ago.[17]

One very major additional change in the role of the media over the past two decades is easy enough to identify: the growth of television to replace the printed press as the principal conveyor of news.

Television is very much more graphic than the newspapers, and this may make for a more imposing message on the death and destruction of any war. The producers of television news programs are moreover very much guided by what camera footage they have been able to obtain. Since cameramen have typically been able to record the operations of one's own troops, but not those of the enemy, the result has been that the home viewer is led to see his own side as inflicting most of the suffering and punishment, doing most of the fighting, bearing the largest portion of the responsibility for the continuation of the war.

A television producer concerned for a maximum contribution to balance and understanding would thus have to eschew some of the footage, to make up for the asymmetries of coverage. Yet hardly any defender of television news operations would ever claim that they have been ready to sacrifice what is entertaining in the interest of objectivity (or that they would be ready to risk losing much of their audience) as part of coming closer to what the printed press has been able to achieve in depth and breadth of reporting.[18]

Indeed, few defenders of the electronic media would ever claim that television has become as profound a source of analysis and coverage as one gets from the printed press at its best. Yet two caveats have to be noted here as well. First, even the printed press is concerned about audience, with only a few U.S. newspapers therefore really being first-rate. Second, the great majority of Americans are no longer relying on the printed press as their primary source of news coverage; rather, they are relying on television.[19] There is basically little or nothing that could be done to turn around this shift in the physical nature of the principal news medium; the concomitant changes in how responsible the media look will be something we have to live with.

One can illustrate the trendiness and shallowness of contemporary media attention easily enough in the Grenada case. As a partial explanation for the U.S. government's slowness in accomodating the press representatives seeking to cover the fighting on the island, it has been noted that a total of 400 such representatives were waiting at Barbados at one point for access to the island, a greater total than the number of reporters covering the Vietnam War at its peak. Given that the total of residents on the island is only some 100,000, this comes to one media reporter for every 250 people, a staggering relationship. Also staggering was the fact that no newspaper or television entity had deemed it worthwhile to have a reporter on the island before the invasion, suggesting at the very least there is a certain trendiness and faddishness as to how the media decide to pay attention, or not pay attention, to any particular area, or any particular flow of news.

VIETNAM, TEHRAN, AND THE FALKLANDS

It is widely conjectured that the press restraints in the Grenada intervention were based on at least two recent experiences. In the U.S. failure in Vietnam, the U.S. press had almost all the access it could have asked for, including easy access for television camera crews, making for what in the end came to be known as the "living-room war."[20] Able to watch the devastation being inflicted on the Vietnamese countryside, and the apparent resilience of the enemy as the guerrilla attacks seemed to persist, an American at home surely did not find his enthusiasm for the war enhanced by what he could see on his television screen. Able to watch and remember the U.S. side of the Vietnam War, the same television viewers were not nearly as able to visualize the treatment meted out to the same villages by the Viet Cong or by the North Vietnamese Army, or a few years later the treatment meted out by Cuban forces in Angola or by Soviet forces in Afghanistan, or by the Vietnamese forces now occupying Kampuchea. The inherent one-sidedness of the visual image and the alleged deliberate one-sidedness of the reporting in the printed press were widely viewed by U.S. field commanders as having eroded the home front support they would have needed to prosecute the Vietnamese War to a successful conclusion.

The British commanders in the Falkland Islands recovery seemed to have accepted this "lesson" from Vietnam, as they went quite far in managing, restricting, and using the press.[21] Direct television access was basically denied, officially on an alleged technical difficulty of getting live signals back to Britain (a lame excuse in the age of satellites); more probable was the reasoning that the visual and graphic picture would instill pessimism at home on the costs being accepted. A fair amount of deliberate misinformation was also put out via the British press, in a few cases again with a view to sustaining home front morale, in a larger number of cases with the intention of confusing the Argentine command as to where the British landings were coming, and as to the general timing and nature of the British attack. The latter use of the press, while somewhat compromising the worldwide reputation of British news services as accurate conveyors of the news, might be regarded as traditional (and far less objectionable) for misleading the enemy and protecting genuine military secrets; this remains an important part of warfare. The former, whereby the British public was presumably given an exaggerated impression of British successes and competence for the short run, so as to maintain their commitment for the longer run, is more worrisome.

The Grenada operation was so swift that very few arguments about "fooling the enemy" could capture any legitimacy, certainly not after the initial surprise attack. Instead we probably have a U.S. government digesting the composite lesson of Vietnam and the Falklands, as live television coverage of casualties and civilian destruction in the early stages was to be avoided, and almost all press commentary which might be critical was to be postponed. Very little can be made of the case here that information was being withheld from the Russians or from the Cubans, whereas in the South Atlantic war it remained somewhat important, until the very end, to withhold information from the Argentines. Rather the information was being withheld from Americans, with the Cuban and Soviet connection coming in only somewhat indirectly, in that Moscow and Havana should not be encouraged to stiffen their commitments or their resistance by any hopes that U.S. public opinion would turn against the administration.

One other episode of U.S. foreign policy had intervened between the Vietnam War and the Grenada operation, again with several relevant analogies to the issues of press relations with the government and military; this was the seizure of U.S. Embassy personnel in Tehran, Iran, and the holding of the some fifty-two people entitled to diplomatic immunity hostage for 444 days.

The press role in the hostage drama was central and truly perverse.[22] U.S television viewers were treated to evening after evening of fresh television coverage of the demonstrations outside the embassy, demonstrations orchestrated almost entirely for the benefit of the cameras of CBS, ABC, and NBC. One literally heard of instances where the demonstrations were delayed for fifteen minutes so that a late-arriving camera crew could get set up. The so-called "student demonstrators" thus aimed their activities heavily at the media links back to the United States, with the media cheerfully cooperating. Walter Cronkite made the situation worse, evening by evening, by reminding television viewers of the exact number of days the hostages had been held, making himself "the most trusted man in America," and leaving Jimmy Carter incapable of winning reelection against Ronald Reagan.

Clearly the media were no longer just reporting the news in the Tehran case, but, by encouraging the Iranians involved to count on an erosion of U.S. home-front resolve, were changing the news, i.e., were making the news by their very presence. A naive U.S. viewer could conclude from watching the evening news that the Iranian man on the street in Tehran was continuously convulsed in a paroxysm of anti-American rage, rather than that the entire operation was heavily theater aimed at the U.S. audience.

If the Iranians had gone through with their occasional threats to exclude the U.S. press, or if television had not yet been invented, the hostage crisis might have taken a very different turn, might have ended much earlier, and Jimmy Carter rather than Ronald Reagan might have been President at the time of the Grenada invasion.

CHANGES IN THE ENTIRETY OF U.S. FOREIGN POLICY

Representatives of the military are quite correct in asserting that the reporters who accompanied the assault forces at Normandy and Iwo Jima were much more inclined to cooperate with the U.S government, in submitting to censorship, in sitting on a story when asked, in accepting on faith a version of events put forward by the U.S. military command. At least two factors have worked to change all this. War has changed since World War II; and--only partially related to these changes from total war to limited war--the U.S. public's perception of foreign policy has also changed.

For a combination of reasons, therefore, the press was enlistable as a "good soldier" in the years until 1967, but not thereafter. The President of the United States could once have picked up the telephone to call the editors of a major newspaper and ask them in "the public interest" to kill a story, with the chances of cooperation being quite good. Reluctant to accept censorship or state interference as any kind of precedent in constitutional principle (although battlefield censorship of the dispatches which might betray "military secrets" had indeed been accepted without real complaint), the press was nonetheless ready to do a fair amount of voluntary self-censorship and self-restraint. Perhaps this came simply in light of the major and horrendous foreign challenges that dictatorships like Hitler's seemed to pose; perhaps instead it was simply the novelty and enormity of the burden Americans were accepting in getting into an active foreign policy in the first place.

By contrast with World War II, however, the United States kept the war in Vietnam limited--limited to fighting on the ground of South Vietnam and air raids against targets in North Vietnam, with no military operations at all against Hanoi's principal supporters, the U.S.S.R. and Communist China. It was quite normal during the war for U.S. reporters to be visiting Hanoi, ducking for cover during U.S. air raids. The U.S. press also had reporters stationed in Moscow on a continuing basis throughout the Vietnam War, of course, and would have had such reporters stationed in China as well, if the Beijing regime had only allowed

it (the admission of U.S. press representatives to China was
indeed one of the most encouraging signs of the 1970 breakthrough
in Sino-American relations).
By comparison it would have been impossible, and unthinkable,
for a U.S. press representative to be interviewing German or
Japanese government officials during World War II, presenting
"their side of the story," recounting their claims about U.S.
atrocities. One of the important consequences of the limiting of
war (a limitation made necessary by the awesome power of nuclear
weapons) is that a continuation of the dialogue between
governments, in part through press interviews and press visits,
has been desirable and necessary; but it has made the press less
of a total ally of the government in wartime. The enemy can no
longer be viewed as a total enemy; the press is no longer a total
ally.
The other major change in government-press relationships
stems instead from the larger breakdown in the consensus U.S.
citizens have felt about the goals and appropriateness of their
foreign policy. For most of our history, including World War II,
the years of the Cold War, and probably until the middle of the
Vietnam War, most Americans shared in an almost subliminal
consensus about America's role in the world, by which we assumed
that our government was doing all it could to help other peoples
attain the same degree of self-rule and government-by-the-consent-
of-the-governed which had worked so well in the United States. It
was only during that painful and unsuccessful endurance contest
with the forces of Ho Chi Minh that we began to entertain strong
doubts about the sincerity of those who had proclaimed this as the
major purpose of the United States in the world.[23]
With students and faculty on campuses often now espousing an
alternative view, by which the economic imperatives and dictates
of a predatory capitalism were the real explanation of U.S.
military ventures abroad--with a few students even shocking their
elders by contending that such base motives had accounted for our
landings at Normandy or Iwo Jima-- the press also accepted a
certain quizzical cynicism here. The discovery that the U.S.
government had very often lied to the public, on the concrete
details of the progress and conduct of the Vietnam War, led the
press to accept a possibility that all of U.S. foreign policy
might have been characterized by deception, and that our central
purposes should similarly be cross-examined.

WORRIES FOR THE FUTURE

Any liberal American concerned about the precedents set with
the barriers on press coverage in the Grenadian intervention might
be worried on two related, but distinguishable, counts.
First, we are generally concerned with whether the press has
a greater or lesser access to the news, whether the continuous
balancing between the powers of government, and the powers of an
alternative to government, gets moved too far in the direction of
executive privilege and alleged military necessity. There are
some very practical problems here, with one of these practical

problems simply being the precedent and pattern set for similar operations in the future.

Second, and of potentially even greater concern, would be any erosion of the fundamental principles of the First Amendment of the U.S. Constitution, this amounting to a qualitative distinction of the first order, rather than any mere quantitative shifting of the balance in one direction or the other. If we concluded that the First Amendment had somehow been violated in the manhandling of reporters on the island of Grenada or the deliberate interference with their means of getting dispatches back to the United States, much more might be at stake; an unchallenged executive decision to ignore the letter of the Constitution would be an opening for a trampling on the rest of the meaning of the First Amendment's protections.

Whether the explicit wording of the First Amendment was violated by the Reagan Administration in the Grenada case will remain open to debate. The Amendment states: "Congress shall make no law respecting an establishment of religion, or prohibiting the free exercise thereof; or abridging the freedom of speech, or of the press; or the right of the people peacably to assemble, and to petition the Government for a redress of grievances."

The wording would hardly require that the United States Armed Forces always invite the press, or offer transportation, or otherwise facilitate the entry of reporters onto foreign battlefields. Yet newspapermen were arrested and prevented from getting their news dispatches back to their editors. Is this not an abridgement?

Our worst fears still lie ahead. No one was precluded from printing editorials and commentary back in the United States disapproving of the Grenadian intervention; indeed, one of our problems is probably that the press much too quickly rushed to be disapproving. Yet a contempt for the press was shown by the Reagan Administration; this could easily read like a contempt for the spirit of what the First Amendment stands for. As military force was used quite openly to deny information to the U.S. public, the relevant commanders indeed took pride in having withheld that information, amid very little reference to withholding information from any foreign enemy.

On this plane, some serious damage to the U.S. constitutional process is at least possible--damage that may have been on its way in any event in the wake of changes in U.S. attitudes about foreign policy, and changes in the nature and style of the press and electronic media--but a damage which cannot easily be brushed off.

There is one more aspect to the sorry exchange here which can also be troublesome for its broader constitutional overtones, as well as for the immediate practical patterns being set. In explaining the restrictions imposed on the press, Secretary of Defense Caspar Weinberger several times made a major point of deferring to "professional military judgement," with the official line being that it had been the uniformed military officers who had decided to curtail the activities of the press, as the civilian Secretary and President "would not dream" of overruling decisions made by admirals and generals.[24] This again echoed the tone of the British in the Falklands War, and reflected the frustrations of the Vietnam War, amid charges of "micromanagement" by civilians, charges actually going back to the arrival of Robert McNamara as Secretary of Defense in 1961.

It was probably inevitable that the pendulum would swing back toward the uniformed military in the continuous debate about how best to manage military campaigns, with the 1960's being the alleged high point of operations research and civilian expertise, and with the Reagan Administration making a greater deference to the professional soldier a part of its overall style.[25] Yet to defer to the military on so important and so domestic an issue as the prerogatives of the press was clearly likely to offend a fair number of Americans who were all too accustomed to uniformed military interferences with liberties in Latin America and in many other corners of the world.

It is, of course, not impossible that Reagan and Weinberger had themselves made the decision to shut out the press (and that Mrs. Thatcher had made the same decision for Britain in the South Atlantic War), but that these civilians had decided to thrust the responsibility for the decision on the military, perhaps thus to make it more plausibly a matter concerning the life and safety of our servicemen. If this paid off in making the decisions more plausible for the short run, however, it might nonetheless exact a longer-term price for the affront to American constitutional tone.

THE PRESS AND FREEDOM

A very traditional American attitude, one that has stood the United States in good stead for its long history, is that government in general should be distrusted. The introduction of the welfare state in the years of the New Deal saw many Americans begin to scoff at such distrust, amid exultations of the marvelous capacities of an active and strong presidency. The malaise of the U.S. foreign policy in the 1960's saw some return to the earlier maxims, however, as Lyndon Johnson and Richard Nixon were, to some extent, reviled for utilizing practices already introduced under Franklin Roosevelt.

It is also traditional for Americans to be dissatisfied with the performance of one newpaper or another, as the years of "yellow journalism" before the Spanish-American War illustrate; but it is a rather new American attitude for us to be distrustful of the entire body of the press.

Such a broad distrust for the press would indeed be a very dangerous lesson to draw from the Grenada intervention, an intervention which otherwise, appears, after only a short period of review, to have been a rather well-taken American military initiative. Despite the early criticism by the U.S. press, it would seem that the United States will draw relatively little criticism from the Grenadians themselves for having deposed the Marxist regime. Yet the press should not draw criticism for being the press if the United States is going to continue being what it has been.

Amid all the doubletalk about what the U.S. motives were for invading Grenada--to rescue U.S. students who might have become hostages, or to preclude the establishment of a Cuban/Soviet military base exploiting the new airport, or to prevent invasions of the neighboring islands which lacked the resources to defend themselves--a much stronger incentive for the intervention tended to be unmentioned by both critics and defenders of the operation: that the government in place was unrepresentative of the people, and that the United States could facilitate the establishment of some government which the people of Grenada would choose themselves.[26]

In the aftermath of Vietnam, the possibility of facilitating self-determination has come to have a hollow ring, as we become doubtful on whether this could work, and suspicious of ourselves as to whether this was what we truly were seeking (rather than markets for our gluts of overproduction, etc.). Our successful post-1945 experiences of steering Germans and Japanese into political democracy--"forced to be free" in the title of one book[27]--might have left us with higher hopes in this regard; but the loss of Vietnam seemed simply the culmination of a long series of failures for political democracy in all the countries freed from colonial rule after World War II. India was the one visible and notable exception, itself passing through a non-democratic interim when Mrs. Gandhi declared her "state of emergency."

Yet hardly noticeable--as are all the Carribean islands--the various microstates physically close to Grenada had managed to maintain political democracy for themselves, demonstrating (if demonstration were needed) that free election systems could indeed function in this part of the world in countries of similar climate and ethnicity and economic situation. The U.S. Armed Forces fought for a good cause in Grenada, and may have done a very good job of allowing the Grenadians to get the kind of government they want, government that they can reject again at the next election if it turns out to be not what they want.

Yet the ultimate irony of the Grenadian operation is that a sine qua non for political democracy, for the kind of government we fought for, is a free and active press, a press that is able to complain and report about the failings of an incumbent administration, with everyone accepting this as its natural role.

If we come back, some five or ten years from now, to assess the overall success or failure of the Grenada intervention, one could propose a very simple benchmark for such a judgement. The operation will have been a success if Grenada by then has a press behaving very much as our press behaved during the rescue operation, demanding to get at the facts, exercising its freedom to be critical, making the government work hard to defend its record in preparation for coming elections. No such freedom was allowed the press of Grenada under the Marxist regime of Maurice Bishop, or under the regime of those who toppled and murdered Bishop with the intent to move the Grenadian system still further leftward. Instead the editors who would have been critical of

Bishop's style of government, along with the intellectuals who would have been critical, had all been put into jail. In all respects of its handling of the Grenada intervention, the Reagan Administration treated the press with greater callousness than is the norm for the U.S. executive branch, perhaps gambling on a popular acceptance or endorsement of this tough attitude if the actual military venture on the island went acceptably well. In terms of evidence of public opinion on the issues, the early returns suggested that the administration got away with this gamble. Yet the public is at the least somewhat fickle on these matters, ready perhaps to blame the press for the loss of Vietnam, but potentially quite ready to trust the press again if anything were to go wrong in the Grenada operation. As a continuing demonstration of how the public wants the government to be watched closely, by the Congress and by the press, the press coverage of the deployment of U.S. Marines to Beirut is a model of this thirst for oversight.

The question thus remains as troublesome as it has always been for concerned liberals in the past. Can a democratic government like that of the United States participate actively in world affairs, contributing "to make the world safe for democracy" without compromising its own freedom, its own prerequisites for a free election system at home? The proper balance of considerations here does not have to tread on the sacred constitutional principles of the First Amendment, but it will always necessarily entail some circumscription of the facilities and prerogatives assigned to the press. Yet it is folly to build up some momentum of zeal for clamping down very hard on these prerogatives and functions of the press, for this may confirm the fear that the defense of freedom will simply mean the loss of freedom to another menace, a menace from within.

NOTES

1. For the extent of confrontations between the military and the press, see Henry E. Catto, Jr. "Dateline Grenada: The Media and the Military Go at It," Washington Post, 30 October 1983, p. C7.

2. A good discussion of the broad relationship of press to U.S. foreign policy can be found in Guneter Lewy, "Can Democracy Keep Secrets?" Policy Review 26(Fall 1983): 17-29.

3. See New York Times, 30 October 1983, p. 21, and "Grenada: All Things Considered," Washington Post, 9 November 1983, p. A18.

4. As an example of this kind of interpretation, by which the administration simply was trying to shield its own reputation, see Anthony Lewis, "What Was He Hiding," New York Times, 31 October 1983, p. 19.

5. The Metcalf comment is reported in the Washington Post, 16 December 1983, p. 10.

6. An example of the kind of criticisms that have been made of the media's coverage of the Vietnam War can be found in Peter Braestrup, Big Story (New Haven: Yale University Press, 1983).

7. For some particularly combative examples from each side, see Joseph Sobran, "When Mounting an Invasion, Why Take Along Enemy Troops," Washington Times, 3 November 1983, p. 1C, and Thomas Collins, "Did Navy Article Foretell U.S. Press Ban on Grenada," Newsday, 11 December 1983, p. 9.

8. A defense of this more complicated and extended category of secrecy is offered in Felix McKnight, "War and Journalists," The Journal of Commerce, 2 November 1983, p. 4.

9. For a comprehensive overview of the British handling of the press in the Falklands War, see Robert Harris, Gotcha: Media, the Government and the Falklands Crisis (London: Faber and Faber, 1983).

10. A good overview of the personal courage of press representatives in recent wars is presented in Robert B. Sims, The Pentagon Reporters (Washington: National Defense University Press, 1983), chapter I.

11. See Stuart Taylor, Jr. "In Wake of Invasion, Much Official Misinformation by U.S. Comes to Light," New York Times, 6 November 1983, p. 20.

12. The resignation of Janka, and threatened resignation of White House spokesman Larry Speakes, his superior, is reported in the Washington Post, 1 November 1983, p. 1.

13. For a discussion of the public's reaction to the restraints imposed on their media, see "Journalism Under Fire," Time (12 December 1983): 79.

14. A discussion of the possible alienation of the media from the public can be found in Heath Meriwether, "The Press Battles Its Own Credibility Problem," Miami Herald, 6 November 1983.

15. Pat Buchanan, "It's the Marines vs. the Media," Washington Times, 2 November 1983, p. 1C.

16. The Jefferson quotation is cited in Les Janka, "Grenada, the Media, and National Security," Armed Forces Journal International 5(December 1983): 9.

17. As evidence for the decline of public confidence in the printed and electronic media, see polls cited in "Journalism Under Fire," Time (12 December 1983): 79.

18. The systematic biases and distortions which accompany the shift from printed newspaper to television news watching are discussed in Austin Ranney, Channels of Power (New York: Basic Books, 1983).

19. For data on the public's reliance on television, see Evans Witt, "Here, There, and Everywhere: Where Americans Get Their News," Public Opinion 4(August/September, 1983): 45-48.

20. Michael J. Arlen, The Living Room War (New York: Tower, 1969).

21. Harris, pp. 61-5.

22. On the media's distorting impact in the Tehran hostage crisis, see Majid Tehranian, "International Communication: A Dialogue of the Deaf?" Political Communication and Persuasion 1 (Spring 1982): 21-46.

23. For a much longer outline of this author's interpretation of the erosion of the United States concensus on foreign policy, see George H. Quester, American Foreign Policy: The Lost Consensus (New York: Praeger, 1982).

24. "An Off-the-Record War," Newsweek (7 November 1983): 83.

25. See Gerald F. Seib, "No More Micromanagement of the Military," Wall Street Journal, 8 November 1983, p. 34.

26. Michael W. Doyle, "Bringing Grenada Democracy," New York Times, 4 November 1983, p. A27.

27. John D. Montgomery, Forced to be Free (Chicago: University of Chicago Press, 1957).

11
Grenada in Retrospect

G. F. Illingworth

Within the last decade the world's three major military powers have for various reasons invaded their neighbors. The Soviets invaded Afghanistan; former Secretary of State Alexander Haig suggested that the Soviet invasion occurred in order to decrease the centrifugal forces at work in and out of the Soviet periphery--to create, in effect, a firebreak in Afghanistan to counter the spread of the Islamic fundamentalism which flared in Iran, spread to Pakistan, and which might ignite among the large Soviet Islamic population in the Moslem Soviet republics.

The Chinese invaded North Vietnam to deter them from continuing their advance across Kampuchea to Thailand. (The Chinese military commander of the attacking forces later asked General Haig if the Americans realized that China was the living deterrent to the Domino Theory being executed in Southeast Asia.)

Lastly, the United States intervened in Grenada for much the same reason that the Soviets invaded Afghanistan: to create a firebreak (this time against the spread of Marxist revolution and destabilization). Since the official after-action reports remain classified, discussion and analysis of events in Grenada must derive from entirely open sources (unclassified published materials). The Soviet Union stated that it went into Afghanistan at the request of the Afghan government and people in order to restore the situation; the Americans said that they went into Grenada at the request of the people (Governor General Sir Paul Scoon, through the OECS), to restore the situation and protect American lives. The Chinese did not make any excuses; they said that they went into Tonkin to teach the Vietnamese a lesson.

When the United States acted in Grenada following the island's self-imposed destabilization, Americans were both confused and angered by the almost universal condemnation of the U.S. move. This condemnation saw a rare agreement between, for example, NATO and Warsaw Pact states, and between those blocs and the Third World in general (including, by and large, the Organization of American States).

Many people saw little fundamental difference between the Soviet invasion of Afghanistan, for instance, and what was called by virtually all but the U.S. Government the American invasion of Grenada. While the dissimilarities are obvious, such as the

130

attitudes of the two native populations to their self-proclaimed benefactors, the fact remains that both were power plays with little prospect of being checked. Both superpower military operations were launched after ostensible appeals from legal native authorities; both target areas were not far from vital oil fields and sea lanes; both were near areas of continuous instability.

Since political states are but collections of people, it is not surprising that states usually act with the same narrow self-interest as a guide. Many kinds of birds and animals, including fish, are territorialists--they claim dominance of an area beyond the immediate limits of their nests or dens; they tolerate lesser creatures, but will fight other competitors which encroach upon their territories. Psychologists state that humans have a sort of personal bubble of about three feet in diameter, into which uninvited intrusions by others normally causes unease. Political states have the same sorts of characteristics; in animals the claimed region of living or hunting space is called territory; in states it is called spheres of influence.

The Helsinki Agreement has not been able to overcome the legacy of Yalta, and states remain free to act as they see fit in their claimed territories or spheres of influence. The disputes between the major powers arise in the great spaces of the neutral ground. Thus the western democracies, particularly the United States, remained helpless in the face of periodic Soviet military repressions of East European populations, and the Soviet Union was unable to resist American pressure on Cuba and the invasion of Grenada.

The United States was unable to do anything to deter Chinese aggression in Tibet, or Indonesian action in Timor, while the Chinese could not restrain Vietnam in Cambodia. In some cases there was no wish to do so. Thus U.S. actions during the Cuban Missile Crisis and in Grenada evoked only rhetoric from the USSR. The danger lies in no-man's land, where each could bring to bear approximately equal amounts of power with relatively equal costs.

Grenada is one of many islands in an American sphere. The importance of its location was illustrated by the fact that a very high proportion of the German submarine fleet--perhaps half--was deployed in the eastern Caribbean and along the northern waters of the South American continent, from which they exacted a fearful toll of Allied shipping. The importance of those sea lanes has not diminished over the years. Rather, with the steady depletion of American mineral resources, American industry--and way of life--have grown increasingly dependent on the minerals and crude oil from Africa and the Persian Gulf. The same dependence exists for the developing and influential nations of the north and northeast South American seaboard. With the advent of the mammoth supertanker the sea lines of communications (SLOCs) around the Cape of Good Hope took on a renewed importance as the Suez Canal could not accomodate these giant oil carriers. (It will be some years before the canal is widened). Therefore the Marxist political successes in Angola and Mozambique must be seen beyond their meaning in Africa itself.

The United States had viewed with growing concern the construction by the Cubans of the Point Salines airfield in Grenada. There was no doubt in the minds of the U.S. officials that this field would facilitate the fomenting of trouble in the region while providing a convenient staging base for further Cuban presence in Africa, an important presence which the United States had long (unsuccessfully) sought to remove.

Behind the Cubans, who were often portrayed as "front men," was seen the larger and more menacing presence of the Soviets, whose increasingly modern navy and growing force projection capabilities were viewed with increasing concern in the United States.

It has been suggested that Grenada would be a useful staging and emergency base for Cuban and Soviet flights to their African interests, specifically Angola, Ethiopia, and Mozambique (the first two being garrisoned by large numbers of Cuban troops). As American use of the Azores shows, such a stopover base would be very useful. Grenada would also be a valuable base from which to direct destabilization efforts in targeted Latin American states.

There is no question of the perceived importance of Grenada to the Soviets. One of the captured documents was a memorandum of a conversation between Soviet Chief of the General Staff Marshal Ogarkov and Einsein Louison, a Grenadian minister who was training in the Soviet Union. The memo stated that "The Marshal said that over two decades ago there was only Cuba in Latin America, today there are Nicaragua, Grenada, and a serious battle going on in El Salvador."[1]

For the United States, there appeared to be little scope for effective action to remove this nearby potential trouble spot without violating a host of international and regional charters. But the ineptness of the factions in Grenada provided the reason for U.S. and regional intervention.

It had been reported that Sir Paul Scoon had earlier tried to get out of Grenada by asking the British to remove him and his family; the British, it is thought, declined to intervene in Grenada's affairs and Scoon withdrew to his stately home and kept quiet. Yet one reason why the United States said it intervened in Grenada was the appeal by the Governor General for regional assistance in restoring order on the island: "The Governor General's appeal carried exceptional moral and legal weight because it came from the sole remaining source of governmental legitimacy in Grenada."[2] But had the Governor General's request to the British to get him out been granted, he would not have remained to call for the restoration of order. Thus it was fortuitous that the British had not helped him to escape.

The Caribbean region has not been the same since the events of late October 1983. The intervention by the combined military forces of the United States and OECS, plus Barbados and Jamaica, has to an extent left an altered regional political situation in its wake.

Much controversy was aroused over this military action by

anti-communist states fearful of the seemingly growing Marxist political and military influence in the area (to include Central America).

In the eyes of many--particularly those in academe and the media--the Administration's case for military intervention in Grenada was weak. There is no argument about the American medical students being frightened. Whether or not they were truly in danger was debatable. The chancellor of the medical school of St. George's at first hotly denied any danger to the students, saying he had been personally assured by the coup leaders that they meant to guarantee the safety of the students. Later, for whatever reason, he changed his mind and agreed, if less than wholeheartedly, that the students may have been in danger.

For the United States to say that it acted to save American lives because no effective government existed after Bishop's execution may have been grounds for intervention, but there are many who saw this as a perilous procedure. Had the United States intervened in every country in which existed a similar situation--violent changes of government in countries which contained American citizens, many of greater number than found in Grenada--the Americans would have been intervening and fighting continuously, all over the globe, for nearly the last half century (as suggested by Britain's Prime Minister Margaret Thatcher).

For the American strategist, events in Grenada pointed to a propitious time for action. The indigenous government had collapsed, the Prime Minister and cabinet members had been executed, dozens of citizens had been slaughtered, and Americans were potentially in danger.

The profound stupidity of the Grenadian revolutionaries deserves comment. As noted in the captured documents, rarely have the Soviets and Cubans had such intellectually inert clients, who caused much frustration for their erstwhile sponsors. And as soon as the first bullet entered Maurice Bishop's body the Grenadian revolution was over.

No major power would tolerate such a fledgling, but potentially troublesome, challenge on its doorstep. With the creation of what would have been a power vacuum, the United States had to move swiftly before the Coard/Hudson group could consolidate its power--as it would have done.

Many have suggested that the fact the U.S. operation went far beyond the safeguarding of the American citizens proves that their security was only an excuse for mounting a long-desired operation against the budding communist island regime.[3] But other factors obviously came into play, involving timeless principles of national security. Here is the sort of dilemma which may never be resolved. How does one reconcile the United Nations' principle of non-intervention with a perceived, potentially serious threat next door?

There unarguably exist two major world orders which in the past have had great difficulty in coexisting peacefully. Both are endowed with a Messianic belief in the righteousness of their systems, and in their inevitable triumph. The Marxist revolution

is 150 years younger than the American revolution, and to the
Soviets their red star is brighter and still rising. They see the
West as a tired, unequal system composed of extremes of rich and
poor, with each of these conditions being perpetuated. Man's
spiritual and material salvation lies in a socialist order, which
they see as inevitable.

American antagonism towards the Grenadian socialist state
surfaced almost immediately after the New Jewel Movement came to
power. As early as 1979 the United States had tried to undermine
the Grenadian economy--first by attempting to discourage some OPEC
and West European countries from helping the Grenadians to build
their new airport and then by forcing international banks to stop
lending money to Grenada.[4] So desperate was Grenada that by 1983
they were talking about following the Cuban example and working up
two sets of financial books--one a "cooked" book to satisfy the
International Monetary Fund's stiff requirements.

Seven months before the U.S. military intervention the State
Department had warned that "the steady evolution of the (Soviet)
front affiliations since 1979 suggests that Moscow hopes to use
its Grenada foothold for future front activities in the
Caribbean."[5] Yet the State Department also wrote, "How active and
effective these organizations have been on the island is
uncertain."[6]

Academics, in particular, have raised some difficult
questions about the U.S. action in Grenada. Legally, Grenada was
not guilty of any offense against any neighboring state and only
the lone American veto prevented a United Nations Security Council
censure, while the General Assembly overwhelmingly condemned the
American action. This U.N. vote cannot be lightly dismissed as
customary Third World anti-Americanism. If so much of the rest of
the world appears to dislike the United States, why is this so and
why does this persist?

Clearly, a dangerous practice is continued when one nation
invades another because it does not like what it thinks the other
state may eventually do. Grenadians, including non-Marxists, have
denied that the U.S. medical students were in danger, and
sovereign states have the right to choose their own friends and
make their own alliances.

Not much should be made of the allegations that Grenada was
planning to build an army far larger than it needed--one which
would be the largest small island army in the region. The fact is
that Grenada was a Marxist state, and Marxist states have
relatively large armies. Is there anyone in Washington who is not
yet familar with Mao Zedong's famous dictum which says that
political power grows from the barrel of a gun? The security
apparatus makes the whole thing work. Nicaragua has a large army;
Cuba has a large army; Vietnam has a large army; the Soviet Union
has a large army, as do China, North Korea, and the like.

Clearly, the airfield at Point Salines--the building of which
was followed closely every day in the United States--was the focus
of American concern, given the rush to Marxism by the agitated
Grenadians in power and the growing destabilization (from the

right and the left) of Central America. The arguments over the true purpose of Point Salines were best illustrated in the correspondence section of The Times (London), although there was no doubt in the minds of the Americans that it would be used to advance the communist cause wherever necessary.

One observer on Grenada, a retired British lieutenant colonel, supported U.S. suspicions in reporting that the Russian fuel tanks (erected by an American firm) were roughly the capacity of the facilities on Barbados; between fifty and sixty aircraft a day (including ten jumbo jets) were refueled daily on Barbados.[7]

Barbados had 10,000 hotel beds for tourists, compared to the 400 tourist beds on Grenada. According to Lieutenant Colonel Cave, the Bishop government planned on increasing this to 700 beds in 1985. Thus the 7,000 cubic meters of fuel capacity created at Point Salines appeared to be vastly out of proportion to the demand of expected tourist traffic. The 10,000 foot runway at Point Salines would have been able to service the largest Soviet aircraft, and Cuban oil tankers could reach Grenada in half a week.

The opposite view, supporting the Grenadian claim that the airport was to be used to increase tourism, was provided by the Managing Director of Plessey Airports Limited (U.K.), which helped to build the airport.[8] The Plessey executive denied any military purposes for the airfield by pointing out the vulnerability of the fuel storage facilities erected above ground. He explained the noticeably acute shortage of tourist beds by asserting that hotel developers were holding back until the airport was completed.

The fact, as so often happens, is that both men were right. Non-Marxist Grenadians have since stated that the new airport was vitally needed if the economy of Grenada was to show any growth. At the same time there was little doubt--and the post-invasion discovery of caches of communist-made arms near the airport have shown--that the airfield would indeed have been an important base for communist regular and unconventional military operations.

Following their revolution, the Grenadian Marxists became increasingly wrapped in the trappings and jargon of the new liturgy. The Grenadians were plunged deeper into a seemingly endless circle of generally unproductive meetings of various sorts. Like communists everywhere, copious notes were taken and kept of these endless and dull meetings. Diaries captured by U.S. troops recorded the increasing despair of the note-takers, who wondered if their fellow Grenadians would ever become politically aware enough to appreciate the revolution. Grenadian Marxist leaders themselves were ignorant of a precedent of leadership by troika.

As V.S. Naipaul wrote, it was a revolution that ran on words, words which in correspondence were frequently misspelled and sometimes not fully understood. The revolutionaries, conscious of their blackness, wanted to be taken seriously by the socialist world and buried themselves under the jargon of Marxist doctrine. But while they held endless meetings the Central Committee never got much done, despite the presence of a cadre of a couple of hundred "internationalist workers," including a number from the United States. However, Naipaul observed, "The apparatus was absurd. But the power was real."[9]

Charles Krauthammer noted that Grenada's revolution and its expectations were a matter of scale.[10] For when many of the Third World states seek aid they think of expensive weapons systems, dams, and the like; Grenada's idea of foreign aid was more modest--a Grenadian official scoured the U.S. in order to raise a couple of thousand dollars to buy a word processor. Even then, the American donor demanded that his donation qualify as tax deductible, so the Grenadians had to find an organization (the American Friends Service Committee in Philadelphia) which could launder the money.

Some academics have asserted that Grenadian Marxists were determined to proclaim and maintain their total independence, yet the mass of captured documents--weighing twenty-five thousand pounds--reveal a very different story of a backward little island, unsure of its ideological anchors, hurling itself at the Soviets and Cubans. And while the Point Salines airfield was said to be a symbol of Grenadian self-reliance, in fact the Grenadians had practically nothing to do with planning and building it. This was a Soviet-encouraged Cuban enterprise.

Yet it is an exercise in futility for the United States to keep on pointing out that Bishop was getting aid from the Soviet bloc. Where else was he to get it? It is practically universally accepted by analysts that once we get by areas like the Middle East there is not enough money left in the U.S. Treasury to adequately promote American interests elsewhere in the world, including the Caribbean and Central America.[11] The Western Europeans increasingly want cash on the barrel for their goods and services.

A number of secret agreements were signed between Grenada and other nations, particularly the Soviet bloc countries. This was seized on and publicized by U.S. officials, but again we should not make too much of this. What nation does publicize every agreement it makes? Since the Grenadian revolutionary leadership was avowedly Marxist, why should anyone be surprised that agreements of various sorts existed with other Marxist states, all of which are notoriously secretive?

Agreements and proposals covered such areas as cooperation between Soviet and Grenadian youth organizations, the sending of modest numbers of cadets and military personnel to the Soviet Union for training, a request to join the Soviet "Intersputnik" satellite communications network, and some requests for some military equipment and spare parts. Grenada was also to be given an executive An-26 aircraft; it was to be supplied by the Soviet Union, but supported and maintained by Cuba.[12] Other equipment to be delivered to Grenada included a few armored personnel carriers and small arms and ammunition.

Bishop, his treasury desperately short of money, went around the world begging (like so many) for help. In North Korea, in April 1983, he signed an agreement which would provide Grenada with technological and agricultural assistance, and two boats and fishing fleet equipment. East Germany would help out with the security forces. The Czechs offered scholarships for Grenadian students to study science and construction. The Vietnamese offered to take some Grenadian military personnel for training in tactics, weapons, chemical warfare, and propaganda; the Vietnamese were very good at these things.

Although the Grenadians had earlier welcomed the ousting of Eric Gairy and the triumph of the New Jewel Movement (a party founded in 1972 by Maurice Bishop and his colleagues), conditions in Grenada became steadily worse as intraparty squabbling grew amidst Marxist sloganeering and a barely understood ideology. By late 1983, the revolution was in real danger of falling apart. The public, rather than enthusiastically supporting the revolutionary movement, was sullenly apathetic. Significant internal differences in philosophy had broken open between Maurice Bishop and Bernard and Phyllis Coard and their respective followers.

Coard, though earlier removed from the ongoing Political Bureau business, remained an eminence grise and retained influence through his domineering Jamaican-born wife, who remained active in NJM Party meetings. Bishop was eventually shouldered aside and finally put under house arrest. Bishop had wanted real grass roots involvement in the running of the country--modeled loosely on the African village tradition. Coard wanted the reverse, a system of highly centralized control on the Soviet model.

Things came to a head in 1983. In August, Minister of Mobilization Selwyn Strachan warned that the rebellion within the party would "turn into open rebellion if we do not address it now," and "it will be resolved in a petty burgeois (sic) way."[13]

On September 14-16, 1983, the Central Committee met to address the perceived impending political disintegration of the NJM, and the meetings began with criticisms of the leadership (Bishop): "All programs of the Revolution are in a very weak condition...."[14] Mass organizations were doing less, and the people were drawing the wrong conclusions from the shooting down of the Korean aircraft and the Soviet invasion of Afghanistan. The militia was "non-existent, the army demoralized... If this is allowed to continue the party will disintegrate in a matter of five to six months." It was charged that "Comrade Leader (Bishop) has not taken responsibility, not given the necessary guidance,... is disorganized very often, avoids responsibilities for critical areas of work..."[15] This is an interesting document, and the party's despair over the nonexistence of the militia, the demoralized state of the small army, and the impending collapse of the political system must be compared to the official U.S. Defense Department description of the Grenadian military defense: "U.S. forces were met by a well-organized centrally commanded and controlled military force."[16]

Bishop may have seen the impending collapse, for it has been suggested that he was reevaluating his relationship with the Soviets and Cubans and moving to some sort of rapprochement with the United States. This may have cost him his life; there have been few successful escapes from the Marxist camp. Leonid Brezhnev articulated what had long been a fact of life: that socialist revolutions were irreversible facts of life. This philosophy leaves only violence as the means by which socialist/marxist governments may be changed.

The party was restructured and Bishop became, in effect, a figurehead; the real power now seemed by many to have apparently shifted to Bernard Coard. Internal party conditions worsened, and the Central Committee met on October 12, 1983. Bishop, who had recently been on a trip to Czechoslovakia, Hungary, and Cuba, challenged the committee, but lost again. His followers had begun to agitate on his behalf, and this time he was placed under house arrest and expelled from the party he had founded.

Oddly, Coard reportedly dropped out of sight after this meeting, and was not seen again until captured by U.S. forces, suggesting that the military commander, General Hudson Austin, may have made a move to the top. On October 17, Austin went on the radio to explain why Bishop had been removed, but that he was safe. At about this time the United States reportedly offered to fly Bishop out of the country, for reasons which are still not clear. On October 18, after days of fruitless effort on Bishop's behalf, five ministers still faithful to the former Prime Minister resigned.

Some of the masses were beginning to stir in Bishop's behalf. On the following day thousands of people went to Bishop's house and freed him. It has been written that Bishop's house arrest had been a difficult time for him. He may not have eaten for three days prior to his release by the crowd, and when they came to his house they found him naked and strapped to his bed, possibly drugged by injections from Cuban doctors. They then marched to the former Fort George, now renamed Fort Rupert (after Bishop's father), and after some confusion heavily armed soldiers drove up in armored personnel carriers and blasted the crowd. When it was all over several unarmed civilians were dead; soon after Bishop himself, plus Ministers Whiteman, Creft (Bishop's mistress), Bain, and two union leaders were shot. Bishop's last known words, as reported by V.S. Naipaul, came as the army was set loose: "My God, they've turned the guns on the people."

There must have been no doubt in his mind that he was next-- and he was.

Bishop was the lesser of evils on Grenada. His prisons held political prisoners, and many prisoners were tortured. He responded to these observations by noting that unlike other revolutions at least his revolution had not shot anyone.

Although Bishop's body was said to have remained undiscovered, most Grenadians have already placed him in their pantheon of heroes--at present he is the sole occupant. There is considerable feeling among Grenadians that the Point Salines airfield when completed should be named the Maurice Bishop International Airport in recognition of the monumental project pulled off virtually through the efforts of this leader of a very

small and poor state. Most of these Grenadians detested his
Marxism, but managed to separate Bishop from his political
philosophy. Even the United States, in its efforts to de-
communize Grenada, has, because of Bishop's already solid place in
Grenadian history, carefully refrained from critizing, attacking,
or degrading his memory as they have the rest of the former
Central Committee members. These had been rounded up, jailed,
paraded in their underwear, and photographed practically naked
and/or manacled and guarded. But not even a superpower can take
on the memory of Bishop, and the U.S. Army's 1st Psychological
Warfare Battalion has bent over backwards to avoid tarnishing his
memory. In death it appears that he looms larger than life--as is
so often the case.

When Bishop, his mistress (the Minister of Education), other
cabinet officials, and an as yet undetermined number of civilians
were shot by the Marxist army soldiers, the shock waves resounded
far beyond Grenada's shores. To rapidly change governments was
not a new phenomenon in the region; the slaughter accompanying
this transfer of power was new, and it caused revulsion and anger
throughout the eastern Caribbean.

There was no secret that a U.S. intervention was at hand, and
the Marxists on Grenada had enough warning to appeal to Cuba for
help. It has been stated by an academic that Fidel Castro refused
to commit forces to take on the United States, and in fact reached
an agreement with the United States whereby American forces would
bypass pockets of Cubans in order to avoid clashes and
casualties.

On October 19, an emergency meeting of the OECS was held in
Barbados; attending were the OECS member states plus two, Jamaica
and Barbados. John Compton of St. Lucia summed up their feelings
when he told a television news reporter that they "were not going
to tolerate it!" They meant it, and a decision was made to ask
the United States (via secret message) to join in the
intervention, since the OECS nations did not possess sufficient
military force to do the job. Following a late night meeting of
the OECS plus two in the early hours of October 22, a message was
sent through the U.S. Ambassador to the region (who resided in
Barbados) to President Reagan; the U.S. decisionmakers were
aroused, and consultation began long before dawn. The President
and Secretary of State were in Georgia, and a cross-country
conference was conducted. The decision was made to ask the OECS
to put the request in writing, and a draft letter was rushed from
Washington to Mrs. Charles, the OECS leader and Prime Minister of
Dominica. She signed the letter, and the Americans now had the
request in writing.[17] The rest is history.

Some academics have questioned the three listed reasons for
the U.S. intervention. These were the concern for the safety of
U.S. students and citizens, the OECS intervention request signed
by Mrs. Charles, and the alleged appeal for help by the Governor
General, Sir Paul Scoon (a retired schoolmaster).

On October 20, portions of a U.S. fleet were diverted to the
Caribbean; these forces included U.S. Marines bound for Lebanon.

The Joint Chiefs of Staff were reported by some academics to have been putting the final touches to the military contigency plan. The U.S. military operations have been described elsewhere, but there are phases of the operations which deserve further analysis.

From a technical standpoint, one should not read too much into the Grenada operation. The disparity in power was emphasized by some embarrassing post-mission statements, particularly by the admiral commanding the U.S. naval task force, who said to the press that "we blew them away."[18]

The operation was not without its problems, most of which remain classified.[19] All requests by non-military analysts to examine the operational after-action reports were denied. But the press has publicized the bombing of U.S. troops by their own aircraft and the leveling of a mental hospital, among other things. Indeed, the press has suggested that a high proportion of U.S. casualties may have been caused by "friendly fire," and two helicopters ran together during an assault. The U.S. Marine Corps study reported that faulty intelligence almost caused the Marines to attack the Venezuelan Embassy.

What gives one cause to pause over this operation is that these missions were carried out in a more benign environment than U.S. forces would face were they opposed by the Soviet Union, or even Cuba or Nicaragua. No hostile naval and air forces were encountered. So we cannot judge how far the U.S. military establishment has gone in improving its professional performance, so tarnished after Vietnam, Iran and Lebanon; this was not the test of sufficient difficulty that would provide such a measurement. Yet it was a victory of sorts in that it went some way to politically restoring U.S. credibility, which has been seriously questioned by friend and foe alike.

The apparent intelligence failures in Grenada, and in recent U.S. history, are particularly disturbing and potentially fatal. For example, although the rescue of the U.S. medical students was the primary publicly-stated reason for the intervention, U.S. troops had no idea that there were two campuses;[20] thus over a full day passed after one of the campuses was secured before the U.S. forces were informed (by students) that there were over a hundred students waiting in the other campus at Grand Anse. This, more than anything, may have called into question for many the alleged dangers to the students, for this was the time when a vengeful Grenadian Marxist people's army could have killed the unprotected students. But they were unharmed.

Another intelligence fault was the failure to identify the mental hospital which was mistakenly bombed by U.S. aircraft, with dreadful results to the patients. An American general's five foot long map of the tiny island did not have the hospital annotated, or plotted. If so, this is an incredible omission, given the resources for "overhead imagery" available to both superpowers. It is also difficult to believe that knowledgeable Grenadians were not brought into the preoperational intelligence gathering process. One must look to the highly publicized intelligence failures in Vietnam, Iran, and the Middle East in order to put things into perspective.

It is difficult to avoid comparing the Grenada military operation with the British recapture of the Falklands (a far more difficult operation against much stiffer opposition). The British intelligence officers sought out former Falkland Islands residents, and the intelligence provided by these civilians--about roads, geography, places--was absolutely vital to the successful outcome of the military operation. Historically, the Americans--relying more on computers, technology, and machines--have not been as imaginative as the Europeans, and the U.S. military operations always seem to lack that personal touch of the operational commander.

It could be said that there is a sort of technological version of the Brezhnev Doctrine extant in the United States--that where technology and computers have taken over, the situation is irreversible. How else can one explain the spectacle of seven C-130 Hercules troop transports flying around in circles--in what the Army major general commanding called "an aerial wagon train"[21] --unable to proceed with the planned parachute assault because a single special inertial navigation set (an electronic black box in the lead airplane) had malfunctioned? Why could not the second or third aircraft have assumed the position of mission leader? Where were the human navigators, and why were they paralyzed by the loss of a black box? Were all seven aircraft radar sets broken? Were all the stopwatches broken? The result of all this helpless circling was that the Point Salines airfield defenders were warned and more prepared than they would otherwise have been.

Several written sources have drawn attention to the differences between official Pentagon and independent reports of the military action. The media remember the official briefings in Saigon during the Vietnam war. A confident military force would not have excluded representatives of the press from the initial assaults, notwithstanding the media's unquestionably miserable, biased, and often incompetent reporting in Vietnam.

A report prepared by William S. Lind (a Senate staff official and member of the Military Reform Institute) for the Congressional Military Reform Caucus implied that "turf" battles had been fought in the Joint Chiefs by stating that "the Army wasn't included until the last minute; furthermore, once committed, the army's advance was too slow."[22]

The survivability of helicopters in battle was again brought into question by the report, which criticized this problem with helicopters and the performance of the various service elite commando units. Concerning the latter, four Navy SEALS drowned when apparently given a bad weather forecast, and the unit also attacked the wrong target when going after Radio Grenada. The Air Force Times reported that the Army's super-secret, elite Delta force appeared to have conducted the least imaginative attack possible when trying to assault by helicopter the Richmond Hill fort. After being driven off by fire, the Army tried exactly the same tactics on the following day, and failed again. On the third day some newsmen simply walked into the prison and declared it captured, the defenders having withdrawn.[23] Of the hundred helicopters committed in Grenada, nine percent were destroyed and "several more" were damaged, giving relatively high overall casualty rates for helicopters against fairly light opposition (no heavy defenses). One would have thought that the Vietnam experience would have sobered those intoxicated with heliborne assault, but the lesson (again) was not learned. As a senior Army commander in Grenada stated, "I think we learned once again that the helicopter is a very vulnerable object when it goes against a well-organized air defense system."[24] The implications here are sobering, given the traditional Soviet emphasis on strong, layered, and integrated air defense systems.

In Grenada, the defense was neither _relatively_ strong nor well-organized.[25] All that the defenders had were a few automatic weapons--no heavy anti-aircraft artillery (AAA), no radar-directed guns, no surface to air missile system, no air defense fighters. The U.S. Army has _never_ faced a coordinated, well-organized air defense system, and _its_ heavy helicopter losses to relatively lightly armed forces in Vietnam and Grenada should be of concern. It does not get any easier from here.

Military reform movement members in the Congress have noted the questionable performance of some U.S. forces on Grenada; to wit: the Army reportedly got in at the last moment in order to justify its request for a third Ranger battalion and Ranger regimental headquarters; the invasion was originally planned as a Navy/Marine team effort (so successful in the Pacific in the Second World War); it was stated that the operation turned into "a pie-dividing contest among all the services," a standard JCS approach to military operations "which allowed the enemy to put on a reasonably good show."[26]

The military elite units reportedly did not give elite performances. Criticism arose over the slow Army movement (suggesting that the increasingly discredited attrition style of warfare is still alive and well in the Army despite all the new talk about maneuver warfare); other criticisms emerged on the reliance of helicopter assault tactics.[27] Only the 2nd Marine Division was praised. None of these criticisms was denied by the Defense Department, which brings us back to the obvious question: who in Washington can fix these problems?

The _Armed Forces Journal_, no enemy of the armed forces or a strong defense establishment, outlined what it termed "The Grenada Map Fiasco."[28] Despite the fact that a naval task force was diverted to the Caribbean several days before the OECS asked the United States to intervene in Grenada, the Marines on board the ships had no maps of the island until nine o'clock in the evening before the Marine assault occurred--or seven hours before the attack. If true--and it has not been refuted--this violates the most basic rules of war (sound planning and resting troops before battle). How could the Marines get the proper rest when their maps arrived at nine in the evening and they were scheduled to make an assault at 4:15 a.m. the next morning?

The map lockers on board the initial assault ships contained no maps of Grenada; the map in the Grenada file was a map of Guyana. The map in the Guyana file was also of Guyana.[29] The Armed Forces Journal (AFJ) noted what this writer had earlier noted:

> This nation spends billions of dollars for the world's most exotic intelligence collection systems, and we can't distribute a map to men whom we've asked to go to war in a few hours? What good is all of that intelligence in the National Military Command Center or at the Headquarters of the Commander-in-Chief, Atlantic, in Norfolk, VA, if we can't fly a map to an aircraft carrier or transmit one electronically to our ships at sea?[30]

The "maps" which did arrive were photos which had to be glued together on the ships, and which turned into a jellified mess when the Marines were soaked by a rain squall as they boarded their helicopters.

Writing for the AFJ, Benjamin Schemmer made a valid point: "The US is spending $16.7--billion this fiscal year (1984) on command, control, and communications (c^3, or C-cubed)--and even in a benign environment, we can't communicate to the troops who need them most a few smidgens of the billions of dollars worth of intelligence we collect and analyze so painstakingly." Schemmer noted that the United States has "10 defense communications satellites and four Navy/Air Force Satellites in orbit--and we had to fly the maps to our Grenada task force..."[31]

The Grenada operation seems to have reinforced the positions of those (including a former Chairman of the Joint Chiefs of Staff)[32] who advocate major reforms in the U.S. armed forces structure, particularly the reformation of the Joint Chiefs of Staff. In the views of many, the position of service chiefs and members on the Joint Chiefs of Staff must be separated so that no officer can be a service chief and a JCS member simultaneously.

The problems of the U.S. military forces are well known to defense analysts; much has been written, and is being written, of the perceived weakening of the whole military system (read the works of Record, Lind, Gabriel, Savage, and Luttwak, for example), and the most severe if publicly silent critics are many U.S. officers themselves.

Given what the military reform caucus in Congress called the barely adequate U.S. performance in Grenada, one may consider the implications of heavier military involvement against stronger and better organized opponents; a superpower could not find a more benign environment in which to conduct military operations than a place like Grenada, which can be completely sealed from the rest of the world, and which leaves little maneuvering room for defensive forces, and whose relatively scarce defenders fielded neither air nor naval forces, nor even any large caliber guns.

Many of the most hawkish U.S. military officers are now coming to the realization that these left-right political problems are not as simple as they once seemed and can no longer be treated as black-white, clear-cut problems. Many now finally accept that poverty and injustice are the root causes of not only Caribbean and Central American regional unrest, but are of growing concern within the United States as well.

The credibility of the Defense Department was damaged seriously in Vietnam, and the public again must weigh opposing statements regarding Grenada. On the one hand the top Defense Department officials and service chiefs have all announced their great satisfaction with the outstanding performance and clockwork precision of U.S. military forces. Yet criticism of U.S. military performance on Grenada has surfaced from numerous quarters, from the Military Reform Institute to pro-military publications such as the Armed Forces Journal. What is the public to think?

Two U.S. groups again clashed in Grenada, for a uniquely U.S. symbiosis now occurs with every military intervention--a little war (between the American government and its own press) is grafted onto the main event. By its own excesses and abominable reporting during the Vietnam War the U.S. press had earned the loathing of a large segment of the U.S. military establishment. So when the press was finally let into Grenada they went after their own Department of Defense rather than the story of the Grenadian operation itself.

V.S. Naipaul, himself from Trinidad, has written of the relationship between the U.S. press and their own government. These remarks can be taken with Dr. George Quester's study of this uneasy relationship.[33] The press appeared little interested in the real story of Grenada, the history, the revolution, the aftermath, or implications for the future. They wanted to ferret out U.S. mistakes and possible abuses with which to attack their own government.

The Grenada affair left considerable debris in its wake. For the British, it was a "sticky wicket." Unable for a number of reasons to intervene directly in the internal affairs of a Commonwealth nation, they became an unfortunate partner in a comedy of errors. When their regional High Commissioner cabled with urgency the news that an invasion of Grenada was imminent, his cable was missent to the post office of a factory. The factory officials discovered this Top Secret cable addressed to the Foreign Office, and they sent it on to the proper address. When it finally reached the Foreign Office one of their bureaucrats directed it to an "In" basket, and there it sat while the British complained of being surprised by the operation. Had the South Atlantic campaign been so conducted the Falklands would now be the Malvinas.

A great many rifts developed over the Grenada affair; how serious and long-lasting they are remains to be seen, but the little island was the subject of major international disagreements. Differences of opinion developed between the United States and the United Kingdom, between the United States and its major European allies, between the United States and Latin America, among the Commonwealth countries, between many

Commonwealth nations and the United States, and between some Commonwealth states (notably the OECS nations) and the United Kingdom.

The position of The Times (London) is revealing. On October 26, 1983, its position was somewhat ambivalent, reflecting the whole British position. Its editorial said that "There is no getting around the fact that the United States and its Caribbean Allies have committed an act of aggression against Grenada. This is in breach of international law and the Charter of the United Nations."[34]

After thinking about it for two weeks its position shifted. Sir Philip Goodhart, a member of Parliament, responded by drawing attention to the other side of the coin in stressing the geopolitical aspects of the Grenada intervention. In writing to The Times (London), Sir Philip articulated what some professional officers have long thought. He noted that in the last twenty years both Labour and Conservative governments had given independence to about twenty mini-states, some with populations of less than 100,000; none of them could adequately defend itself.

Sir Philip noted that "Three of these mini-states, Grenada, the Seychelles, and Zanzibar, have already been hi-jacked by small bands of armed men not much larger than that gang that carried out the great train robbery."[35] In a fourth case, The Gambia, only the fortunate presence of a couple of men of the SAS (Special Air Service)--Britain's elite and secretive commando troops--held the takeover in check until the neighboring Senegalese Army could intervene and crush the coup attempt.

Sir Philip's letter, in fact, was a response to an earlier editorial by The Times, whose position had changed and had declared that it had had enough of these hi-jackings of small states. In applauding the U.S. intervention The Times now suggested that rather than apologizing for the intervention, Grenada should be but a first step in a Western approach to the problem. "A more important task for the West now is not to feel hang-dog about this rescue, but to develop a coherent and multilateral approach to further rescues. If it could not have been done for Grenada, could anybody have had hope? From this small beginning, a strategic initiative should be seized." If not, asked The Times, "so who is to look after those members of the United Nations who, like Grenada, are to all intents unable to defend themselves from a group of thugs?"[36]

It was noted that up to the U.S. intervention in Grenada the West had watched impotently while "nation after nation had become prisoner of this rhetoric." (The doctrine was the Brezhnev Doctrine). Most of these socialist states, noted The Times, were "ruled by military dictatorships, which often call themselves People's Democratic Republics with neither popular consent, nor democracy, nor the republican ideal anywhere in evidence." Furthermore, regarding the U.S. condemnation by the United Nations, noted The Times, "Less than 50 of the 158 nations in the UN could in any way be considered democracies--the vast majority of members of the United Nations are dictatorships of one kind or another, but all of the kind which is ultimately legitimized only by the barrel of the gun...." The final sharp point was reserved for those states condemning the intervention: "How ironic, then, that the majority of unelected dictatorial governments which voted to condemn the East Caribbean States and the United States called for early elections in Grenada--a privilege they deny absolutely or in all but name to their own citizens. Not the Soviet Union and its allies, though; even they could not quite stomach that recommendation."[37]

All of this raises a significant question: if the Soviet bloc can arbitrarily enunciate a doctrine which says "once a prisoner, always a prisoner," why cannot the West repudiate this and say that where practically possible, "once free, always free?" Furthermore, this need not be a "white only" concern; states like Kenya, for example, would not wish to see regional states destabilized and captured by Marxist thugs.

Finally, noted Sir Philip, there are international agreements concerning the hi-jacking of airliners; why not such agreements concerning the hi-jacking of small, free mini-states? In the light of the turnabout in Grenada it may be time to take a hard look at this idea.

Sir Geoffrey Howe, the British Foreign Minister, also recognized this problem of defenseless mini-states. But Britain is in some ways a victim of its unrivalled imperial past; its former possessions are now independent and many are run by the sorts of dictators deposed by the US/OECS intervention in Grenada.

Finally, of Grenada one must ask: are the seeds of revolution still there? There are some who think that they are, that many of those who rose with the revolution will not be able to go back to what they were before it. Of the prisoners in the U.S. detention facility, V.S. Naipaul wrote, "The eyes that held mine still transmitted power and conviction."[38] Few Third World nations have had success with democracy; in Grenada, only time will tell if history will repeat itself here.

NOTES

1. Grenada, A Preliminary Report, Joint U.S. State Department/Department of Defense Report, 16 December 1983, cover.

2. Ibid, p. 2.

3. Since this was written, the Air Force Times, after having obtained a "heavily censored" Grenada report under the Freedom of Information Act, reported that "American forces who invaded the Caribbean island of Grenada were sent to assist in reestablishing a democratic government, not just to rescue American civilians as administration officials had first suggested. (Air Force Times, 4 February 1985, p. 4).

4. British Broadcasting Corporation Report, 31 October 1983. Economic threat is a commonly used tactic by the U.S. government

146

to enforce desired behavior. In the last thirty years such nations as the Soviet Union, France, Great Britain, and Grenada have been subjected to actual or threatened economic warfare with a view to weakening the targeted state and its monetary system.

5. Grenada: Soviet Front Organizations, U.S. State Department Report 581-AR, 21 March 1983. Some of their organizations were the World Peace Council, International Organization of Journalists, International Union of Students, World Federation of Democratic Youth, and the Women's International Democratic Federation.

6. Ibid.

7. The Times, Letter from Lt. Col. F. Cave, 2 November 1983.

8. The Times, Letter from Mr. D.S. Collier, 8 November 1983.

9. V.S. Naipaul, "An Island Betrayed," Harpers (March 1984): 63.

10. Charles Krauthammer, "Grenada and the End of Revolution," The New Republic, 30 January 1984.

11. Public Broadcasting (Radio) System, the Stanley Foundation's "Common Ground" panel discussion by foreign aid analysts (Wasserman, Newman, et. al.), 25 January 1985, KBIA, Columbia, MO.

12. Department of Defense, Document Exploitation Interim Report, Document 107385-103286, 7 December 1983.

13. Grenada: A Preliminary Report, p. 31.

14. Ibid, p. 32.

15. Ibid.

16. United States Military Posture for FY 1985, Report by the Organization of the Joint Chiefs of Staff, p. 95.

17. Remarks made by a visiting professor at the University of Missouri-Columbia, 14 March 1984.

18. Richard Harwood, "Tidy U.S. War Ends: We Blew Them Away," Washington Post, 6 November 1983, p. A1.

19. The Air Force Times, in its story on page 4, 4 February 1985, suggested that the lessons of the Iranian desert disaster have still not been learned (Tom Burgess, "Grenada Report Critical of Tactical Communications").

20. Charles Doe, "Grenada Rescuers Unaware of Students at 2nd

Site." Air Force Times, 12 March 1984.

21. Washington Post, 9 November 1983, p. A3.

22. Air Force Times, 23 April 1984, p. 49.

23. Ibid.

24. Washington Post, 9 November 1983, p. A34.

25. John Burgess, "Recruits Describe Disintegration of People's Revolutionary Army," Washington Post, 6 November 1983, p. A20; and Ibid., "U.S. Overwhelmed Uninspired Defense," pp. A1, A20.

26. Rick Maze, "Report Faults Military Performance in Grenada," Air Force Times, 23 April 1984, p. 49.

27. Ibid., quoting William Lind.

28. Benjamin F. Schemmer, "Grenada Highlights One of DoD's Major C^3 Problems But Increased Funding is Bringing Solutions," Armed Forces Journal (February 1984): 50-52.

29. Ibid, p. 52.

30. Ibid. (The same sort of comments were heard during the Vietnam War.)

31. Ibid.

32. General David C. Jones (USAF, Ret.), "Why the Joint Chiefs of Staff Must Change," in Understanding U.S. Strategy, Terry L. Heyns, ed. (Washington, D.C.: National Defense University Press, 1983). See also, Tom Burgess, "Study Asks Restructuring of Joint-Staff Programs," Air Force Times, 11 February 1985, p. 14.

33. V.S. Naipaul, p. 68.

34. Lead editorial, The Times (London), 26 October 1983.

35. The Times, 7 November 1983.

36. Ibid., lead editorial.

37. Ibid.

38. V.S. Naipaul, p. 67.

A Chronology of Events Concerning Grenada

Lawrence S. Germain

August 15, 1498
The island which we now call Grenada was "discovered" by Christopher Columbus on his third voyage to the new world.

April 1, 1609
A group of 203 British landed on Grenada intending to establish a settlement but failed due to the opposition of the Carib Indians and the environment.

June 1650
A group of about 200 Frenchmen from nearby Martinique led by M. du Parquet established a settlement.

1674
Grenada became a possession of the French Crown.

1700
A census showed a population of 257 whites, fifty-three free colored and 525 slaves.

1763
The British took possession of Grenada under the Peace of Paris. However, this only formalized the capture of the island by a British fleet the previous year. The island then had eighty-three sugar estates.

October 6, 1767
Henri Christophe, later King Henri I of Haiti was born in Grenada and lived the first ten years of his life there.

1778
The French regained possession of Grenada. A French force of 10,000 under the command of Comte d'Estaing overwhelmed the British garrison of 540.

1783
The British were granted Grenada by the Treaty of Versailles.

March 2, 1795

A revolt of freemen and slaves led by Julien Fedon, son of a slave mother and a French father, attacked Grenville on the eastern coast of the island and eventually gained control of most of the island except for St. George's. British reinforcements of 2,000 men under the command of General Ralph Abercromby finally defeated the rebels after the rebels had held most of the island for fifteen months and had killed Governor Ninian Home and fifty other British prisoners.

1807

The British banned the slave trade.

December 2, 1823

President James Monroe sent a message to Congress declaring that European powers had no right to extend their system to the new world.

1833

The British banned slavery by the Emancipation Act of 1833.

1843

Frank Gurney brought nutmeg from the island of Banda in the Dutch East Indies to Grenada. Today, Grenada grows one third of the world's supply of nutmeg.

1922

Eric Matthew Gairy was born.

1932

Theophilus Albert Marryshow, having founded the Association of Grenadian Workers, led a protest demonstration of 10,000 people against an official decision to increase import duties.

May 29, 1944

Maurice Rupert Bishop was born in Aruba in the Dutch Antilles where his father was working in the Standard Oil refinery.

July 1950

Eric Gairy, having returned from the island of Aruba where he had worked in the oil refineries, formed the Grenada Manual and Mental Worker's Union.

February 19, 1951

Gairy called a general strike.

February 22, 1951

Gairy and his lieutenant, Herbert Blaize, were arrested at a demonstration at the offices of the Legislative Council in St. George's and imprisoned on the island of Carriacou.

March 5, 1951

Gairy was freed.

March 15, 1951
Gairy was allowed to speak on the radio in an effort to convince the people to stop their protests.

October 1951
The Grenada People's Party, organized by Gairy, won seventy-one percent of the vote in the election defeating the opposition led by Marryshow and taking six of the eight seats on the Governor's Legislative Council.

September 1954
The Grenada People's Party, now reorganized as the Grenada United Labour Party (GULP) took seven of the eight seats in the Legislative Council even though its share of the vote fell to forty-six percent.

1955
Hurricane Janet brought extensive damage to Grenada.

September 1957
Gairy was opposed in the elections by the Grenada National Party organized by his former lieutenant, Herbert Blaize. GULP received fifty-two percent of the vote but won only two of the eight seats on the Legislative Council.

August 1961
Gairy was back in power as Chief Minister with a majority of eight of the ten seats in the Legislative Council.

1970
Maurice Bishop returned from London where he had studied law at Gray's Inn and worked for a while in the British civil service.

Grenada participated in the Miss World contest with Jennifer Hosten of Grenada emerging as Miss World of 1970-71. Gairy had been a member of the jury.

March 11, 1973
The New Jewel Movement (NJM) was formed by the merger of the Movement for Assemblies of the People founded by Maurice Bishop and Kenrick Radix, and JEWEL (Joint Endeavor for Welfare, Education, and Liberation) led by Unison Whiteman, Selwyn Strachan, Sebastian Thomas, and Teddy Victor.

April 5, 1973
The telephone, electricity, and water workers called a strike.

April 20, 1973
Jeremiah Richardson was shot and killed outside the De Luxe Cinema in Grenville by Gairy's police. In response, demonstrators closed down Pearls Airport for three days.

November 18, 1973

With a general strike pending, several opposition leaders met at the home of Grenville businessman H. M. Bhola. With the order "Get them dogs," Inspector Innocent Belmar had his forces raid the meeting. Maurice Bishop, Unison Whiteman, Selwyn Strachan, Hudson Austin, Simon Daniel, and Kenrick Radix were all severely beaten and jailed. This and other incidents were investigated by a commission of inquiry under a Jamaican lawyer, Sir Herbert Duffus. The commission said that Belmar should be removed from the police force. Gairy responded by promoting Belmar.

January 1, 1974

The dock workers called a strike which was to last three months.

January 21, 1974

Rupert Bishop, the father of Maurice Bishop, was shot at point blank range and killed at Otway House, the headquarters of the Seamen and Waterfront Workers Union.

February 7, 1974

Grenada became an independent nation with Eric Gairy as Prime Minister. The British Government was represented at the lowest possible level by Peter Blaker, a Parliamentary Under-Secretary at the Foreign and Commonwealth Office. The Queen was also represented at a low level by Governor Major Leo de Gale, one of the richer white citizens of the island. He had been appointed governor only a few days before, when Dame Hilda Bynoe resigned.

December 7, 1976

Maurice Bishop was elected to parliament in Grenada and became leader of the parliamentary opposition of six seats, three of them held by NJM members. Gairy's Grenada United Labor Party held nine seats.

July 19, 1977

A meeting of the General Assembly of the Organization of American States (OAS) was held in Grenada with Cyrus Vance, the U.S. Secretary of State, as the featured guest. The New Jewel Movement called a mass meeting to coincide with the meeting of the OAS. The NJM acquired a martyr in the form of seventeen year old Alister Strachan who dived into the sea as Gairy's police fired at him. His body was later washed ashore.

October 2, 1977

A Chilean Hercules transport plane landed at Pearls airport and unloaded material labled medical supplies. Bishop said the cargo was arms.

September 1978

Sir Paul Scoon was named Governor General of Grenada by Queen Elizabeth II following the resignation of Major Leo de Gale.

March 12, 1979

Gairy left Grenada for Barbados and met with American Ambassador Frank Ortiz on the first leg of a journey to the U.N. in New York.

March 13, 1979

Maurice Bishop seized control of the Government of Grenada. Only one soldier was killed in what has been called a bloodless coup. About fifty NJM supporters (only eighteen of them armed) seized the defense force barracks at True Blue at about 4 a.m. and burnt it to the ground. Gairy's men fled without firing a shot. Radio Grenada was quickly captured. Police at their headquarters at Fort George held out until 4 p.m. before surrendering. Maurice Bishop was named Prime Minister. By the end of the day, NJM had about fifty people in custody.

March 25, 1979

Maurice Bishop announced the suspension of the 1974 constitution.

April 14, 1979

Grenada established formal diplomatic relations with Cuba. Julian Torres Rizo was assigned as charge d'affaires for Cuba in Grenada.

April 1979

The following weapons were received from Cuba: 3,400 rifles with 3 million rounds of ammunition; 200 machine guns with 500,000 rounds of ammunition; 100 pistols with 66,000 rounds of ammunition; 100 shoulder-fired rocket launchers with 4,000 rockets; 12 82mm mortars with 4,800 mortar shells; and 12 12.7mm anti-aircraft guns with 237,000 rounds of ammunition.

October 10, 1979

Julian Torres Rizo was promoted to full ambassador.

October 13, 1979

The Government of Grenada closed the weekly newspaper, Torchlight.

November 19, 1979

Prime Minister Bishop announced that Fidel Castro had personally authorized Cuban aid to construct a new international airport in Grenada. Cuba was to provide services valued at $40 million supplemented by $2 million from Syria, $2 million from Iraq, $6 million from Libya, and $2 million from Algeria. A pilot team of thirty-six Cuban construction workers had arrived in Grenada by the end of November.

March 1980

The Soviet Union began overt relations with Grenada with a visit by Admiral of the Fleet of the Soviet Union Sergei Gorshkov.

The Cuban merchant ship <u>Playa Larga</u> arrived in Grenada with 136 construction workers and heavy construction equipment.

May 1980
Grenadian Deputy Prime Minister Bernard Coard paid his first official visit to Moscow. Coard signed a treaty with the Soviet Union which granted landing rights in Grenada to Soviet Tu-95 <u>Bear-D</u> long-range reconnaissance aircraft. Coard, the son of a prosperous St. George's merchant had graduated from Brandeis University and had worked at the Institute of Development Studies at the University of Sussex.

October 27, 1980
A secret military assistance agreement between the Soviet Union and Grenada was signed in Havana. It called for the delivery of 5 million rubles of arms and ammunition to Grenada without charge. Delivery was to be made via Cuba.

October 1980
Grenadian forces were sent to Nicaragua where some were reportedly killed in actions against the Miskito Indians.

November 1980
The number of Cubans involved in building the Point Salines airport had reached 300.

March 13, 1981
Maurice Bishop delivered a speech to a mass rally in St. George's. In his introduction he addressed "Your excellency Sir Paul Scoon, Governor General of Grenada," indicating that he still recognized Sir Paul in this role.

December 1981
In a speech to the Worker's Party of Jamaica, Selwyn Strachan, Grenadian Minister of National Mobilization, said that the Soviets and Cubans would have access to the new international airport.

March 11, 1982
A new radio transmitter was dedicated by Maurice Bishop. Radio Grenada had been renamed Radio Free Granada and the one kilowatt replaced by a seventy-five kilowatt transmitter using Soviet equipment and installed by Cuban and Soviet technicians. Radio Free Grenada was controlled by Phyllis Coard, Jamaican-born wife of Bernard Coard. Plump, bespectacled and a strong feminist, she was a member of the wealthy Evans family who are large shareholders in the company which produces the Tia Maria coffee liqueur.

July 27, 1982
Prime Minister Bishop was invited to Moscow. Bishop emerged from the meetings with the promise of considerable Soviet aid. In addition, the Soviet Union agreed to fund and construct a new port on Grenada's east coast. Soviet ships would be granted

recreational calls at the facility. In a secret part of the agreement, the Soviets promised to provide 10 million rubles in arms to Grenada without charge. This was to include fifty armored personnel carriers.

July 1982
    Bernard Coard resigned from the Central Committee, attributing his decision to slack and weak functioning of the Central Committee and the Political Bureau.

August 25, 1982
    It was reported that a Cuban ship docked at St. George's, the capital of Grenada, and unloaded six Soviet BTR-60 armored personnel carriers, seven 130mm artillery pieces, and other weaponry.

September 1982
    The Soviet Union established an embassy in Grenada with a staff of twenty-six headed by Gennadiy I. Sazhenev. They chose a location for the embassy at Morne Rouge, about five miles from St. George's, but very close to Radio Free Grenada.

October 1982
    Prime Minister Bishop made a state visit to Surinam at the invitation of Desi Bouterse, the ruler of Surinam.

December 15, 1982
    The minutes of the Grenadian Politburo of this date show that Barbara Lee, an aide to Rep. Ronald V. Dellums (D., Calif.) had arrived in Grenada. Dellums had recently been in charge of a congressional investigation into whether the Salines Airport was designed for military use. The investigation decided that it was not. Ms. Lee's mission was to ask Bishop whether any changes in the report were "deemed necessary."

December 1982
    Major Einstein Louison, Army Chief of Staff, left Grenada for a six-month training course in the Soviet Union.

March 10, 1983
    Einstein Louison met with N. V. Ogarkov, Chief of the General Staff of the Soviet Union.

March 1983
    Prime Minister Bishop flew to the Seventh Summit of the Non-Aligned Nations in New Delhi, India, in the company of Desi Bouterse and Fidel Castro.

April 14, 1983
    Maurice Bishop visited P'yongyang, North Korea where North Korea and Grenada announced a five-year development program for Grenada. North Korea was to build a 15,000-seat stadium, a party headquarters building, a fruit-processing factory, two fishing boats, and an irrigation system. In addition, in a secret

agreement, North Korea agreed to supply small arms, ammunition, and equipment to equip a force of more than 1,000 men. The equipment valued at about $12 million, was to include 1,000 assault rifles, eighty machine guns, fifty portable rocket launchers, two coast guard boats, 6,000 uniforms, and ammunition.

April 20, 1983
        A meeting of the Politburo was held. One of the agenda items was a discussion of methods to keep Sir Paul Scoon in line since he had been making statements contrary to government policy.

May 1983
        Bernard Coard visited the Soviet Union, ostensibly for health reasons. On his return he passed through London and addressed the West Indian Committee and the Institute of Education of London University. These lectures were well received.

June 4, 1983
        Maurice Bishop announced the establishment of a five-member commission headed by Allan Alexander, a lawyer from Trinidad, to draft a new constitution for Grenada.

June 7, 1983
        Maurice Bishop visited the United States where he met with National Security Advisor William P. Clark and Deputy Secretary Kenneth W. Dam.

July 13, 1983
        A plenary session of the Central Committee of the New Jewel Movement, which extended through July 19th, expressed dissatisfaction within the party.

July 21, 1983
        Acting Commissioner of Prisons Justin Roberts stated under oath that the Government of Grenada was then holding seventy-eight persons without charge at the Richmond Hill Prison.

        A construction agreement was signed by Cuba and Grenada calling for Cuban assistance in constructing thirty miles of road, fifty-seven bridges, an ice plant, and a national convention center.

August 26, 1983
        The Central Committee met again and raised misgivings concerning the beginning of a disintergration of the party.

August 31, 1983
        As of this date the Government of Grenada was as follows:

        Governor General   Sir Paul Scoon
        Prime Minister   Maurice Bishop
        Deputy Prime Minister   Bernard Coard
        Minister of Agriculture   George Louison

Minister of Communications, Works and Labor	General Hudson Austin
Minister of Defense and Interior	Maurice Bishop
Minister of External Relations	Unison Whiteman
Minister of Education, Youth and Culture	Jacqueline Creft
Minister of Health	Christopher De Riggs
Minister of Housing	Norris Bain
Minister of Industrial Development and Fisheries	Kenrick Radix
Minister of Land and Forestry	Unison Whiteman
Minister of Justice	Kenrick Radix
Minister of National Mobilization	Selwyn Strachan
Minister of Tourism	Lyden Ramdhanny
Minister of Women's Affairs	Jacqueline Creft
Attorney General	Richard Hart

Additionally, the members of the Central Committee of the New Jewel Movement were: Maurice Bishop, Chairman, General Hudson Austin, Selwyn Strachan, George Louison, Unison Whiteman, Phyllis Coard, Major Leon Cornwall, Lt. Col. Liam James, Lt. Col. Ewart Layne, Christopher de Riggs, Chalkie Ventour, Kamau McBarnette, Tan Bartholomew, Fitzroy Bain, and Ian St. Bernard.

September 14, 1983
       The Central Committee again met, the meeting lasting until Sept 16th. Bishop's leadership was attacked by Lt. Col. Ewart Layne, Chalkie Ventour, and Phyllis Coard, among others. A proposal, introduced by Liam James, was adopted which called for shared leadership. Maurice Bishop would remain as Prime Minister but his responsibilities would be limited to the public aspects of the party and government. Bernard Coard would become a member of the Central Committee and essentially the executive officer of the government. The proposal was passed by a vote of nine to one with three abstentions: Maurice Bishop, Unison Whiteman, and General Hudson Austin. George Louison voted nay. Austin abstained because he had just returned from a visit to North Korea and had missed much of the meeting. By a vote of nine against three abstentions it was agreed that the masses would not be informed of the new leadership arrangement.

September 17, 1983
       Bishop, Whiteman, Jimmy Emmanuel, Permanent Secretary at the Ministry of Foreign Affairs, and Don Rojas, Bishop's press secretary, went to Basseterre to attend the celebration of independence of St. Kitts-Nevis.

       The nine anti-Bishop members of the Central Committee met in Grenada. Coard agreed to return to the Central Committee and the Political Bureau if Bishop agreed. September 23rd was set as the date by which Bishop was to give his final decision about joint leadership.

September 23, 1983
    Bishop sent the Central Committee a message that he was sick, but that he would appear the next day.

September 25, 1983
    A meeting of the entire membership of NJM (only about seventy people) was called. Bishop failed to attend saying he had reservations about the issue of joint leadership. After a delegation demanded his attendance he agreed to attend. He finally agreed to the joint leadership proposal for the sake of party unity.

September 26, 1983
    Maurice Bishop departed for Czechoslovakia and Hungary. The Czechs agreed to supply electrical generating equipment.

October 9, 1983
    The Bishop party landed in Havana where they were given a high level reception. Bishop had also visited Moscow and East Berlin.

October 10, 1983
    Maurice Bishop returned to Grenada. He was accompanied by Unison Whiteman and George Louison, two of his strongest supporters. Only one member of the NJM, Selwyn Strachan, was at the airport to meet Bishop when he landed.

October 12, 1983
    At 1 a.m., Major Keith Roberts called together members of the security forces who were known not to be personally committed to Bishop and told them to take orders only from the Central Committee and to take no further orders from Bishop. At 7 a.m., all full members, candidate members, and applicants of the NJM in the Army (fifty-eight in all) passed a resolution claiming that Bishop and Louison were trying to reverse the earlier Central Committee decision and demanded that they be expelled from the party. Liam James led the attack on Bishop. At 9 a.m., the Central Committee met and charged George Louison with failing to support the Central Committee's position on joint leadership in discussions with Grenadians while in Budapest. Discussions lasted until 10:30 p.m., before they voted to strip Louison of his membership on the Politburo and the Central Committee. They also charged Bishop with spreading the rumor that Bernard and Phyllis Coard were plotting to kill him. The charges were denied, but Cletus St. Paul, Bishop's security chief, was arrested nonetheless. Major Einstein Louison, Army Chief of Staff, and brother of George Louison, as the highest officer not in the Coard faction, was suspended "for his opposition and petty bourgeois behavior in this issue" and placed under house arrest.

October 13, 1983
    The Central Committee placed Prime Minister Maurice Bishop under house arrest at his official residence on Mount Royal. Unison Whiteman, returning from the U.N. to Grenada, was contacted

by Tom Adams, Prime Minister of Barbados, as Whiteman was passing through the Grantly Adams Airport in Barbados. Adams warned Whiteman of the troubles in Grenada and offered him political asylum. Nonetheless, Whiteman proceeded to Grenada.

About 250 people attended a NJM party meeting at which the Central Committee explained its actions. The meeting was so anti-Bishop that Bishop supporters were afraid to speak up.

October 14, 1983
    Bernard Coard resigned as Deputy Prime Minister, reportedly to dispel rumors that he had been involved in a plot to kill Prime Minister Maurice Bishop. Meanwhile, Selwyn Strachan went to the offices of the Free West Indian newspaper to explain the Central Committee position. He was chased out of the building. Strachan, and Bernard and Phyllis Coard were not seen in public again until after the U.S. invasion.

    The Cuban Ambassador offered to meet with the Central Committee of the NJM. Coard refused the offer.

October 15, 1983
    Tom Adams, Prime Minister of Barbados, said that a Barbadian military official "reported to me that he had been tentatively approached by a U.S. official about the prospect of rescuing Maurice Bishop from his captors and had made an offer of transport."

    Kenrick Radix and Fitzroy Bain led street demonstrations demanding the release of Bishop and his reinstatement as Prime Minister. George Louison and Unison Whiteman talked for two and a half hours with Coard and Strachan, trying to find a resolution to the worsening situation.

    Fidel Castro sent a message to the Grenadian Central Committee expressing the principle of total non-involvement in the internal affairs of Grenada.

    Maurice Bishop's mother was allowed to visit her son.

October 16, 1983

    Victor Nazi Burke, an economist, was named to succeed Bernard Coard as Finance and Trade Minister, but not as Deputy Prime Minister.

    Louison, Whiteman, Coard, and Strachan met for five hours.

October 17, 1983
    A task force of U.S. naval ships sailed from Norfolk, Va., later stopping at Morehead City, N.C. to pick up marines from nearby Camp Lejeune.

An inter-agency group met in Washington D.C. to discuss the repercussions of the arrest of Bishop.

Louison, Whiteman, Coard, and Strachan met for another five hours.

October 18, 1983
Radix led a second street demonstration. He was jailed by Coard backers. Whiteman announced that he, Louison, Norris Bain, Lyden Ramdhanny, and Jacqueline Creft had all resigned from the government. George Louison was jailed. A crowd of two to three thousand people demonstrated in the streets of Grenville.

October 19, 1983
A crowd gathered at Mount Royal demanding Bishop's release. Major Leon Cornwall attempted to silence the crowd by shouting "Maurice Bishop has betrayed the masses." He was booed until he withdrew. Then a machine gun opened fire over the heads of the crowd causing panic. A nineteen year-old student, Thompson Cadore, led a group to the rear of Mount Royal and succceeded in forcing their way into the room where Bishop was being held. They found Maurice Bishop and Jacqueline Creft bound to two beds. Bishop appeared to have been without food or water for over a day. This may have been self-imposed, since he told his mother that he feared poison. Bishop proceeded to Fort Rupert (named in honor of Bishop's father) via the marketplace. He took over the fort's central office. Troops converged on the fort, employing three armored personnel carriers commanded by Lieutenant Iman Abdullah, Lieutenant Raeburn Nelson, and Officer Cadet Conrad Meyers. Meyers was in charge of the operation because of his three years of service in the U.S. Army, some of it in the West Berlin garrison. They fired into the crowd, causing about fifty casualties. Bishop was captured, taken into the courtyard of the fort, and executed. Also executed were Unison Whiteman, Jacqueline Creft, Norris Bain, Fitzroy Bain, Keith Hailing, Evelyn Bullen, and Evelyn Maitland. Labor leader Vincent Noel had been killed in the first shooting.

All residents of the island were placed under a 24-hour shoot on sight curfew. The Cubans halted work on the Point Salines airport during the curfew. Diplomats from the U.S. Embassy in Barbados attempted to travel to Grenada but were turned back because the Pearls Airport was closed. A Leeward Islands Air Transport (LIAT) commercial flight was turned back and all subsequent flights were cancelled.

October 20, 1983
Radio Free Grenada said that a sixteen-member military council headed by General Hudson Austin had taken power in Grenada. The other members of the council were Lieutenant Colonels Leon James and Ewart Layne, Majors Leon Cornwall, Tan Bartholomew, Chris Stroude, Keith Roberts, and Basil Gahagan, Captains Lester Redhead and Huey Romain, First Lieutenants Ashley

Foulkes, Rudolph Ogilvey, and Iman Abdullah and Second Lieutenants Kenrick Fraser and Raeburn Nelson.

John Compton, Prime Minister of St. Lucia, telephoned Tom Adams, Prime Minister of Barbados, and proposed that there be a multinational move to intervene in Grenada to restore law and order and to lead the country to an early election.

A statement by Cuba said that "the death of Bishop and his comrades ought to be clarified, and if they were executed in cold blood, those responsible deserve exemplary punishment."

October 21, 1983
The ten ship U.S. Navy task force which had left Norfolk, Va. for Lebanon on October 17th, was diverted toward Grenada. The task force included the aircraft carrier USS Independence (CV-62) and 1,900 Marines, some of whom were to relieve American members of the multinational force in Lebanon.

Tom Adams, Prime Minister of Barbados, met with G. L. Bullard, British High Commissioner, and told him that the British would be invited to participate in an intervention in Grenada. He "told the same thing" to the American Ambassador, Milan D. Bish. He also met with Noble Power, High Commissioner for Canada, but issued no invitation to join.

Meeting in Bridgetown, Barbados, the members of the Organization of Eastern Caribbean States (OECS), Dominica, St. Lucia, Montserrat, St. Christopher-Nevis, Antigua and Barbuda, St. Vincent and the Grenadines, and Grenada, called for intervention in Grenada by unanimous vote (Grenada was not represented). They asked for assistance from Barbados, Jamaica, and the United States.

The 24-hour curfew in Grenada was lifted for four hours to permit Grenadians to buy food.

October 22, 1983
U.S. envoys Linda Flohr and Ken Kurze, along with David Montgomery, the British Deputy High Commissioner, left Barbados for Grenada presumably to check on the safety of U.S. and British citizens on the island. There were over 1,000 U.S. citizens in Grenada, about 600 of them students and employees of St. George's University School of Medicine which has offices in Bay Shore, Long Island. At least 200 of these students were from New York State and seventy-five were from Long Island.

Radio Free Grenada announced that the Pearls Airport would reopen on October 24th, and that the curfew would be reduced.

Cuban Ambassador Torres Rizo told General Austin that Fidel Castro had said that sending Cuban reinforcements to Grenada was impossible and unthinkable.

A special meeting of Heads of Government of the Caribbean Community was held in Port of Spain, Trinidad and discussed the possibility of punitive actions against the rulers of Grenada. They voted eleven to one, with Guyana dissenting, to impose sanctions against Grenada. None of the nations outside the OECS (Guyana, Trinidad and Tobago, Belize, and Bahamas) approved the use of force.

October 23, 1983
The United States received a formal request from five members of the Organization of Eastern Caribbean States to assist in a joint effort to restore order and democracy on the island of Grenada.

A U.S. diplomat met with Major Leon Cornwall, who denied that there was any need for an evacuation and demanded that anyone leaving use commercial carriers. However, commercial carriers were not flying to Grenada. Another charter plane brought in two additional diplomats, including the Consul General from Barbados, who continued conversations with Cornwall. They concluded that he was stalling for time and seeking to impede an orderly evacuation.

Radio Free Grenada broadcast a heavily edited tape by Einstein Louison, in which he apparently took the blame for organizing and arming the people.

Joint Task Force 120 was activated with Vice Admiral Joseph Metcalf III, Commander Second Fleet, in command.

October 24, 1983
Although four small chartered planes carrying about thirty people departed, the military government in Grenada kept the airport closed to commercial traffic. This was in spite of the fact that General Hudson Austin had told Dr. Geoffrey Bourne, Chancellor of the medical school, on October 22nd, that the airport would be opened on October 24th. A chartered plane, which was sent to pick up Canadian citizens, was unable to land.

Colonel Pedro Tortolo Comas Carlos Diaz Larranaga, Cuban expert on Grenadian affairs, arrived in Grenada from Cuba aboard a Soviet-built An-26 transport aircraft. Tortolo had commanded the Cuban military mission in Grenada from 1981 until May 1983. His mission was to advise the Cubans as to what to do in case of an attack and to inform the Grenadians that the Cubans would not attack U.S. troops, but would defend themselves and the perimeter of their work area.

Navy SEALS went ashore on the northern beaches of Grenada. They reported that beach conditions were marginal for amphibious assault vehicles and unsuited for landing craft.

A small group of top Congressional leaders were briefed about the impending "invasion" of Grenada.

Prime Minister Margaret Thatcher intervened by telephone with President Reagan in an effort to stop the invasion.

October 25, 1983
   Three AC-130H Spectre Lockheed gunships flew non-stop from Hurlburt Field in Florida, arriving in Grenada before dawn. Using low-light-level television cameras and infrared sensors they discovered vehicles and construction equipment parked on the runway of the Point Salines airfield. At dawn, Pearls Airport on the northeast coast of Grenada was seized by 400 Marines who went in by helicopter. The first landing south of the airfield drew antiaircraft fire which was later suppressed by AH-1T Cobra gunships. The Marines then moved on the town of Grenville. A half hour later, about 350 Rangers attacked the 10,000 foot runway of the international airport at Point Salines. The Rangers then pushed toward the capital of St. George's and toward the True Blue campus of the medical school. By midday the True Blue campus was secure and about 500 prisoners had been taken. As soon as the American forces achieved their initial goals, 300 troops from six Caribbean nations were moved in.

A special Navy commando (SEAL) team approaching Richmond Hill prison came under fire from a building flying the flag of the People's Revolutionary Army. An air strike by a single. A-7 attack aircraft was called. The pilot reported receiving fire. It later developed that the building was a hospital and that twenty-one civilians had been killed. SEAL teams in St. George's were pinned down and awaited relief. A SEAL team guarding Governor General Sir Paul Scoon was surrounded. Two gunships were called in and provided relief from three armored personnel carriers which were approaching the Governor General's house. Cobra gunships subsequently engaged antiaircraft sites but were shot down.

Shortly before dark, 250 more Marines came ashore with M-60 tanks and armored amphibious vehicles, and units of the 82nd Airborne Division began to land.

The strength of the Grenadian Army was about 600, supplemented by a militia estimated to be over 2,500.

Congressional reaction was plentiful and vocal. Congressional statements included:

Rep. Phil Gramm (R., Texas): "We must end the open season on Americans which has been declared by every terrorist and criminal element in the world."

Senator Steve Symms (R., Idaho): "This could be Ronald Reagan's "Falkland Islands" victory. It is the first time in 20 years that we have tried to enforce the long neglected Monroe Doctrine."

Speaker Thomas P. O'Neill Jr. (D., Mass.): "Now, when our Marines are in action, is not the time to be critical."

Senator Daniel Patrick Moynihan (D., N.Y.): "I don't know that you restore democracy at the point of a bayonet."

Rep. Bill Alexander (D., Ark.): "Step by step, war by war, the president's foreign policy is leading our nation into a face-off with the Soviet Union."

Rep. Olympia J. Snowe (R., Maine): "I am dismayed we are involved in Grenada, especially on the heels of Beirut. The two events raise a lot of concerns about exactly what we are doing. To what extent are we involved in so many situations that we could get into a war?"

Rep. Paul Simon (D., Ill.): "The military solution seems to be an automatic reflex with this administration and that is a deeply disturbing characteristic of the White House's foreign policy formulation."

Rep. Ronald V. Dellums (D., Calif.): "Cowboy mentality."

Charles R. Modica, Chancellor and founder of St. George's University School of Medicine criticized the U.S. action as "very unnecessary" and said that the President had "acted on the wrong advice" and "should be held accountable."

Nicaragua and Cuba requested an urgent meeting of the U.N. Security Council to discuss the invasion of Grenada.

The chief Cuban representative to the U.N., Dr. Raul Roa-Kouri, met with the Soviet chief delegate, Oleg A. Troyanovsky. Dr. Roa-Kouri condemned the invasion and said that the Cubans in Grenada were "heroically resisting the invasion."

The Soviet press branded the invasion of Grenada "an act of undisguised banditry and international terrorism." "Peace-loving mankind demands that the interventionist troops of the United States and its puppets be pulled out of Grenada."

The U.S. embassy in Moscow assured the Soviet Foreign Ministry that steps were being taken to insure the safety of Soviet personnel in Grenada. Soviet press dispatches made no mention of Soviet advisors on the island. No Soviet protest was lodged with the U.S. embassy. Richard Jacobs, Grenadian Ambassador to Moscow said, "It will be another Bay of Pigs. The Americans will be pulverized."

The Senate of Mexico voted to condemn the invasion and called for the withdrawal of all foreign troops from the island. Ambassador Fernando Salazar of Bolivia said, "Today it is Grenada, tomorrow it will be another country. This looks very much like what happened in the Dominican Republic."

Lt. Col. Desi Bouterse, the military leader of Suriname, ordered Cuban Ambassador Osvaldo Cardenas to leave Suriname within six days and suspended all agreements with Cuba. He asked Cuba to lower the diplomatic status of its embassy to a charge d'affaires. He stated "the leadership of the Suriname revolution is convinced that a repetition of developments in Grenada should be prevented here."

October 26, 1983
    About 800 members of the 82nd Airborne Division were flown into Grenada. Resistance continued at Fort Fredrick, Grenada's military headquarters above St. George's, and at the Richmond Hill Prison, overlooking the waterfront. Secretary of Defense Caspar Weinberger reported U.S. losses as six killed, eight missing, thirty-three wounded, and three helicopters shot down. U.S. strength ashore was reported to be about 3,000.

    Marine forces relieved the SEALS and rescued thirty-three persons, including Sir Paul Scoon from the Governor General's residence. Paratroopers from the 82nd Airborne met considerable resistance in approaching the Grand Anse campus of the medical school. Rangers, using marine helicopters, landed in the middle of the campus and evacuated 224 students. In the action, one Marine Ch-46 helicopter was shot down. General John W. Vessey Jr., Chairman of the Joint Chiefs of Staff, reported that, "We got a lot more resistance than we expected" in Grenada.

    A vast quantity of Soviet-made weapons were reported seized at Frequente near Point Salines Airport. There were six warehouses at the site: one for arms, one for ammunition, and four for quartermaster items, spare parts, and vehicles.

    Dr. Francis Alexis, President of the Grenada Democratic Movement and Professor of Law at the University of the West Indies in Barbados, asserted, "This is not an invasion of Grenada. We call it a freedom mission, a liberation from criminal dictatorship that is welcomed by the vast majority of the people of the Caribbean."

    Sixty-nine American students who had been attending St. George's University School of Medicine arrived in Charleston, South Carolina aboard an Air Force C-141 transport plane. Some knelt and kissed the ground. Charles L. Modica, Chancellor and founder of the school, reversed his statements of the day before by saying that President Reagan was justified in ordering the invasion.

    Democratic presidential candidates commented on Grenada:

    Senator Alan Cranston (D., Calif.): "We have a trigger-happy president, Ronald Reagan who has recklessly landed the U.S. into two civil wars."

    Former Vice President Walter F. Mondale: "I hope every conceivable step is being taken to protect our people there."

Senator John Glenn (D., Ohio): "If our mission there is to protect American lives, then we should evacuate those who want to leave quickly and remove our forces. If there is a larger strategic mission, then the President should inform the Congress and the American People."

Congressional comments continued:

Senator Thomas F. Eagleton (D., Mo.): "The notion that American nationals were endangered is flimsy, illusory and hypothetical."

Rep. Jim Leach (R., Iowa): " It may be easy for foreign troops to land in Grenada but it could prove very difficult for them to leave."

Organized demonstrations against the U.S. action in Grenada were started.

The Rev. Herbert Daughtry, leader of the Black United Front, speaking to a rally of about 2,500 people near the U.N. building in New York said, "This is a sad day for me because we have learned that Cubans have died in Grenada." He called for the immediate withdrawal of U.S. troops.

At a news conference held in New York by the Committee in Solidarity with Free Grenada, David Hood, the only Grenadian who spoke at the conference, said, "My people are being butchered."

Speaking to 400 people at the Federal Building in San Francisco, Gus Newport, the mayor of Berkeley, California, called the Grenadian action "pure propaganda to get Lebanon off the front page."

At Wells College in Aurora, New York, Bernardine Dohrn, a former leader in the radical Weather Underground, told the audience, "We have a problem figuring out who is the enemy in all these countries. Who are we supposed to oppose? What possible justification can there be?"

The news media were upset by the restrictions placed on them in covering the action in Grenada. Seymour Topping, Managing Editor of the New York Times, said, "We have strenuously protested to the White House and the Defense Department about the lack of access to the story in Grenada by our correspondents who are waiting in Barbados. We are also disturbed by the paucity of details about the operation released by the Pentagon at a time when American people require all the facts to make judgments about the actions of our Government."

Foreign reactions also contiued:

Italian Defense Minister Giovanni Spadolini said, "We are

against military intervention as the solution of international controversies."

The Chinese Government issued a statement "China is deeply concerned about the situation in Grenada and is keeping a close watch on developments there. The Chinese Government has always maintained that the affairs of a country should be settled by its own people free from interference."

The Russian news agency Tass rejected the American justification for the intervention by stating, "What can be more cynical and hyprocritical than such statements when under the pretext of concern for human rights an attempt is being made to drown in blood the right of a whole people to free and sovereign existence....What is happening in reality is outright armed aggression against a peaceloving people of a small country that is not threatening anyone with anything."

The Cuban Government released the text of a note which they received from Kenneth N. Skoug Jr., the Director of the Office of Cuban Affairs in the State Department. The note said in part, "As we have told the Cubans from the beginning, we have taken fully into account a desire for the safety of Cuban personnel on the island. There would be no problem in the first place·between us if the Cubans in Grenada had not fired first against out forces." The note expressed a willingnesss to talk to the leader of the Cuban forces in Grenada "but we don't know who he is. If he will identify himself to us, we are prepared to arrange for an immediate cessation of hostilities followed by the repatriation of Cubans, even armed ones, in Grenada."

A resolution condemning the American invasion of Grenada sponsored by Nicaragua and Guyana was circulated to members of the U.N. Security Council.

Prime Minister Eugenia Charles of Dominica told the U.N. Security Council that the British appointed Governor General of Grenada, Sir Paul Scoon, had asked for aid after the assassination of Prime Minister Maurice Bishop. She said she could not disclose through what channels Sir Paul had made the request.

The Marine Corps reported that for every potential recruit who wanted to back out for fear of going to war, three new recruits stepped forward to volunteer.

October 27, 1983
      U.S. troops overran Richmond Hill Prison where Cubans and Grenadian soldiers had been holding out. The Grenadian Army Headquarters at Fort Frederick had already been captured. Fighting was reported continuing at Calivigny Point, about two miles east of Point Salines Airport. Paratroopers had surrounded the Calivigny barracks, which was bombarded by navy guns, fighter-bomber aircraft, and gunships. The barracks were finally captured by a Ranger helicopter assault.

Barbados, St. Vincent, and St. Kitts-Nevis sent sixty-eight additional policemen to join their 300-man force on Grenada.

Commenting on documents found at a Cuban military installation in the village of Frequente, an administration official said, "It is clear from these documents and other information we now have that serious consideration was being given to seizing Americans as hostages and holding them for reasons that are not entirely clear, but seem to involve an effort to embarrass the United States and, more immediately, to forestall American military action in Grenada."

By midday, 377 people, most of them students, had been evacuated to South Carolina. Many students were relieved to be off the island. The comments from the students included:

Janet Bause of Detroit: "Lots of our Grenadian friends said before the invasion they hoped the Americans would come in....when the Americans landed some Grenadian soldiers took off their uniforms and hid."

Randall Tressler of Jarrettsville, Md.: "I spoke with a lot of Grenadians and asked if they had faith in the Government. They said they were afraid of it." As for the American intervention, he said, "I don't see how they would have gotten us out otherwise."

However, Gary Solin of Chicago, bursar of the medical school disagreed. "Our safety was never in danger." He had met with General Hudson Austin on October 24th and said that the General had guaranteed the safety of the students.

Cuba announced that it had accepted the offer of Belisario Betancur, President of Colombia, and Filipe Gonzalez, Prime Minister of Spain, to mediate the return of Cubans taken into custody in Grenada.

President Reagan gave a thirty-minute televised address to the nation on Lebanon and Grenada.

The House Foreign Affairs Committee adopted legislation declaring that the War Powers Resolution pertained to events in Grenada. This would require the President to withdraw troops from Grenada within sixty days unless Congress authorized their continued presence. Deputy Secretary of State Kenneth W. Dam commented that it was highly unlikely that troops would remain in Grenada for sixty days and the Administration felt it was not necessary to apply the War Powers Resolution.

Public comment continued:

Senator Gary Hart (D., Colo.): "Frankly, I don't trust them. We are dealing with an Administration that is not inclined to obey the law. They can always find an excuse to stay in Grenada and they clearly do not want to be bound by the sixty day limit."

Rep. Peter H. Kostmayer (D., Penn.): "The Administration has not demonstrated their action was necessary, and they have not demonstrated, morally or ethically, that it was right....I haven't seen a single shred of evidence that American lives were in danger in Grenada.

Rep. Howard Wolpe (D., Mich.): "We play directly into the hands of those who want to portray the United States as an imperial power. In the end that compromises our political position."

Senator Charles H. Percy (R., Ill.): "I am concerned about the impact of such an operation on world opinion and the legal justification for our intervention."

On the other hand Rep. William S. Broomfield (R., Mich.): was "very elated" and said the action could prove to be "one of America's finest hours."

Rep. Dante B. Fascell (D., Fla.): "I have concluded that it was absolutely essential for the President to take the action he took."

Senator Lawton Chiles (D., Fla.): offered an amendment to the debt ceiling bill that would urge the President to bar the return of Cuban prisoners seized in Grenada until Cuba agreed to take back undesirable refugees sent to the United States during the 1980 boat lift.

Senator Daniel Patrick Moynihan (D., N.Y.) issued an invitation to William J. Casey, Director of the Central Intelligence Agency, to meet with senators because the role of the CIA in Grenada "has been widely reported and discussed on the Senate floor."

Former Vice President Walter F. Mondale: "They may have an argument, but if they do, we haven't heard it."

The Rev. Jesse Jackson: "Americans should feel a sense of outrage and disgrace over the invasion of Grenada."

Former Secretary of State Henry A. Kissinger: "I think this was a strong, wise, and important decision made by the United States Government."

Michael N. Manley, former Prime Minister of Jamaica and leader of the opposition People's National Party, said that Grenadian Deputy Prime Minister Bernard Coard had won then lost the support of the army in moving against Prime Minister Maurice Bishop.

Fourteen demonstrators were arrested at the United States Mission to the United Nations. Calling themselves the Emergency Committee Against the Invasion of Grenada, they chanted "U.S.A. out of Grenada" and "U.S.A. out of Nicaragua." One of those arrested was Marilyn P. Vasta, a member of the Committee in Solidarity with the People of El Salvador. She said, "We see this as a real danger, especially given the U.S. involvement in Central America."

Fifteen reporters, none of them from daily newspapers, were flown from Barbados to Grenada on a C-130 transport plane. They returned to Barbados the same day. They were representatives of ABC, CBS, NBC, United Press International, Reuters, Associated Press, and U.S. News and World Report. There were at least 300 reporters in Barbados trying to cover the situation in Grenada. Walter Cronkite, former CBS News anchorman commented on this situation: "This nation is founded on the belief that people have the right to know and that we participate in our Government's actions. These are our Marines, our Rangers down there. This is our foreign policy and we have the right to know precisely what is happening, and there can be no excuse in denying the people that right."

Prime Minister Margaret Thatcher told the House of Commons that Britain would look sympathetically on any request to join other Commonwealth nations in a peacekeeping force in Grenada. She also said that no request for intervention from Sir Paul Scoon had passed through British channels.

West German Foreign Minister Hans-Dietrich Genscher said that West Germany had told the United States that it hoped "the hostilities are halted without delay and all foreign forces withdrawn from Grenada." The remarks were made at a session of parliament called by the Green Party. Mr. Genscher added, "We would have advised against the intervention."

A new resolution sponsored by Guyana, Nicaragua, and Zimbabwe was offered to the Security Council of the U.N. It used softer language than the provisions resolution sponsored only by Guyana and Nicaragua. It "deeply deplores the armed intervention in Grenada" rather than "strongly condemns." It also "called for an immediate cessation of the armed intervention and the immediate withdrawal of all foreign troops from Grenada." Charles M. Lichenstein, the deputy permanent representative of the U.S. delegation, challenged the right of Ian Jacobs to represent Grenada. He cited a letter from Sir Paul Scoon saying "In our present situation, no person or group is authorized to speak before the United Nations without the expressed permission of the Governor General or until a new Ambassador is appointed for Grenada. I have given no such authorization to any group at this time." The Security Council President, Abdullah Salah of Jordan, ruled that Mr. Jacobs would not take his seat pending a final decision on the question by the Secretary General. Caldwell Taylor, Grenada's representative at the U.N., emerged from five days of hiding, saying his life was in danger. "The only way the butchers, those who murdered Maurice Bishop, the Pol Pots, can escape the judgment of history is if George Louison is killed, Kendrik Radix is killed, and if I am killed." "When a man's country is invaded, the only man who can applaud the invasion is a Quisling and I am not a Quisling." He said that he would not participate in any interim government that would "destroy the mandate given to us by Maurice Bishop. Just as I am opposed to the invasion of my country I am opposed to those who slaughtered Maurice Bishop." Mr. Taylor engaged in heated discussions with his deputy, Ian Jacobs and they were joined by three members of the Cuban delegation. When the Security Council convened, it was Mr. Jacobs and not Mr. Taylor who occupied the seat for Grenada.

October 28, 1983
        Some Cuban and Grenadian troops had taken positions in the central and northern mountains of Grenada, leading to fears on the part of some U.S. military leaders that they might attempt to conduct an extended guerrilla campaign.

        Admiral Wesley L. McDonald, U.S. Atlantic forces commander, said that there were about 6,000 U.S. troops on the island. He also said that captured documents revealed that the Cubans planned to place a force of 341 officers and 4,000 reservists in Grenada. U.S. casualties were given as eleven dead, seven missing, and sixty-seven wounded. No casualties were suffered by the forces contributed by Caribbean nations. The U.S. naval task force consisted of the USS Independence (CV-62), USS Richmond K. Turner (CG-20), USS Coontz (DDG-40), USS Caron (DD-970), USS Moosebrugger (DD-980), and USS Clifton Sprague (FFG-16). Amphibious lift ships included the USS Guam (LPH-9), USS Trenton (LPD-14), USS Fort Snelling (LSD-30), USS Manitowoc (LST-1180), and USS Barnstable County (LST-1197).

        Col. Ken Barnes, Commander of Jamaican forces on Grenada, explained their role and said, "We are not trained to fight battles. Our duties for the most part will center on internal security, mostly police activity, searches, patrols, and interrogations." Caribbean troops were said to be guarding 638 Cubans and seventeen Grenadians.

        Three Air Force planes carrying 211 evacuees from Grenada landed at Charleston, S.C., bringing the total number evacuated to 645. Four East Germans were flown from Grenada to Charleston where they booked commercial flights to East Berlin. They said that they were tourists and wanted to leave the island.

        By a vote of sixty-four to twenty, the Senate adopted an amendment to the bill raising the debt ceiling declaring that the War Powers Act applied to the fighting in Grenada. Senator Charles F. Percy (R., Ill.) commented, "The implication of this resolution is that we take the War Powers Act seriously. It is the law of the land and we ought to abide by it."

Other comments included:

Rep. Dick Cheney (R., Wyo.): "A lot of folks around the world feel we are more steady and reliable than before."

Senator Howard H. Baker Jr. (R., Tenn.) "I applaud the President for what he did. It is manifestly in the best interest of the country."

Thomas P. O'Neill, Speaker of the House: "To be honestly truthful, his policy scares me. We cannot go the way of gunboat diplomacy. His policy is wrong. It is frightening."

The Senate adopted as a non-binding resolution the language proposed by Senator Lawton Chiles to the effect that no Cuban prisoners should be repatriated until Cuba agreed to take back the undesirables who had been sent to the United States via the Mariel boatlift.

Les Janka, a Deputy White House Press Secretary for Foreign Affairs, resigned, citing damage to his credibility as a result of the Administration's handling of the invasion.

The U.N. Security Council approved a resolution "deeply deploring" the "flagrant violation of international law" by the Grenada invasion. The vote was eleven to one, the one being the U.S. veto. Britain, Togo, and Zaire abstained. France, the Netherlands, and Pakistan, nominal allies of the United States, voted for the resolution.

Porfirio Munoz Ledo, Mexico's chief delegate commented, "What we have here is a clear violation of the rules of international law."

Sir Paul Scoon called Javier Perez de Cueller, Secretary General of the U.N., to reaffirm that he had closed all of Grenada's foreign missions and that "no one was authorized to speak for Grenada at the U.N...."

The Soviet Union accused U.S. planes of firing on the Soviet embassy and wounding a member of the staff. The charge was denied by the U.S. State Department. The population of the Soviet embassy was apparently considerable. There were forty-nine Soviet citizens including some dependents. In addition, twenty-four North Koreans had taken refuge in the embassy as well as some Bulgarians and East Germans.

Concerning the number of Cubans on Grenada, Cuban Deputy Foreign Minister Ricardo Alarcon said, "The total number of Cubans is less than 800. Taking into account every person born in Cuba including diplomatic personnel and children, it is about 790."

October 29, 1983
　　Deputy Secretary of State Charles A. Gillespie was named charge d'affaires for the U.S. Embassy in Grenada.　He was reported to be in St. George's.

　　Most of the 1,200 Marines were to be replaced and would proceed to Lebanon.　Most of the 700 Army Rangers had been relieved.

　　Bernard and Phyllis Coard, Selwyn Strachan, and Liam James were captured by U.S. Marines.

　　Sir Paul Scoon said in a radio broadcast that he planned to appoint a "representative body of Grenadians to assist as an interim measure in administering the country."

　　A Cuban ship, the Vietnam Heroico, that had been asked to leave St. George's harbor when the invasion began, was still anchored twelve miles offshore.　The ship, 430 feet long with a capacity of 13,000 cubic feet of cargo and 218 passengers, had made a number of trips to Angola during the early Cuban involvement there.

　　Alister Hughes, a Grenadian journalist and a reporter for the Caribbean News Agency and The Associated Press who had been arrested on October 19th but later freed by fellow prisoners at the Richmond Hill jail, said, "I don't regard it as an invasion, but a rescue operation.　I haven't met any Grenadian who has expressed any other view."

　　Senator Robert C. Byrd (D., W.Va.) suggested a fact finding mission to Grenada by legislators.　Senator Howard H. Baker (R., Tenn.) described it as a good idea.　Senator Donald W. Riegle (D., Mich.) offered an amendment to the debt ceiling bill declaring "restrictions upon the press in Grenada shall cease."　It passed fifty-three to eighteen.　Further congressional comment included:

　　Senator Rudy Boschwitz (R., Minn):　"An important extension of our national will."

　　Senator Lawton Chiles (D., Fla.):　"At some stage there has to be some feeling that the United States is not totally impotent."

　　Senator Paul S. Sarbanes (D., Md.):　"I think the most disturbing thing is the unprecedented treatment of a free press. The implications of that, if it becomes a pattern, are enormous."

　　Senator Paul E. Tsongas (R., Mass.):　"A lot of people believe the reason they went in was political."

　　Senator Daniel Patrick Moynihan (D., N.Y.):　"We simply do not know enough yet to draw any firm conclusions about Cuba's role or intentions. Nothing has been discovered so far that would show with any certainty that Cuba was planning to take over Grenada."

Senator Alfonse M. D'Amato (R., N.Y.): "America has a responsibility not to allow people to shoot their way to power, not in this area which is so important strategically. The worst of this thing was the rush to politicize it and to go after the President before they knew the facts."

Grenada's Ambassador to the Soviet Union, Richard Jacobs, met with Georgi M. Korniyenko, a First Deputy Foreign Minister.

The Cuban Government announced that there were 784 Cubans on Grenada. Of these, only forty-three were members of the armed forces, twenty-two army officers, and the remaining twenty-one were translators. Since the United States had taken 638 prisoners and there were eighty-five Cuban citizens in the Cuban Embassy, there were only sixty-one left.

The ABC news program "Nightline" sponsored a telephone call-in survey. They registered 279,323 calls favoring the invasion of Grenada and 33,483 calls against it.

Newsweek Magazine was barred from further participation in the Grenada press pool trips after a photographer working for the magazine failed to return with the group. The photographer, J. Ross Baughman, was believed to still be on Grenada.

October 30, 1983
The Department of Defense reported casualty figures for the U.S. forces in Grenada as sixteen killed, seventy-seven wounded, and three missing.

Marine forces swept the northern end of the island with support from Cobra gunships, Navy close air support, and naval gunfire. Army elements continued to sweep the southern end of the island.

General Hudson Austin was captured at Weatherhaven Point by units of the 82nd Airborne Division after his location was revealed by Grenadians. He was found inside a house with two members of the Grenadian People's Revolutionary Army and with two white men of unknown identity. They were all flown to the USS Guam.

Vice Admiral Joseph Metcalf, III, USN, assumed responsibility for the restrictions placed on the press. The restrictions were eased with more reporters allowed to go to Grenada and to stay overnight. A total of 168 reporters and photographers were flown to Grenada from Barbados and told they were free to stay as long as they wished. The numbers permitted on previous days had been: October 27th, fifteen, October 28th, twenty-four, and October 29th, fifty.

The Cuban Government said it had been told by John A. Ferch, Chief of the United States Interests Section in Havana, that fifty-nine wounded Cubans were receiving medical treatment from American armed forces personnel. Castro indicated that he wanted to use the Cuban ship Vietnam Heroico to return the Cuban prisoners.

The oil field workers union in Trinidad called for the immediate withdrawal of American combat forces.

October 31, 1983
    Caches of weapons were found by U.S. forces including enough rifles to outfit two brigades (about 8,000 men). Some were old weapons but about eighty-five percent were modern combat rifles. Many weapons were in boxes labled "granola" and "rice." Six trucks full of ammunition were found in the hills after residents told U.S. troops about the site.

The peak number of U.S. military personnel on Grenada was reached this day at 7,335.

The American Society of Newspaper Editors protested to the Department of Defense over its refusal to permit reporters to cover the first stages of the invasion of Grenada. The protest was in the form of a telegram to Secretary of Defense Caspar W. Weinberger.

Rep. Thomas S. Foley (D., Wash.) was named to lead a group of representatives to tour Grenada in connection with the War Powers Resolution. Some Republicans saw this as indirect criticism of President Reagan's actions. Rep. Gerald B. H. Solomon (R., N.Y.) defended the President: "God bless the President of the United States for doing what he did."

Canada and Trinidad/Tobago agreed to take part in a plan for a Commonwealth security force for Grenada. Foreign Minister William G. Hayden of Australia, said that Australia did not contemplate participating in any peacekeeping force. He added that his government would have advised against the United States invasion of Grenada had it been consulted. Prime Minister Robert Muldoon of New Zealand said that his government wanted foreign troops withdrawn from Grenada and that it was prepared to take part in a peacekeeping force of Commonwealth nations.

U.S. representative Jose S. Sorzano challenged the right of Caldwell Taylor to sit as the representative of Grenada in the United Nations. The President of the General Assembly, Jorge Enrique Illueca of Panama ruled that the Grenadian representative could keep his seat until the General Assembly credentials committee ruled on the challenge.

West German spokesman Peter Boenisch hinted that the Bonn Government was having second thoughts about its original criticism of the Grenada invasion.

November 1, 1983

Edward Seaga, Prime Minister of Jamaica, claimed that General Hudson Austin was warned of the impending invasion by a Caribbean head of government following a regional summit meeting in Trinidad. It is believed his comments were aimed at Forbes Burnam, the President of Guyana.

U.S. Marines made a pre-dawn landing from helicopters and landing craft on the island of Carriacou north of Grenada. They found no resistance. Seventeen Grenadian soldiers surrendered and a cache of arms was found.

Charles A. (Tony) Gillespie who was acting as U.S. charge d'affaires in Grenada, met with Sir Paul Scoon, Governor General of Grenada, to discuss arrangements for establishing an interim government and preparing for general elections.

Governor General Scoon broke diplomatic relations with the U.S.S.R. and Libya.

November 2, 1983

The aircraft carrier Independence along with five destroyers and cruisers and five transport and amphibious ships carrying 1,800 Marines departed Grenada for Lebanon where the Independence would relieve the Eisenhower.

Nine combat ships including the aircraft carrier America were ordered to sea from east coast ports to conduct a training exercise in the Atlantic.

Eight U.S. Air Force A-10 attack aircraft were deployed to the Caribbean, some to operate out of Barbados, and some out of Puerto Rico.

U.S. losses in Grenada were placed at eighteen killed and ninety-one wounded.

Fifty-seven wounded Cubans along with ten medical workers were returned to Cuba. They were flown to Bridgetown, Barbados in a C-130 Hercules, and from Bridgetown to Havana in a DC-8 chartered by the Red Cross from the Swiss charter company Balair.

Peter McPherson, Administrator of the Agency for International Development, said that $3,375,000 had been allocated for relief and restoration in Grenada.

David Brinkley, Senior Correspondent for ABC News, John Chancellor, a commentator for NBC News, and Edward M. Joyce, President of CBS News, criticized the barring of news reporters from Grenada in a hearing before a House Judiciary subcommittee.

A resolution "deeply deploring" the armed intervention in Grenada was adopted by the U.N. General Assembly with only the United States, Antigua and Barbuda, Barbados, Dominica, El Salvador, Israel, Jamaica, Saint Lucia and Saint Vincent, and the Grenadines dissenting. The resolution, which was presented by Nicaragua and Zimbabwe, was essentially the same as the one which had passed the Security Council and had been vetoed by the United States. An amendment offered by Belgium called for "the holding of elections as rapidly as possible." South Yemen raised a motion that no action be taken on the Belgian amendment. That motion, which was supported by Libya and Guyana, was defeated and the Belgian amendment was passed by a vote of seventy-one to twenty-three. The representative of South Yemen, Abdalla Al-Ashtal, proposed a motion curtailing debate which passed sixty to fifty-four, so the resolution was adopted without debate.

The invasion of Grenada was praised by Adolfo Calero Portocarrero, head of the Nicaraguan Democratic Force, an anti-Sandanista group who said that the invasion was proof that "the United States is not only powerful but willing to use its power."

November 3, 1983
The aircraft carrier _America_, which had departed Norfolk, Va., was en route to training exercises to be held near·Guantanomo Bay Naval Base, Cuba. In addition to the _America_, the force contained the nuclear-powered guided missile cruiser _Mississippi_, the guided missile destroyers _Luce, Conyngham_, and _Dahlgren_, the destroyers _Thorn_ and _Peterson_, the frigate _Aylwin_, and the ammunition/fuel ship _Platte_.

Sixteen Libyan nationals, four of them diplomats, departed for Bridgetown, Barbados aboard a U.S. military plane.

Gail Reed, the Chicago born wife of Cuban Ambassador Julian Torres Rizo, said in an informal through the fence interview that "the killing of Bishop was not authorized."

Cuban exiles in Miami pointed to the arrival of Col. Tortolo in Grenada following the death of Maurice Bishop as evidence that the Cubans intended to overthrow the government of General Hudson Austin.

Carlos Romero-Barcelo, the Governor of Puerto Rico, supported the invasion of Grenada saying, "I think the President had no other choice but to intervene."

John Chancellor admitted that his mail in response to broadcasts criticizing the President for excluding the press from Grenada had been running 10-to-1 against the NBC News position.

United Nations Under Secretary General Diego Cordovez was in Barbados en route to Grenada at the request of Secretary General Javier Perez de Cuellar.

November 4, 1983
The remaining 126 occupants of the Soviet Embassy in Grenada were flown to Merida, Mexico in a Navy DC-9. The group included fifty-three Cubans, forty-nine Soviet citizens, fifteen North Koreans, six East Germans, and three Bulgarians. There were also Libyans on the flight. Although the Russians had specifically agreed that they would take no weapons, their luggage was found to contain three crates with thirty-eight AK-47 automatic rifles.

Fifteen U.S. Congressmen arrived in Grenada on a C-130 military transport from Barbados to begin a three-day fact-finding mission. Rep. Thomas S. Foley (D., Wash.) was the leader of the group. Rep. Ronald V. Dellums (D., Calif.) expressed interest in finding whether "the use of force was employed as a last resort or whether it was a matter of preference."

The U.S. State Department made public five treaties which showed commitments to deliver arms to Grenada. According to the agreements the Soviet Union was to supply 4,000 submachine guns, 2,500 rifles, 7,000 mines, 15,000 grenades, and sixty armored-personnel carriers. According to a treaty dated April 14, 1983, North Korea was to provide arms including 1,000 automatic rifles with 360,000 rounds of ammunition, fifty light machine guns, thirty heavy machine guns with 60,000 rounds of ammunition, fifty rocket-propelled grenade launchers with 500 rounds of ammunition, 200 hand grenades, two coast guard boats, 6,000 uniforms, and 6,000 knapsacks.

November 5, 1983
Comments by members of the Congressional delegation visiting Grenada included:

Rep. Don L. Bonker (D., Wash.): "I think we are just plain confused about why the United States went in. What we're finding is impressive in terms of Cuban and Eastern European military equipment, but when the President announced his reasons for the invasion, all he said was that we were going to save American lives and end the political chaos here. Nothing about Cuban weapons."

Rep. Michael D. Barnes (D., Md.): "It's remarkable how little we knew before we went in here. The Administration was beating the drums on Grenada for months and when we launched the invasion all we had were tourist maps."

CBS News conducted a poll which sampled 304 Grenadians in thirty locations on the island. They found that ninety-one percent of those polled were "glad the United States troops came to Grenada" while only eight percent wished they had never come. Similarily, eighty-five percent said they or their families were in danger while General Hudson Austin was in power while only eleven percent said they were not. Even under Maurice Bishop, thirty-three percent said they believed they were in danger while forty-eight percent said they were not.

November 6, 1983
    General Hudson Austin and former Deputy Prime Minister
Bernard Coard and his wife, Phyllis, were flown from the USS
Saipan to the Queens Park football stadium in downtown St.
George's and then taken to the Richmond Hill jail, which was under
the control of the Caribbean security forces.

    The Congressional delegation investigating the Grenada
invasion and aftermath flew back to Barbados. Michael D. Barnes
(D., Md.) a member of the group commented, "I came down here very
skeptical, but I've reluctantly come to the conclusion that the
invasion was justified." The leader of the delegation, Thomas S.
Foley (D., Wash.) said, "Some Americans here who were, to say the
least, not supportive of the President on many issues, said that
they felt their lives were very much in danger."

    General John W. Vessey Jr., Chairman of the Joint Chiefs of
Staff, announced the formation of a panel to review the news
restrictions imposed in the initial days of the Grenada invasion.
He named Winant Sidle, the director of public relations for the
Martin Marietta Corporation and a former Deputy Assistant
Secretary of Defense for Public Affairs, to head the panel.

    Since October 25th, the Military Air Command had flown 750
missions involving 18,000 passengers, 8,800 tons of cargo, and
500 aircrew.

November 7, 1983
    Guy Farmer, the Chief U.S. Government spokesman on Grenada,
placed U.S. losses at eighteen killed, ninety-seven wounded, and
twenty-nine otherwise injured. He placed Cuban losses at forty-
two killed. However, Cuba has put the number of its dead at
twenty-seven. Mr. Farmer, also said that about 1,800 members of
the Grenadian militia and People's Revolutionary Army had turned
themselves in and that about 200 of these were being held for
questioning. An estimated 400 members of the army and 350 members
of the militia had not come forward or surrendered their weapons.

    The credentials committee of the U.N. General Assembly
adjourned without making a decision on the U.S. challenge to the
credentials of Grenada. Until such a decision is made and
approved by the General Assembly, Caldwell Taylor will continue to
represent Grenada. The Credentials Committee is chaired by Olara
Otunnu of Uganda. Diego Cordovez of Ecuador, Under Secretary
General for Political Affairs, returned from Grenada with copies
of a proclamation by Sir Paul Scoon closing all Grenadian
diplomatic missions abroad.

November 8, 1983
    After hearing the report of the Congressional delegation
which had visited Grenada, Speaker of the House Thomas P. O'Neill
Jr. (D., Mass.) said, "The delegation has now returned with the
information that at the very minimum a potentially life-
threatening situation existed on the island with regard to

American citizens. Since this was the case, I believe that sending American forces into combat was justified under these particular circumstances." Thomas S. Foley (D., Wash.), leader of the group, said, "The majority--and I would say, the very large majority--feels that under the circumstances the President acted correctly to protect American lives." However he added "If I conceived this to be a precedent for other interventions, I would be frightened." Representative Robert G. Torricelli (D., N.J.) acknowledged, "There's a strategic retreat going on."

However, not all members of the delegation were convinced. Ronald V. Dellums (D., Calif.) said, "This invasion was not about students. They were a convenient vehicle for the further militarization of American foreign policy. As an American citizen, I was appalled by the U.S. invasion of Grenada, which I consider and undeclared act of war in violation of the Constitution, and the U.N. and O.A.S. charters." Louis Stokes (D., Ohio) complained that U.S. forces "are engaging in illegal searches and seizures of people and homes." Dellums and Stokes said that the twenty-one member Black Caucus had endorsed their report, which challenged the decision to invade.

The Caribbean airline LIAT resumed regular flights to Grenada for the first time since October 17th. They took sixty-five people to Grenada, while twenty-two departed the island.

November 9, 1983
     Sir Paul Scoon, Governor General of Grenada, named a nine member interim government to be headed by Meredith Alister McIntyre, 51, presently Deputy Secretary General of the United Nations Conference on Trade and Development. Mr. McIntyre who was educated at the London School of Economics and Nuffield College, Oxford, must be released from his U.N. responsibilities by the Secretary General of the U.N. before he can accept the position in Grenada. In his absence, the Advisory Council will be headed by Nicholas Braithwaite, 58, former head of the Commonwealth Youth Center based in Guyana. The other members of the Council appointed were Arnold M. Cruickshank, senior manager of the agricultural division of the Caribbean Development Bank; James DeVerre Pitt, Director of the Grenada Science Council; Patrick Emmanuel, senior research fellow at the Institute of Social and Economic Research at the University of the West Indies in Barbados; Alan Kirtin, a permanent secretary in Jamaica's Civil Service; Chris Williams, a welfare and youth worker; Joan Purcell, the local director of the Canadian Save the Children Fund; and Raymond Smith, former manager of a radio station.

November 13, 1983
     Cuba declared five days of mourning in memory of the Cubans who were killed resisting the invasion of Grenada.

November 14, 1983
     Fidel Castro delivered a speech in Havana to honor the Cubans

181

killed in Grenada. Several comments in the speech show great
regard for Maurice Bishop, but little regard for Bernard Coard and
Hudson Austin. "Unfortunately, the Grenadians themselves
unleashed the events that opened the door to imperialist
aggression....Hyenas emerged from the revolutionary ranks. In
spite of our profound indignation over Bishop's removal from
office and arrest, we fully refrained from interfering in
Grenada's internal affairs. ...This group of Coard's that seized
power in Grenada expressed serious reservations toward Cuba from
the very beginning because of our well known and unquestionable
friendship with Bishop."

November 15, 1983
      The Governor General of Grenada swore in five members of the
interim governing council. The other four members including the
chairman designate Meredith Alister McIntyre were not able to be
present. Anthony R. Rushford, a legal advisor to Sir Paul Scoon
and a retired British Foreign official, has been named as an ex
officio member of the advisory council.

      Costa Rica's Foreign Minister, Fernando Volio, resigned from
his post, citing his country's vote in the U.N. condemning the
invasion of Grenada as "the straw that broke the camel's back."

November 18, 1983
      The U.S. forces remaining on Grenada numbered 1,030 combat
troops and 1,693 support troops.

November 19, 1983
      A private press reestablished in Grenada with the publication
of the Grenadian Voice, a publication whose editors had been
jailed in 1981. The editorial in the first edition offered
President Reagan the paper's "Order of Valor" for the "rescue
mission."

November 21, 1983
      President Reagan notified Congress (who had just adjourned)
that he would allocate $15 million to train and equip a 350-man
Caribbean security force. Another $15 million, originally
intended for Syria, would be used to assist economic development
in Grenada.

November 29, 1983
      A week long meeting of the Commonwealth nations ended in New
Delhi, India, with a declaration saying that this was a time for
"reconstruction, not recrimination" in Grenada. They called for
the departure of "foreign military forces" but refrained from
condemning the United States. The declaration followed much
heated debate between the Caribbean nations which favored the U.S.
intervention and African nations which feared that it created a
precedent which might be followed in South Africa.

December 6, 1983
   Anthony Rushford, retired British Foreign Service officer and legal advisor to the Advisory Council, resigned the latter position reportedly following disagreements over the pace of institutional restoration.

December 8, 1983
   As of this date, the Advisory Council named by the Governor General to serve as an interim administration until elections could be held was as follows:

   Nicholas Braithwaite, Chairman, health, education, youth and community development, and sports;

   Dr. Alan Kirton, Deputy Chairman, civil services and secretary to the Advisory Council;

   Arnold Cruickshank, agriculture, natural resources, and industrial development;

   Dr. James Pitt, construction, housing, environmental matters, and science and technology;

   Patrick Emmanuel, foreign affairs, civil aviation, and tourism;

   Mrs. Joan Purcell, labor, employment, and women's affairs;

   Christopher Williams, without portfolio;

   Raymond Smith, telecommunications, information, and postal services; and

   Randolph Mark, without portfolio.

   Alister McIntyre, who had been asked to Chair the Advisory Council, was forced to decline due to health problems.

About the Editors and Contributors

Editors

Colonel PETER M. DUNN, U.S. Air Force, is Commander, U.S. Air Force ROTC Detachment 440, University of Missouri. He was formerly Assistant Provost for Research at the Defense Intelligence College. Colonel Dunn is a veteran of three tours of duty in Vietnam. Among his publications are works on the beginnings of the Indochina conflicts. Colonel Dunn, who holds a Ph.D. in History from the University of London, is coeditor of The Military Lessons of the Falkland Islands War (Westview, 1984) and Military Intelligence and the Universities; A Study of an Ambivalent Relationship (Westview, 1984). He is currently coediting a book on the Soviet Navy, which will be published by Westview in 1985.

Commander BRUCE W. WATSON, U.S. Navy, is the Director of Publications at the Defense Intelligence College and is an Adjunct Professor in the School of Foreign Service, Georgetown University. Dr Watson is the author of Red Navy at Sea: Soviet Naval Operations on the High Seas, 1956-1980. He has also edited several books, including The Military Lessons of the Falkland Islands War (coedited with Peter M. Dunn), and Military Intelligence and the Universities (also coedited with Peter M. Dunn). A contributor to the U.S. Naval Institute Proceedings, the U.S. Naval War College Review, and the Air University Review, Dr. Watson is currently coediting three books on the Soviet Navy; all will be published by Westview Press in 1985. In addition, he is coauthoring a study on Soviet, Cuban, and U.S. interests in the Caribbean Sea with Dr. James L. George, which will be published by the Hoover Institute in 1985. Dr. Watson currently serves as the Chairman, Comparative Foreign Policy Section, International Studies Association.

Contributors

STEPHEN J. ANDRIOLE, President of International Information Systems in Marshall, Virginia, is formerly the Director of the Defense Department's Advanced Research Projects Agency's Cybernetics Technology Office (DARPA/CTO), where he was also a Program Manager. He has taught international relations, national security analysis, and applied methodology at the University of Maryland, the Johns Hopkins School of Advanced International Studies, and the George Washington University; he was also a

183

Research analyst and Project Manager at Decisions and Designs, Incorporated. Dr. Andriole is the author, coauthor, editor, or coeditor of sixteen books and over seventy-five articles.

CAPTAIN DOROTHEA M. CYPHER, U.S. Army, is a career military intelligence officer, and has served in several operational billets, including as a military intelligence aviator attached to the Eighth U.S. Army in the Republic of Korea. She holds a Master of Science degree in Strategic Intelligence from the Defense Intelligence College.

LAWRENCE S. GERMAIN is a staff member on the Weapons Program, Los Alamos National Laboratory, where he is researching the history of nuclear weapons technology. Dr. Germain is most concerned with the history of nuclear policy. He is well published and recently prepared a chronology on the Falklands War in the Westview monograph on that subject. His chronology of the Grenadian operation is based on intensive analysis of that subject.

CYNTHIA GILLEY is an international consultant specializing in population and development policy. She has travelled extensively throughout Latin America on assignments with the Agency for International Development, the U.S. House of Representatives, the World Bank, and the Battelle Memorial Institute.

COURTNEY D. GLASS is a Research and Program Assistant at the Defense Intelligence College. Before moving to the College in early 1984, she worked an as Intelligence Research Specialist at the Defense Intelligence Agency. She has a Master's degree in Latin American Studies from the University of Alabama, and has travelled extensively throughout Latin America.

GERALD W. HOPPLE is Senior Analyst at Defense Systems, Inc. Previously, he was a faculty member at the Defense Intelligence College, where he designed courses and taught in the areas of advanced methods for intelligence production, the intelligence research process, and the psychology of intelligence analysis. He has also been affiliated with several private research organizations and has taught at George Mason University and the University of Maryland. In addition to a recent article in World Politics on intelligence and the Falklands conflict, he is the author or coauthor of eight books (including National Security Crisis Forecasting and Mangement, Westview Press, 1984, and Revolution and Political Instability: Applied Research Methods, St Martin's Press and Frances Pinter Publications, 1984).

G. F. ILLINGWORTH is associated with the University of Missouri, has a sustained interest in national security affairs and has accomplished exhaustive research on the Grenadian operation.

ROBERT A. PASTOR is Professor of Political Science at Emory University in Atlanta and Director of the Latin American and Caribbean Program at the Carter Center. In 1985-86, he is on leave as the Fulbright Professor of U.S. Foreign Policy at El Colegio de Mexico City. Dr. Pastor taught at The University of Maryland (1982-85), where he also directed a research project on Migration and Development in the Caribbean. He was the Senior Staff Member in charge of Latin American and Caribbean Affairs on the National Security Council from 1977-81, and the Executive Director of the Linowitz Commission on U.S.-Latin American Relations from 1975-76. Dr. Pastor received his Ph.D. in Government from Harvard University, where he also taught.

GEORGE H. QUESTER is Chairman, Department of Government and Politics, The University of Maryland. Professor Quester's areas of specialization include military strategy and arms control, American foreign policy, and international politics. Prior to coming to the University of Maryland, he had taught at Cornell University, the National War College, U.C.L.A., and Harvard University. He is the author of American Foreign Policy; The Lost Consensus, Offense and Defense in the International System, and The Politics of Nuclear Proliferation, along with a number of journal articles on international security issues and other issues. He served three years as an officer in the United States Air Force, and is a member of the International Institute for Strategic Studies and the Council on Foreign Relations.

FRANK UHLIG, JR. is editor of Naval War College Press and Naval War College Review. He is also assistant director at the War College's Center for Naval Warfare Studies. Prior to assuming these positions, Mr. Uhlig served as editor and then senior editor at the U.S. Naval Institute, and was founding editor of the Institute's annual Naval Review. A prominent commentator on naval matters, he has written for a wide variety of magazines, newspapers and books. In 1970 he was awarded the Navy League's Alfred Thayer Mahan Award for Literary Achievement.